Getting Excited About Data

SECOND EDITION

Getting Excited About Data

SECOND EDITION

Combining People, Passion, and
Proof to Maximize Student
Achievement

EDIE L. HOLCOMB
Foreword by Tony Wagner

CORWIN PRESS
A Sage Publications Company
Thousand Oaks, California

Foreword Copyright © 2004 by Change Leadership Group

For information:

Corwin Press
A Sage Publications Company
2455 Teller Road
Thousand Oaks, California 91320
www.corwinpress.com

Sage Publications Ltd.
1 Oliver's Yard
55 City Road
London EC1Y 1SP
United Kingdom

Sage Publications India Pvt. Ltd.
B-42, Panchsheel Enclave
Post Box 4109
New Delhi 110 017 India

Printed in the United States of America

Library of Congress Cataloging-in-Publication Data

Holcomb, Edie L.
Getting excited about data : combining people, passion, and proof to maximize student achievement / by Edie L. Holcomb.—2nd ed.
     p. cm.
Includes bibliographical references and index.
ISBN 0-7619-3958-X (Cloth) — ISBN 0-7619-3959-8 (Paper)
   1. Educational indicators—United States. 2. Educational evaluation—United States. 3. Education—United States—Statistics. 4. School improvement programs—United States. 5. Academic achievement—United States. I. Title.
LB2846.H56 2004
379.1´58—dc22

                                        2003022997

This book is printed on acid-free paper.

04   05   06   07   08   10   9   8   7   6   5   4   3   2   1

Acquisitions Editor:	Robert D. Clouse
Editorial Assistant:	Jingle Vea
Production Editor:	Julia Parnell
Copy Editor:	Stacey Shimizu
Proofreader:	Toni Williams
Typesetter:	C&M Digitals (P) Ltd.
Cover Designer:	Tracy E. Miller
Graphic Designer:	Lisa Miller

Contents

List of Figures

Foreword

Tony Wagner

Edie Holcomb has written a wise and exceptionally user-friendly book—now made even more so in this updated and expanded second edition. She clearly communicates the importance of using a variety of student data to guide both school and district improvement, and she provides a wealth of valuable advice, strategies, and tools for engaging adults in the discussion and use of data in a nonthreatening environment. Edie's book should be on the shelf of every school administrator and teacher leader in America—not for show, but rather as the first tool to reach for in the change process.

Data helps us do many things in schools: understand where we are, define where we want and need to go, measure progress along the way. It is indispensable information that is best used internally, as Edie stresses, for the development of shared accountability. Sadly, most of our use of student and school data in America today is punitive, not informative. Data is used by politicians and the media to decry the "failure" of our public schools, to ferret out "underperforming schools," and, increasingly, to impose harsh sanctions on students, teachers, and schools who do not "measure up" or "make adequate yearly progress."

Using data in this fashion as a crude device for imposing summary judgment creates a climate of fear and victimization, and it is unlikely to produce the desired improvements. More and more students, who are required to pass high-stakes tests for promotion or graduation, talk about how they've grown to dislike school, with the unrelenting focus on test preparation and the intense anxiety that the tests engender. With the increasing frequency of tests and severity of the sanctions for "failure," the dropout rate has steadily increased in many districts. Teachers, too, feel victimized, because they are being held accountable for increasing student achievement and, in most cases, do not know what they should do differently to get better results. The fallback position for many is to blame the parents for poor student performance—or to retire early. Meanwhile, after nearly a decade of increased emphasis on accountability, reading and writing scores for secondary students continue to decline while elementary scores are up only marginally, according to the most recent National Assessment of Educational Progress (NAEP) tests.

The heart of the problem is that we do not know how to educate all students to the new higher learning standards now required for learning, work, and citizenship in a so-called knowledge society. It's not as if we once knew how to do this and forgot or got lazy—it's not a matter of "failure." The challenge, as Edie and I both see it, is to create new knowledge about how to systemically improve teaching and learning for all students. More testing does not necessarily improve teaching. Improvement efforts, driven by data, are essential, but we must understand more clearly all of the steps required for raising the level of instruction in *every* classroom.

My colleagues and I at Change Leadership Group in Harvard's Graduate School of Education work with change leaders to improve their effectiveness at implementing systemic improvements in their schools and districts. As a part of this effort, we've researched strategies for improving teaching in those districts that have dramatically raised the level of student achievement for the lowest quartile of students—including those from the most at-risk populations—and have identified seven practices that appear to be central to any successful effort at instructional improvement. What we call "The 7 Core Tasks for Improving Teaching and Learning" should not be seen as a blueprint, but rather as an outline of both a process and a description of a set of intermediate goals that are most likely to significantly improve student achievement. They are listed briefly below, and, beginning with the graphic organizer in Chapter 1 of *Getting Excited About Data*, Edie provides guidance that will support schools and districts in replicating these core practices:

1. The district/school creates *understanding and urgency* around improving *all* students' learning for teachers and community, and they regularly report on progress. Data is disaggregated and transparent to everyone. Qualitative data (e.g., focus groups and interviews) as well as quantitative data are used to understand students' and recent graduates' experience of school.

2. There is *a widely shared vision of what good teaching is*, which is focused on rigor, the quality of student engagement, and effective methods for personalizing learning for all students.

3. *All adult meetings are about instruction* and are models of good teaching.

4. *There are well-defined standards and performance assessments for student work* at all grade levels. Both teachers and students understand what quality work looks like, and there is consistency in standards of assessment.

5. *Supervision is frequent, rigorous, and entirely focused on the improvement of instruction.*

6. *Professional development is primarily on-site, intensive, collaborative, and job-embedded and is designed and led by educators who model best teaching and learning practices.*

7. *Teams of teachers use data diagnostically at frequent intervals to assess each student's learning and to identify the most effective teaching practices.* They have time built into their schedules for this shared work.

We at Change Leadership Group have learned that these 7 Core Tasks are not a "buffet," from which a district can choose one or two for implementation without regard to the others. Rather, they represent an interdependent systems approach to the improvement of instruction. While not all may be implemented at once, none can be skipped. For example, few may feel the need to define good teaching if there is no urgency for change. Moreover, definitions of good teaching are incomplete if they do not include data about student work. Finally, effective supervision requires a shared vision of good teaching and standards for student work and is driven by a variety of informative data. This same data also informs planning for effective professional development and the content of school and district meetings.

In the analysis of high-performing schools and districts, use of data comes up again and again. *Getting Excited About Data* is an indispensable guidebook for navigating this new and vital world of shared accountability for the learning of all our students.

Tony is currently Co-Director of the Change Leadership Group at the Harvard Graduate School of Education. His most recent book, *Making the Grade: Reinventing America's Schools*, has just been released in paperback by RoutledgeFalmer. Tony can be reached through his Web site, www.newvillageschools.org.

Preface

The Preface to the first edition of *Getting Excited About Data* began like this:

> It doesn't seem so very long ago—except when I get things in the mail like invitations to 25-year reunions. But there are days when it seems like light-years. I'm referring to the "good old days" when I was a classroom teacher and my *opinion* counted. I could answer parents—or even principals—with a *subjective* statement in a sincere, confident voice, and I would be believed. Not so these days. It seems as if Missouri has taken over the union with everyone crying, "Show me." Professional judgment isn't enough; people want proof. In short, they want to see the data.

That book was written for all the teachers, school administrators, staff developers, and advocates of public education who wanted to be proactive and responsive to their community. They were voluntarily learning and implementing new processes and practices so they could better understand their learners and evaluate their work.

This second edition, written just five years later, emerges in a different context. President George W. Bush and Secretary of Education Rod Paige just celebrated the first anniversary of No Child Left Behind, a major overhaul of the Elementary and Secondary Education Act requiring annual testing in Grades 3–8 in reading and math, and once again in high school, with "adequate yearly progress" to be made by all groups of students. Leaving no child behind—the act, not the Act—is exactly what the data volunteers of five years ago had in mind, but few of them came to the NCLB birthday party. The threats of takeover and further diminished resources through parent exodus to other so-called choices have turned idealism into legalism.

The career that didn't seem so long has now entered a new century, and more memories surface. Once, as young teachers, we greeted "the dawning of the age of Aquarius." Now, we gasp for breath, drowning in the age of accountability.

For public education to survive, all schools and districts must develop the skills and processes needed to gather, display, analyze, interpret, make decisions, and take action with data. For those who are just taking up that challenge, this book remains simple and basic—a starting point. For those who have already come a long way, creating school portfolios, setting data-driven goals, and adopting research-based strategies, this second edition adds new material on using formative classroom assessment; aligning instructional improvement work at the district, school, and classroom levels; and monitoring both implementation of new practices and the resulting impact on student learning. The three P's of people, passion, and proof are more consistently emphasized throughout, and a new final chapter on leadership adds three R's for leaders: reflection and relentless resilience.

What This Book Is *Not*

Even with the new material, there are still a number of things this book is not.

This is not a statistics book. The uses of data recommended in this book require the ability to count, calculate averages and percentages, and construct simple graphs. Students who meet the fourth-grade benchmarks of Washington State's Essential Academic Learning Requirements in the probability and statistics strand of mathematics would be able to assist with the data work discussed here. Regression formulas and correlation coefficients are omitted. Here, the term *significance* isn't represented as $p < 0.05$. It refers instead to what the *school* defines as significant—that is, as important, relevant, and useful to know.

This book is not comprehensive. If psychometricians describe this book as simplistic and basic, we will know we've been successful. There are legitimate reasons why most educators are uncomfortable with the use of data. The purpose of this book is to raise comfort and interest levels so readers will become ready, willing, and able to explore more sophisticated uses of data. My intent is simply this: to meet people where they are and help them take their next developmental steps into this standards-based, data-driven age of accountability.

This book is not bureaucratic and impersonal. Reading it and implementing its recommendations won't turn anyone into an accountant, auditor, or undertaker. Its purpose is to affirm and build on the nurturing nature of teachers, adding the support of objective information to their usually accurate professional intuition. Stories, such as the one in Chapter 12, illustrate how the use of data can stimulate greater sensitivity to the needs of students, not turn them into numbers.

This book is not a quick fix for the achievement gap. Almost every chapter highlights some equity issue I have experienced myself or encountered in schools and districts—urban, rural, and suburban—in over 30 states and several countries. These experiences began over 35 years ago, when I taught in an Alabama school that had just experienced forced desegregation, and my class of third graders spanned 11 grade levels in reading. The experiences became even richer 20 years ago, when I became principal of a school with racial and socioeconomic diversity. The state department of education came to conduct an audit of our Title I program, because the fall-to-spring normal curve equivalent gains we reported were suspect. The gains were validated, and state officials described our elementary school as "the best kept secret in the state."

In my latest position, I have spent four years working with urban schools in Seattle, Washington, including those with a majority of students of color, large numbers of English language learners, and 60%–70% qualifying for free or reduced-priced lunches. During this span of time, I have learned with pride that the best of classroom teaching and assessment most dramatically impacts challenged learners and accelerates their progress. I learned with frustration that schools most in need of stability and sophisticated instructional expertise suffered constant teacher turnover due to rigid salary schedules and seniority-based transfer policies. And I learned with humility that I need to partner with leaders of color, because learning cognitively, listening compassionately, and becoming culturally competent are not the same as "knowing" the realities of the achievement gap, especially for African American males.

In this book, I share what I can say with confidence from my own experience and observation. For more in-depth insights on closing the achievement gap, I highly recommend Ruth W. Johnson's *Using Data to Close the Achievement Gap* (2002), as well as publications of the Education Trust and other resources listed in the Reference section, which have enlightened me.

This book is not written in jargon. For this book, I have intentionally chosen a casual, conversational style. My purpose is to use plain English to describe simple things I've done with real people that have created interest and opened doors. Because these activities have helped my colleagues and clients, I trust you will find them useful also.

I'm aware that the pronouns *I* and *we* are frequently interchanged throughout the book. I have let this inconsistency stand because it feels natural, because none of these activities could have occurred without the cooperation of others, and because I hope you will read as an active participant in mental dialogue with me.

What This Book *Is*

The purpose of *Getting Excited About Data* is better captured by the subtitle: *Combining People, Passion, and Proof to Maximize Student Achievement.* Collecting more data for the sake of having more data is an exercise in futility unless it engages people by connecting to their deep and authentic passions for teaching and learning. People who work incredibly hard because they care need the proof of their efforts to encourage and sustain them and to help them gain the respect they so deserve. The goal is not to be a more research-based, data-driven school. The goal is to increase student success.

The focus of *Getting Excited About Data* is the human element— hopes and fears, prior knowledge, beliefs about student potential and professional practice, and current needs. This book offers a variety of tools and group activities to create active engagement with data and interaction with peers that will build more collaborative cultures with a shared sense of collective responsibility for all students' learning.

How This Book Is Organized

The content of *Getting Excited About Data: Combining People, Passion, and Proof to Maximize Student Achievement* is organized into five major sections with unique purposes. The first two chapters serve as the knowledge base and foundation for the rest of the book. Chapter 1 is the "what we need to do" chapter. It introduces a visual organizer that illustrates the relationship between components of an aligned plan to impact achievement and highlights the points where data is critical to align and maintain the process. Two high school scenarios are contrasted to illustrate the importance of engaging people, arousing passion, and documenting proof. Chapter 2 addresses "why we should," emphasizing the important role of data in school effectiveness and successful school change over the past two decades.

The next section focuses on the human capacity to work with data. Chapter 3 describes the limited ways in which data are typically used in most school districts and examines "why we don't" use it for more powerful purposes. It acknowledges the barriers that are embedded in the reality of school life and suggests ways to build interest and motivation for greater involvement with data. Chapter 4, new to this edition, describes the organizational infrastructure that needs to be built to engage busy people and explains how structure and process impact the school culture. The passion part of the subtitle is aroused in Chapter 5, which begins with an activity that stimulates reflection on the core values of the school and provokes the search for evidence that the mission is being accomplished.

Four chapters constitute the third section and focus on initial steps to initiate more deliberate and intentional use of data. For schools just embarking on the data journey, a road map is provided. Even schools that are well down the road will find these chapters helpful as a diagnostic review to strengthen their practices. Chapter 6 expands the definition of data beyond "just test scores; recommends types of data useful to elementary, middle, and high schools; and introduces five key questions that help determine the types of proof that will be meaningful and will stimulate curiosity and action. Chapter 7 describes characteristics of user-friendly data, with helpful tips and examples of data displays. The importance of engaging people in collaborative interpretation of data about their school is stressed in Chapter 8, and a professional development activity for this purpose is provided.

Components of the previous chapters are combined in Chapter 9, which outlines a Data Day activity that sends clear signals to staff and community about an increased focus on evidence of results. Even schools who have become accustomed to using data should reassert this practice publicly on a periodic basis, such as when major initiatives or change efforts are being planned, or when staff turnover, a new principal, changes in attendance boundaries, or other factors present a "new picture" of the school.

The activities in the fourth section provide an overview of a school's student characteristics, achievement, and other factors related to staff and community perceptions. The chapters in this section utilize the data to establish priorities and integrate accountability requirements with goals that are data-based, grounded in the school's values, and within the range of maximum optimism. Chapters 11 and 12 actually add to the data and knowledge bases by providing recommendations for the deeper analysis of the data in the established priority areas, the study of strategies with documented success (data) in research and best practice, and more intentional reflection on current practices consistently used throughout the school.

Chapter 13—which opens the final section—intentionally shifts the focus from the school to the district. The deeper analysis of student data, study of research and best practice, and reflection on current practice will generate many ideas, needs, and concerns that are beyond the capacity and scope of authority of the individual school. It describes the alignment and support needed to contribute to successful change at the school level.

Chapter 14 returns to the school-level focus on planning the new work and describes a new type of data collection to verify that plans are being implemented and are having the intended impact on student learning. The challenges of sustaining focus and momentum until the effort shows up in student success are explored in Chapter 15.

Finally, this second edition closes with a new chapter on leadership. Michael Fullan (2003a) stated in a speech in January 2003 that "leadership would be to this decade what standards were to the 90's." The expectations for schools rise, the threats of punishment for "failure" escalate, and the resources diminish. To survive is success; to thrive is extraordinary. As the previous 15 chapters emphasized the three P's of people, passion, and proof, Chapter 16 introduces the three R's of reflection and relentless resilience for leaders in the 21st century.

Acknowledgments

Combining writing with a more-than-full-time job in school district administration is a challenge that can only be met with the support of many—those who inspire the content and those who help with the product.

My friend and colleague Debbie McDonald pushed me to start the first edition, and hasn't let up through this one.

Special thanks for technical help are due to my husband, Lee; my patient typist, Janet Oiness-Kennedy; and artwork creators, Dave Pedersen, Anne Mustappa, Mike O'Connell, Joan Dore, Charlotte Carr, Cindy Backstrom, and Brian Rick. Thanks also to Robb Clouse, Corwin editor, for patience as I tried to pursue this project with persistence, but keep it in proper order of life priorities.

Without the dedication and cooperation of committed educators who have been willing to take risks with me, there would be nothing to write and no examples to share. I am grateful to hundreds of unnamed teachers, principals, and district administrators whose work is represented by the stories shared in this text. Beyond gratitude, I express my admiration for the leadership of the following individuals:

Mr. Dave Adams, Principal, Birchwood Elementary School, Bellingham, Washington

Dr. Brian Benzel, Superintendent, Spokane Public Schools, Spokane, Washington

Mr. Gary Bersell, Director of Instructional Services, Janesville, Wisconsin

Dr. Lois Brick, North Central Association and Wisconsin Department of Public Instruction

Mr. Cal Callaway, Director of Instruction, Oregon, Wisconsin

Dr. Janet Chrispeels, California Center for Effective Schools, University of California at Santa Barbara, Santa Barbara, California

Mr. Steve Clarke, Principal, Bellingham High School, Bellingham, Washington

Mr. Greg Holmgren, Principal, Silver Beach Elementary School, Bellingham, Washington

Dr. Dale Kinsley, Superintendent of Schools, Bellingham, Washington

Mr. Jim Kistner, Principal, Sehome High School, Bellingham, Washington

Dr. Sara Larsen, Director of Instruction, East Troy, Wisconsin

Mr. Rob McElroy, Principal, Happy Valley Elementary School, Bellingham, Washington

Ms. Gigi Morganti, Principal, Kulshan Middle School, Bellingham, Washington

Mr. Steve Morse, Principal, Roosevelt Elementary School, Bellingham, Washington

Dr. Mike O'Connell, Director of Research, Evaluation, and Assessment, Seattle, Washington

Mr. Nick Payne, Principal, Alderwood Elementary School, Bellingham, Washington

Ms. Jean Prochaska, Principal, Sunnyland Elementary School, Bellingham, Washington

Ms. Annita Rao, Teacher Leader, Sioux Falls, South Dakota, and Goldsboro, North Carolina

Dr. Mabel Schumacher, Director of Instruction, Fort Atkinson, Wisconsin

Dr. Sandra Sorrell, Director of Curriculum, Instruction, and Assessment, Fort Collins, Colorado

Dr. Mary Ellen Steele-Pierce, Assistant Superintendent, Curriculum and Instruction, W. Clermont School District, Cincinnati, Ohio

Mr. Walter Trotter, Education Director, Seattle, Washington

Watching these people work with passion is all the proof I need that public education is in good hands.

Edie L. Holcomb
November 2003

Corwin Press gratefully acknowledges the contributions of the following people:

Denny R. Vincent
NASSP, President
  Board of Directors
Principal
Muhlenberg North
  High School
Greenville, KY

Jill Hudson
Facilitator & Webmaster of
  Coalition of Essential
  Schools Northwest
Principal
Madison Middle School
Seattle, WA

Edwin S. Hedgepeth
NASSP, Member,
  Board of Directors
Principal
Farragut High School
Knoxville, TN

Mike Schmoker
Author
Speaker and Consultant
Flagstaff, AZ

Theodore B. Creighton
Author, Professor
Director, Center for Research &
  Doctoral Studies in
  Educational Leadership
Executive Director, NCPEA
Sam Houston State University
Huntsville, TX

Marilyn Day
Principal
Washington Middle School
Seattle, WA

Judy Peterson
Principal
The Center School
Seattle, WA

Deborah H. McDonald
Kentucky State Director
Appalachian Education
  Laboratory
Louisville, KY

Terry Bergeson
State Superintendent of Public
  Instruction
Olympia, WA

About the Author

Edie L. Holcomb currently serves as Executive Director of School Administration in the Bellingham (Washington) School District, where she serves principals, teachers, and students in eight elementary schools, two middle schools, and a comprehensive high school. In her previous work in Seattle, Washington, she coordinated the collaborative work of over 300 teachers in the development of their standards-based learning system, including grade-level benchmarks to match state standards, alignment of curriculum and resources, and development of classroom-based assessments and anchor papers. She represents members at large on the Leadership Council of the Association for Supervision and Curriculum Development (ASCD).

Dr. Holcomb is highly regarded for her ability to link research and practice on issues related to school leadership and instructional improvement. Her background includes teaching at all grade levels and administrative experience at the building and district level in Illinois, Alabama, Minnesota, South Dakota, Iowa, Wisconsin, Colorado, and Washington State. She received the Excellence in Staff Development Award from Iowa ASCD in 1988.

Dr. Holcomb holds a BS in elementary education, an MS in gifted education, and an EdS and PhD in educational administration. Her dissertation on the needs of beginning principals received the Paul F. Salmon Award for Outstanding Education Leadership Research from the American Association of School Administrators in 1990.

She has also served as Associate Director of the National Center for Effective Schools, developing training materials and providing technical assistance throughout the United States and in Canada, Guam, St. Lucia, and Hong Kong. In addition to this book and its first edition, she has authored two editions of *Asking the Right Questions: Techniques for Collaboration and School Change*. She can be contacted directly at elholcomb@ aol.com or by phone at 360-671-1164.

This book is dedicated to my Olsen family—

My husband Lee F. Olsen, partner, coach, and cheerleader
in this work as in all things,

and Bret, Marie, Melanie, Jared, and Ross, kids and grandkids.

Thank you for adding love, balance, and resilience to my life.

Using Data for Alignment and Achievement

"**W**ell, lady, there's good news and bad news. Which do you want first?"

This was not the opening line of a comedian. It was the greeting of the mechanic as he returned from the service bay of the dealership where I had purchased my still-pretty-new red sports car. I asked for the bad news first. "You're going to need four new tires, and the high-performance type you have are not included in the special sale we're running. You also need your front end aligned and your brake pads are nearly shot. You're looking at right around a grand altogether."

My treat-the-mechanic-nice-or-it-will-only-get-worse smile faded as my heart sank and my stomach somersaulted. I could see my little vacation nest egg fading before my eyes. "So what could possibly be the good news?"

I wished I hadn't asked. It was all the spark he needed to fire up a lecture that seemed prerecorded for female customers. "Lady, the good news is that you're alive. I can't figure out why you women can't seem to grasp the importance of basic routine maintenance. You hit something or something hit you and knocked that front end out of line, and instead of getting it checked and fixed right away, you just let it go on and on until your tires are worn all uneven and the right front one could have blown out any time and put you into a skid or a rollover, and with your brake drums affected, too, you'd have a mighty hard time driving your way out of it. Anybody who'd neglect a car like this shouldn't be allowed to have one in the first place. Didn't anyone ever tell you the number one rule of owning a car? Take good care of your car and it will take good care of you! You're just lucky you got in here when you did!"

What an embarrassing, expensive experience for someone who uses the word *alignment* almost daily in her organizational development work! There's no way to calculate the number of school improvement/reform/restructuring/transformation efforts that have gone out of control, rolled over, or skidded to a stop due to lack of alignment. Well-intended but misaligned efforts result in disillusioned educators who resolve, "Never again," disappointed constituents who wonder, "Why can't they get their act together?" and disengaged or disenfranchised students moving through a system of public education without having truly learned.

Figure 1.1, Using Data for Alignment and Achievement, illustrates the relationships that must be in alignment so that investments of human and fiscal resources will pay the dividends of improved student achievement. This figure is a composite of the key components of a variety of change processes used in school districts I have known: Effective Schools models, school accreditation processes, total quality management, strategic planning, and, most recently, school improvement plans required by state accountability systems and demanded by No Child Left Behind, the reauthorization of the Elementary and Secondary Education Act (www.ed.gov/offices/OESE/esea). I have frequently seen one or two of these components done well; however, I have rarely seen a fully aligned system. But I have observed that the districts with the most tightly aligned and data-driven approaches to change and improvement are also those making a difference in student achievement.

The visual organizer of an aligned achievement plan appears twice in this chapter. First, we explore the relationships among the components; then, we describe the essential uses of data at critical points in the school improvement process (Figure 1.2). Scenarios from two high schools are provided as example and nonexample so readers can gain further understanding by comparing and contrasting their approaches to change.

Alignment Between Mission and the School Portfolio

The literature on change is full of materials that stress the importance of an organization having a statement or document that articulates its "passion"—the core values and purposes that guide it. Few authors describe the mission as a set of commitments for which the organization is accountable. The vertical arrow between the *Mission* and the *School Portfolio* in Figure 1.1 demonstrates the need to provide evidence that the mission is being fulfilled.

The term *school portfolio* is used here to describe a collection of data compiled at the individual school level. Chapters 6 and 7 discuss the contents and format of the portfolio. Although it is frequently referred to as a

Figure 1.1   Using Data for Alignment and Achievement

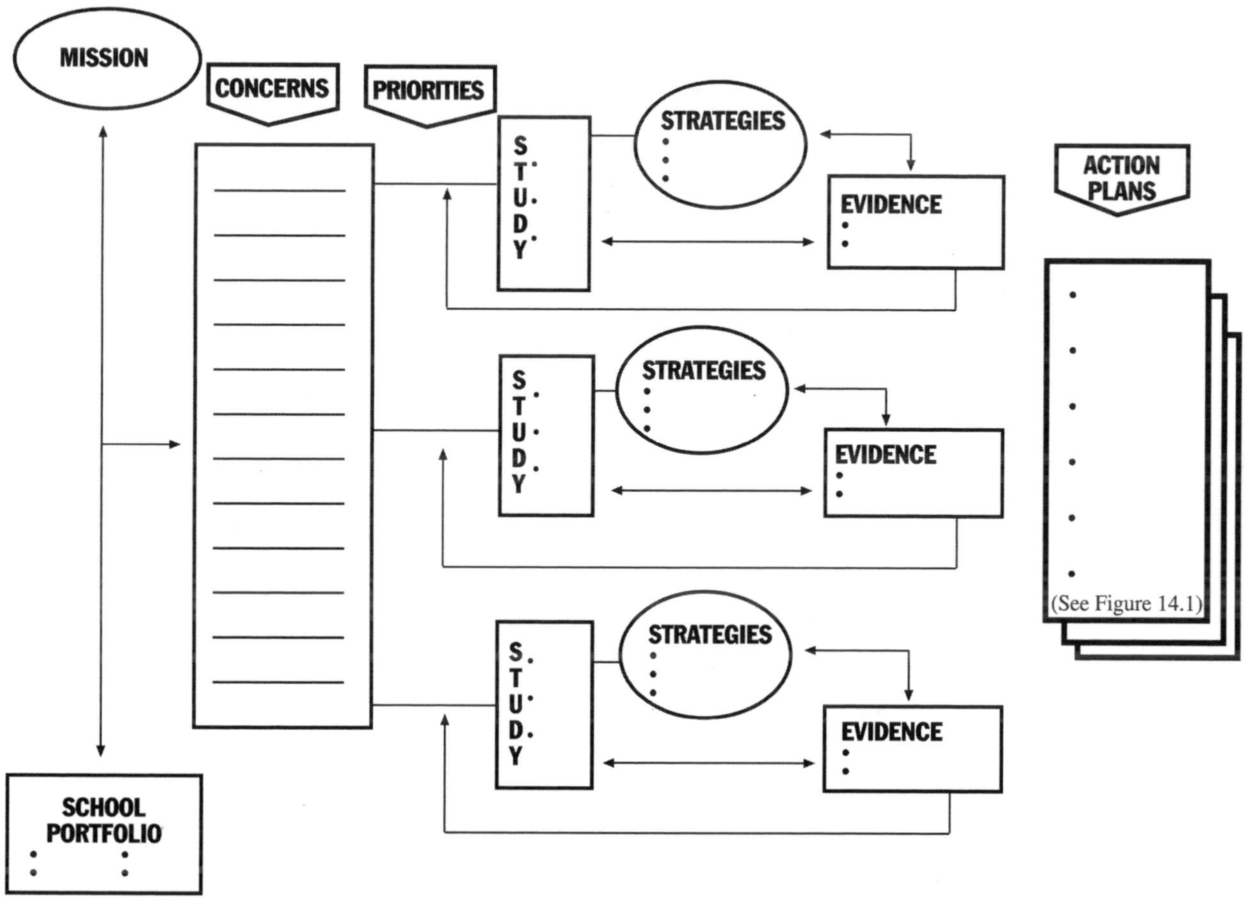

4

Figure 1.2   Aligning the Achievement Plan

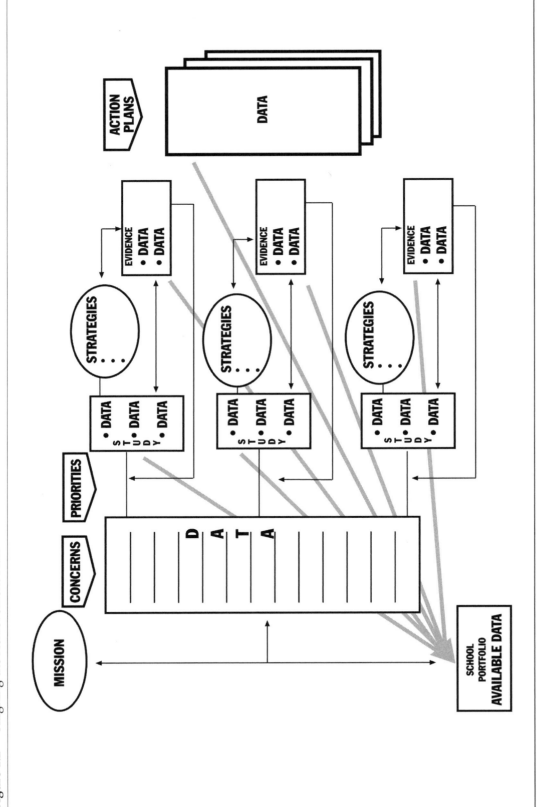

profile, I prefer to call it a school portfolio for three reasons. First, I believe that the comparison to a portfolio of student work is a very fitting reminder that we work in a school context. Second, the term *portfolio* is apt because a student's (or artist's) portfolio is intended to demonstrate three important aspects of his or her work: the range of skills, the very best final products, and artifacts that provide evidence of progress and learning. A school also needs to present the wide variety of needs it addresses, examples of success to celebrate, and evidence of improvement occurring where needed.

Third, I believe one of the reasons school-level data should be compiled as a portfolio is to paint a more complete picture of the uniqueness of that school and its students than the term *profile* implies. Painting a picture requires more than an outline or silhouette. This is not to say that a school portfolio should be a two-ton tome. Chapter 6 will emphasize the need to be intentional about the portfolio's contents, so staff and constituents are not overwhelmed and intimidated by sheer volume.

The relationship between the mission and the school portfolio is that one should provide evidence of the other. In organizational development terminology, it is looking for alignment between our *espoused theories* (beliefs) and our *theories in use* (how we operate on a daily basis); (Argyris & Schon, 1974). When we provide evidence of what we do, how closely does it match what we say? Our integrity is judged by whether we do what we say we will do.

Alignment Between Mission, Portfolio, and Concerns

The length of the vertical arrow between *Mission* and *Portfolio* in Figure 1.1 represents the amount of discrepancy between rhetoric and reality. Awareness of this discrepancy should generate a range of concerns, which Peter Senge (1990) might describe as "creative tension." The horizontal arrow emphasizes that the *Concerns* we begin to address should arise directly from the values we hold dear and the data we examine courageously. In Chapter 10, this list of concerns is also prompted by the question, "What are *all* the things that *anyone* might say *could* be improved in our school?" This inclusive question reminds us that the school portfolio should contain perceptual data from the constituencies that have a major stake in the school: staff, students, and parents.

Alignment Between Concerns and Priorities

If our school portfolio includes a variety of data from a range of sources, many concerns will be identified (see Chapter 6). Only a few can be addressed with the type of substantive, systemic effort needed to change student achievement. The contrast between the many lines in the *Concerns* box and only three spaces for *Priorities* in Figure 1.1 represents the need to focus on a few areas of critical importance and major impact on student achievement. Chapter 10 emphasizes how and why this is so important.

Alignment Between Priorities, Study, and Strategies

Too often, participants in a school improvement process have unrealistic time expectations placed on them. They may be asked to set new annual goals each year and be given just a day to go on retreat and develop the improvement plan. This model yields several unintended, undesired consequences. Significant needs are not addressed as goals because they can't be attained in one year. Strategies for meeting the goals are brainstormed based on the particular experiences and preferences of the group. Important factors in the local context that would inform these decisions are ignored.

The three bullets in the *Study* component of Figure 1.1 emphasize the necessity for deeper analysis of the data, thorough examination of research and best practice, and honest analysis of existing practices within the school. Annual plans must be replaced by multiyear plans, with months of planning time provided for thorough work and adequate engagement of those who will be affected by coming changes. The strategies selected for implementation must be consistent with the school's mission, linked to needs arising from data, and proven effective in other settings.

It is important to note that there are three bullet points in the oval labeled *Strategies*. These bullets do not represent three specific tasks, as the three bullets in the *Study* box do. Rather, they serve as a reminder that there is no "silver bullet" or "magic potion/program" that can solve a complex problem. A powerful combination of effective strategies must be created and coordinated.

Alignment Between Priorities, Strategies, and Evidence

Traditional methods of program evaluation and school improvement have claimed success by reporting evidence that selected strategies were implemented. Glowing accounts are provided of the number of teachers who attended training and the number of new initiatives begun. One reason we so often reported what the adults did, rather than the results achieved for students, is that this is what we *knew how to do*. Individual teachers kept track of students' progress in idiosyncratic ways at the classroom level, but there was little assurance that this data matched schoolwide goals or could be aggregated to show student progress for the school as a whole.

As Figure 2.2 indicates, high-performing schools identify formative assessments they will use to monitor students in a more frequent, more authentic, and less threatening way than the large-scale assessments they also administer and analyze. The two bullet points in the *Evidence* component of Figure 1.1 represent the need to verify *implementation* of the selected strategies and to ensure that this effort has an *impact* on student learning.

The arrows that go back-and-forth and around *Priorities, Strategies,* and *Evidence* in Figure 1.1 illustrate that this activity is cyclical, continuous, ongoing work. The process is not as straightforward as the two-dimensional confines of print make it appear: For example, the two-way arrow between *Strategies* and *Evidence* reminds us that determining what evidence we need and learning how to gather it will also inform what we need to do as strategies so the evidence we seek will be available. When I work with planning groups, it is a challenge to restrain them from making decisions about strategies until they have a good idea of what goal attainment would look like and how that would be documented.

Alignment Between Strategies, Evidence, and Action Plans

The components of *Mission, School Portfolio, Priorities, Strategies,* and *Evidence* in Figure 1.1 represent the major components of the achievement plan. They signal major decisions about what the school's focus will be, what new work the school will initiate, and how the school will determine its effectiveness. This overall "plan at a glance" can be displayed, publicized, and referred to frequently. The big-picture view helps keep leaders, staff, and stakeholders grounded when multiple efforts seem overwhelming and may feel that they are starting to spin out of control.

The achievement plan describes "why" (mission and portfolio), "what" (goals), and "how" (strategies and evidence). But when it comes to putting all this work into place, the devil is in the details. School leaders need more specific, concrete *action plans* to identify "who," "when," "where," and "with what funding." Chapter 15 provides guidance for planning the new work. Figure 15.1 is an example of an action plan. The *Action Plan* blocks on Figures 1.1 and 1.2 are a reminder that more detailed planning is needed to ensure implementation of the strategies that were selected and collection of the needed evidence to document success.

Consolidating Multiple and Existing Plans

For a Summer Institute in 1999, our state department of education created a list of possible plans and/or grants currently in place, including the 46 possibilities shown in Figure 1.3. The list may be shorter now, since

Figure 1.3   Possible Plans Already in Place

<table>
<tr><td>

Building-Level Plans
- Accreditation/Self-Study
- Crisis Response
- Safety Procedures
- Reading Improvement Plans

Grants
- Goals 2000
- State Technology Grant
- Technology Literacy Challenge Fund
- School-to-Work
- Readiness to Learn
- Comprehensive School Reform Designs
- School Security Enhancement
- Washington Reading Corps
- K-2 Professional Development
- Community Network
- 21st Century Community Schools

District-Level Plans
- Strategic Plan
- Assessment Plan
- Transportation
- Facilities
- Asbestos Management
- Budget Development
- Crisis Plan
- Safety Plan
- Staff Development Plans

</td><td>

State-Mandated Plans
- K–4 Reading Improvement Goals
- Student Learning Improvement
- Technology
- Learning Assistance Program
- State Transitional Bilingual Education
- Highly Capable

Federally Mandated Plans
- Even Start
- Title I—Schoolwide
- Title II—Targeted Assistance
- Title II—Eisenhower Professional Development
- Title IV—Safe and Drug Free Schools
- Title IV—Learn and Serve America
- Title IV—Compliance
- Title VI—Innovative Education
- Title IX—Gender Equity
- Carl Perkins—Vocational and Applied Ed.
- Emergency Immigrant
- Homeless Education
- Individuals With Disabilities Education Act
- Migrant Education
- Americans With Disabilities Act
- Class-Size Reduction
- School-to-Work

</td></tr>
</table>

funding for some of those plans has been cut in this time of reduced resources for public education. Some of the plans on the list may not apply in your location. It is, however, highly likely that your school is implicated in and accountable for a multiplicity of plans—some you may not be aware of. This list provides a starting point for your quest.

Questions to be asked as you begin work include the following:

- How many plans are there?
- Where are they?
- What do they require of us?
- Is the school the major focus or is the primary activity and responsibility a function of the district? (See Chapter 13)

Plans that clearly fall within the scope of the school context need to be reviewed and aligned wherever possible within the achievement plan illustrated in Figure 1.1. For example, the existence of a reading improvement plan mandated by the state to the district indicates that one priority area has already been identified as reading, and this priority probably includes some strategies that have already been selected for implementation. These should be reflected in the school's aligned achievement plan, rather than being housed in a separate place and creating the probability that the school will add more strategies, with the potential for overload and fragmentation. In other cases, the existing plan may be a thorough, complete, well-aligned action plan (see Figure 14.1 in Chapter 14). This existing action plan would be integrated into the overall achievement plan by listing its major strategy or strategies on Figure 1.1 and then linking it to the priorities it addresses.

Using Data for Alignment and Achievement

The auto mechanic who worked on my car had a computer and a number of other tools he used to align my front end and get my wheels back in balance. The tool for aligning our efforts to increase student achievement is data. In Figure 1.2, the critical points for use of data are superimposed on the basic diagram from Figure 1.1. The initial version of the school portfolio is clarified as baseline data. Shaded arrows have been added to illustrate how the school portfolio continually expands as more data are acquired and used throughout the process. These arrows show how the regular use of data changes the appearance of a linear process into a continuous improvement cycle.

Data for Initial Review

When most schools make the commitment to become more data-driven, they are panic-stricken about where they are going to find information to include. Then, they discover that there are "mother lodes" of data scattered throughout the school and district that have been as shrouded with mystery as the lost ark and certainly have never been mined. Once people begin to discover what they *can* include in the initial school portfolio, it becomes a challenge to limit its size and scope. Chapter 6 provides ideas for organizing the school portfolio and the shaded arrows on Figure 1.2 illustrate why organization is so essential. Because the school portfolio is a work in progress at all times, there will be ample opportunities to add more information or more detailed analysis as the process continues.

Data to Focus Priorities

The data compiled in the school portfolio will be used as one of three filters to help the school focus on a limited number of priority areas for attention. Chapter 10 describes the critical importance of an objective look at how severe an issue is, as well as its connection to the values of the school and the ability of the school to change it. Using data at this point is also critical for another reason. It establishes awareness that the school portfolio is not just a product to be "finished and done with," but a work-in-progress will be consulted regularly whenever decisions are pending.

Data From Further Study

The three bullets in the *Study* box of Figure 1.2 represent further analysis of the data related to each priority issue or need, investigation of best practices, and review of current programs and instructional practices. When new strategies are being considered, data that substantiate their claims of effectiveness should be a prerequisite. Data on current practice might include documenting the amount of time each teacher devotes to an essential skill or standard. The shaded arrow shows how these data become part of the school portfolio as it is continually updated.

Data for Documenting Results

As improvement goals are crafted into language that will motivate a whole-school effort, the question, "How will we know we're getting there?" should be addressed. Some answers will be very evident, because there are data sources that were available earlier and used in the initial school portfolio—and these can be monitored over time. Standardized tests and state assessments are two examples. Other answers will have to be constructed as professionals discuss what could be measured, observed, or aggregated from information they already keep as individual teachers. Chapter 14 provides examples of data used to document implementation and impact in actual schools.

Plans for Collecting Data

A school's completed version of Figure 1.1 identifies the data that will be used to document progress. Some of this will be test data that automatically comes from the state to the district and on to the school. Other data will be school-specific and must be intentionally collected. The plans for this data collection should be embedded in the action plans. For example, refer to Figure 14.2, which identifies artifacts that would be collected and graphs that would be created to demonstrate the implementation and impact of a monitoring program for chronic absentees. One reason we end up with little to show for our efforts is that we don't plan ahead and take the action needed to get the proof we will want to present.

Two Schools Implement a Major Change

The program at a recent conference on high school reform included a strand devoted to block scheduling. There were "how *to*" sessions—how to vary instructional strategies in the longer time frame, how to develop the master schedule, and so forth. There were also "how *we*" sessions—sessions offered by principals and teachers to describe their various approaches, challenges, and solutions to the problems of this new design.

Because I was working closely with a high school at the time, I wanted to select some successful sites for them to visit. My data gathering involved seeking out these principal-presenters in the hallways, during lunch and in the evening, so I could privately ask them a few questions. The stories of School A and School B illustrate the range of responses I heard. The focus for the reader should not be the specific innovation of block scheduling, and the reader must temporarily suspend personal bias on that specific topic. The scenarios should be read with a focus on the change process itself. How are the components of Figure 1.1 and the data uses of Figure 1.2 revealed (or not) in these two approaches to change?

School A

Author: Hi. I see from the program that you're doing block scheduling at your school. How long have you been at it?

Principal A: Well, it's about a year and a half now. We're into our second year of it.

Author: Why did you make that kind of a change?

Principal A: Well, I'm sure you've heard of our school. Our district is known as one of the most progressive in the state and our board likes to be sure we're on the cutting edge. The superintendent called me in one day and said that the board members were getting on his case because the elementary schools were doing multiage and looping and stuff like that, and the middle schools had these new "houses"—whatever they are—and they wanted to know what we're going to do for restructuring at the high school. So, we did some checking around and went to a national conference, and block scheduling seemed to be the thing that's "hot." So, we came back and started to work on it.

Author: Did you run into any resistance? How did you go about implementing such a change?

Principal A: Well, there were already enough schools doing it that I could call around and find out what the problems seemed to be. A couple of things they all mentioned were the hassles of getting the master schedule put together and trying to explain the whole thing to parents who just had images of the way high school was back when they went to school. So, we decided we'd head off the resistance by just dealing with those right off the bat. I took my department heads to my cabin for a retreat for a couple days right after school got out, and we worked out the master schedule. That way, it would be all in place for teachers when they came back in August, and we wouldn't have to spend weeks worth of meetings trying to iron it out. We did the best we could to make people happy, but we knew there's just no way to please them all. And on the parent thing, I've got a good friend with kids in the school who runs a public relations firm. He volunteered the time to make up a brochure that we could send to all the parents in early August and give them fair warning so they could get used to the idea. It's a good thing I work year-round, because there sure were a lot of people calling in to ask me about it.

Author: Is it working for you? How do you know?

Principal A: Well, like I said, we're in our second year. We had a lot of glitches and some people didn't like it at first—but we just stuck to it and we made it through. The board was real supportive that we wouldn't just give up after one year. And it must be good for the kids. Last week, my assistant principal was getting ready to throw out some old referral slips when he noticed there were only about half as many hallway disciplines as the year before. So, obviously we're doing something right.

School B

Author: Hi. I see from the program that you're doing block scheduling at your school. How long have you been at it?

Principal B: Well, I guess there's two ways I could answer that. If you mean how long we've been using it, I'd say two years. This is our third year. But if you mean how long we've been *working* at it, I'd say three years, because I'd count the year we spent making up our minds and getting ready for it.

Author: Why did you make that kind of a change?

Principal B: Well, now you're in for a longer answer, if you have time. It seems simple at first. We were getting ready for the accreditation people to do a site visit, and we were checking off the stuff they look for—like a mission statement, for example. We remembered we had one from the last time around, and we got it out to review. We actually liked it and decided to keep it, but as we were talking about it, we sort of wondered if it was for real or not. We had things like "critical thinking" and "problem solving" and "having a caring, personal community" in there, but we really hadn't been thinking about whether they were true. So, we decided to make those three things a real priority in the next couple of years. Then we had to get data together—you know, they want a school profile. And we got to wondering if maybe we could find out about critical thinking and problem solving and caring community from stuff in there. Well, we checked, and we didn't like it. On test score measures of problem solving, we weren't very good. When we had teacher focus groups, people were complaining about the poor quality of written work and the shallow answers in class discussions. When we looked at survey data from the students and parents, we were disappointed at how many didn't agree that they had two or three adults to turn to with problems or didn't agree that the school treats each student as an individual, and so on. We started asking "why not," and eventually decided that it's pretty hard to teach to high levels of Bloom's taxonomy and get quality work in 42-minute periods—and pretty hard to know kids as individuals with 170 different faces in front of you every day. That's when we realized that our own structure was keeping us from meeting our goals, and we decided to change it.

Author: Did you run into any resistance? How did you go about implementing such a change?

Principal B: That's a long story, too. We knew we could never make everyone happy, but we wanted to be sure that everyone got to be heard. So we decided to devote two months for study of the various problems and to put everyone on a study group. And we weren't just random about it either. My leadership team and I looked over the staff list, and thought about each person and what might trouble them—like, the math teachers are going to worry about continuity and the PE teachers are going to worry about sports. So, we put them on the group that would deal with their issue, and made sure each group also had some people who were real excited and optimistic. We gradually worked through the issues until we got a schedule that everyone agreed was the best we could do—not their personal best, but overall best. And while the teachers were working, we also had a couple of groups of parents and community members raising their questions and getting ideas and reactions from the people they knew. It helped us decide about communication strategies and gave us some advocates out in the town. Anyway, when school got out for the summer, we had all the plans in place and we had structured our August staff development days as a preparation.

We had three days where experts gave us content in the morning, and then we met as departments in the afternoon and the experts helped teachers restructure their instructional units for September with a variety of teaching strategies. That way, the teachers were ready to go and knew how to modify their lessons as the year went on.

Author: Is it working for you? How do you know?

Principal B: Well, for one thing, we have some new binders in the curriculum office that show how we changed our course syllabi, and we have some sample lesson plans. That's been really helpful for new teachers coming in, and proves we really did follow through on the changes in instruction. And then, last spring, we did the same surveys as three years ago. The students and parents sure gave us better ratings for personalization and caring. And our test scores are up across the board—so, I guess our emphasis on higher-level thinking and sticking to our standards for quality work has really paid off. I think you'd have a real tough time getting this crowd to go back to the old way.

Two A's and Three Powerful P's

This chapter introduced Figures 1.1 and 1.2 to illustrate the two A's of using data: *alignment* and *achievement*. School A had no sense of mission unless it was "to be progressive" and no particular priorities except perhaps to "keep the school board happy." At no time did they review their achievement data or use it to guide their planning or to analyze their effectiveness. School B, on the other hand, started with a sense of mission, tested it against the reality shown in their data, established priorities based on the evidence, and aligned their efforts with student achievement in mind.

The subtitle of the book captures three powerful P's that were also present at School B. Their approach to change engaged the *people* who would be affected by change and responded to the voices of the students expressed through the surveys. They acknowledged and tapped the *passion* of individual staff members and gave them opportunities to be heard and to influence decisions. And, when this group gave their conference presentation, they were clearly excited about their data, as they displayed the *proof* of their efforts in pre- and post-test scores and survey results.

Making It Public

Schools that stand out in my mind have made their change process and data work transparent. For example, some have enlarged Figure 1.1 to poster size and used it as a worksheet to guide their planning year.

One school filled a huge bulletin board in its foyer with the components from Figure 1.2. Staff members created a beautiful poster of their mission statement and displayed it on the top left corner of the bulletin board. In the lower left corner, they posted the executive summary of their conclusions from analysis of the data in their school portfolio. The priority goals they set were lettered in calligraphy on sentence strips. Strategies for each goal were connected by strings of yarn, which gave them the ability to connect several strategies to more than one goal area. Their combined master plan was illustrated with a series of laminated monthly calendars that highlighted the events from their action plans.

Any visitor to this school knew what was happening and why. Any new idea or grant opportunity had to pass the acid test of proving where it would fit on that crowded, colorful bulletin board.

Schools with many existing plans or initiatives already underway have started "in the middle" of Figure 1.1, filling in the strategies they had adopted and backtracking to check alignment with questions such as the following:

- What goals were we trying to meet with this?
- How carefully did we research this program?
- What data established the need for this and will provide evidence of its success?
- Is it consistent with the values stated in our mission?

Future chapters in this book will include other suggestions for communicating about the data work and keeping it visible. Communication and visibility are powerful ways to engage staff and stakeholders, and transparency reduces the anxiety of those who may wonder what the data work is revealing.

On the Road Again

My tires are now replaced and balanced, my front end is aligned, and my car is tracking straight down the road. If the components of school improvement are aligned with data, the school should also be able to move ahead and see its forward progress. In the next two chapters, we'll explore how the use of data is becoming more and more essential and why it is so hard to "get excited about" the use of data.

2

Understanding the Importance of Proof

It was the summer of 1984 and I had just been appointed to my first principalship. I stopped at the district office and asked for any materials I should pick up that would help me prepare for the coming school year. I was given a large wad of keys of all sizes and three notebook binders of district policy and procedures—each one 4 inches thick, covered with light blue canvas cloth, threadbare at the corners, with ravelings along the spine. As I headed for my car, the heavy, pointed keys tore through the lining of my suit pocket and fell to the ground. As I bent to retrieve the keys, the stack of notebooks in my arms became unbalanced, tumbled to the ground, and nine rings popped open, fanning their contents across the parking lot like a deck of cards in the hands of a gambler. I was not off to an auspicious beginning. I never found the locks to match some of those keys, and the time it took to reassemble the policy books exceeded the total number of times I opened them in the next three years.

My Data Roots

The only other thing the district had given me was a registration form for some Effective Schools training. That small brochure turned out to be the real key that unlocked doors for me and provided principles of leadership that have guided me for 20 years.

I was assigned to a school with students who were Caucasian, Native American, Vietnamese, Cambodian, Hmong, and African American. Their parents were blue-collar workers at the nearby meatpacking plant or state prison, or lived with assistance in low-income housing projects and on the reservation. Their test scores were the second lowest of the elementary schools in a district of 47,000 students. In the Effective Schools training, I was delighted to learn that Ron Edmonds and other researchers in the United States and England had found schools where student achievement exceeded the levels typically associated with their demographic profile. These schools were characterized by seven factors that became the beacons to light my way. They were

- Strong instructional leadership
- A clear, focused mission
- A safe, orderly environment
- Teaching oriented to time-on-task and opportunity-to-learn
- High expectations for student success
- Frequent monitoring of student progress
- Home-school communication and parent involvement

I was excited about the potential for strengthening these characteristics at my new school, but I was the only one who knew about them. I lacked an ally and I had a Title I certificated position to fill. With only three days to go until the start of school, my ally and Title I teacher moved into town. We began to study together and to look at how Title I services had been delivered in our school. It was a typical program, with small groups of students pulled out of the classroom for remedial skill drills delivered by instructional aides and supervised by the certificated teacher. There was almost no interaction between the Title I aide and the classroom teacher, except an occasional note in the staff mailbox that would read this way: "Suzie Student needs to work on. . . ." Or "Peter Pupil is failing in. . . ."

Annita Rao, my ally, and I went to work. (This was before I had learned the other two P's—engaging all the *people* and tapping their individual *passion*s to develop the collaborative culture.) With varying degrees of support, we changed from "pull-out" to "push-in" programs and assigned the aides to work in the classrooms. We identified a set time each week for the classroom teacher to conference with the Title I teacher about the content that would be taught in the coming week. We switched from "fix after failure" to "prime the pump" and helped students review their prior knowledge and practice prerequisite skills in advance of the whole-class instruction.

Some teachers were resistant to having another adult in the room, or, as some admitted, didn't like having "those" children in their rooms the whole day without a break from them. Some students became uneasy because their stereotypes were being challenged. One day, a sixth grader made an appointment with me to discuss the cheating that was going on in class. He claimed to be representing a "lot of us" who think the teachers are giving away the tests to certain kids. His "evidence" of the crime was that "There's some kids who never got anything but D's and F's and now they're getting B's, and there's no way that could be." Even the state department of education became suspicious when we reported normal curve equivalent (NCE) gains from fall-to-spring a year after those changes. They came for an audit, validated the gains, and declared Bancroft Elementary "the best kept secret in the state."

That is the simple story of how I learned the importance of proof. How could staff, students, or the state argue with the data? Our results allowed us to continue with our change process, and, in turn, raised our expectations of student capability.

Data to Close the Achievement Gap

Ruth Johnson's (2002) work with data to close the achievement gap arose from the same roots and has been reinforced with 30 years of additional research. As she states,

> There is evidence from as early as the 1970s (Edmonds, 1979) and beyond . . . that describes how schools with large populations of low-income students and students of color mitigate perceived achievement barriers. Some of the major factors are the following:
>
> - High goals, high standards, high expectations, and account-ability for adults and students ("Better Balance," 2001; Haycock et al., 2001; Kahle, Meece, & Scantlebury, 2000; Kim et al., 2001; Olson, 2001)
> - Whether or not students receive well-qualified and cultur-ally competent teachers (Darling-Hammond, Berry, & Thoreson, 2001; Ferguson, 1997, cited in Haycock, 1998; Haycock, 1998; Kain & Singleton, 1996; Ladson-Billings, 1994; National Commission on Teaching and America's Future, 1996)
> - Curriculum content and rigor (Adelman, 1999; Gamoran & Hannigan, 2000; National Center for Education Statistics, 1995; National Commission on the High School Senior Year, 2001; Office of Education Research and Improvement, 1994; Valverde & Schmidt, 1998)
> - Continuous inquiry and monitoring through the use of data (Johnson, 1996a; Olsen, 1996; Sandham, 2001a). (p. 6)

Johnson goes on to describe a school in which

> teachers, counselors, administrators, and parents came to understand the power of data to make improvement in the achievement of all groups of students. They began to "own"

the data and to take leadership in the use of data at their sites. Some results included upgrading curriculum, strategically focusing on students' academic needs, highlighting institutional barriers and discrimination, revising the report cards to align with standards, designing and implementing computer systems to retrieve student-level and teacher-level data, and creating a data culture. (p. 34)

Note: references cited above are from original work.

Use of Data Highlighted in National Research Reports

In an effort to assist schools with their work to increase student achievement, the Washington State Office of the Superintendent of Public Instruction (OSPI; Shannon & Bylsma, 2003) recently reviewed and reported on the 25 national and state studies listed in Figure 2.1. Some were reviews of other research conducted over a period of years on the same topic. Others examined high-performing schools with specific populations and settings. Nine characteristics emerged as themes in multiple studies:

- Clear and shared focus
- High standards and expectations for all students
- Effective school leadership
- High levels of collaboration and communication
- Curriculum, instruction, and assessment aligned with standards
- Frequent monitoring of teaching and learning
- Focused professional development
- Supportive learning environment
- High levels of family and community involvement

When I reviewed these findings, my first reaction was awe at the uncanny similarity between this 2003 set of characteristics and the seven correlates of effective schools that first began to light my way. The first three elements on this list are almost identical to the earlier one. Alignment with standards is a 1990s way to phrase "opportunity to learn" the necessary skills. Frequent monitoring and family involvement also resurface.

My second reaction was indignation that we continue repeatedly to identify the same factors in study after study after study, and yet they still are associated with exemplary (not typical) practice. After 30 years of knowing what is needed, these descriptors should have become universal! My third reaction was to notice again the importance of having data and using it to monitor what occurs for staff and students in classrooms across the country.

One of the studies included in the OSPI review reported on 16 elementary schools that are outperforming their demographics. The Washington School Research Center at Seattle Pacific University examines

Figure 2.1 Synopsis of National Research Reports

RESEARCH BASE
Summary

Characteristics of High Performing Schools

National Reports	Clear & Shared Focus	High Standards & Expectations	Effective School Leadership	High Levels of Collaboration & Communication	Curriculum, Instruction & Assessment Aligned with Standards	Frequent Monitoring of Teaching & Learning	Focused Professional Development	Supportive Learning Environment	High Level of Family & Community Involvement
Comprehensive School Reform	X			*	X	*	X		X
Dispelling the Myth		X			X	X	X		X
Educational Reform and Students at Risk	X		*	X	*	X	X	X	*
Hawthorne Elementary School	X	X	X	X	*		X		X
Hope for Urban Education	X	*	X	X	X		X	X	X
Key High School Reform Strategies		X		X			X		X
Leave No Child Behind	X	X	X	X	X	X	X		X
Org. Characteristics of Schools that Successfully Serve ...	X	X	X	X	X		X	X	X
Profiles of Successful Schoolwide Programs	X	*	X	X	X	*	X	*	X
Promising Practices Study of High-Performing Schools	X	*	X	*	*	X	X		
Promising Programs for Elementary and Middle Schools	X				X	X	X		
Schooling Practices That Matter Most	X		X		*	X	*	X	X
Schools that Make a Difference	X	X	X	X	X	X	X	X	X
Stories of Mixed Success	X		X	X	X		X		X
Successful School Restructuring	X	*	X	X	X	*	X	X	*
Toward an Understanding of Unusually Successful ...	X	X	X	X	X	X	X	X	X
Turning Around Low-Performing Schools	X	X	X	X	X	X	X	X	X
Washington Reports									
Bridging the Opportunity Gap	X	X	X	X	*	X	X	X	X
Make Standards Meaningful	X	X						*	
Make Standards Stick	X	X	*	X	X	X	X		X
Make Standards Work	X			X	*		X		X
Organizing for Success	X	X	X	X	X	*	X		X
Reality of Reform			O	*				O	O
School Restructuring and Student Achievement in WA	X			X			X		X
Washington State Elementary Schools on Slow Track ...	O		O	O	O		O		
Total	**22**	**16**	**18**	**21**	**21**	**15**	**23**	**12**	**21**

X   Explicitly identified as key finding or in discussion of findings
*   Inferred or identified indirectly in descriptions
O   Identified as important by noting the absence or lack thereof

Shannon, G.S. & Bylsma, P. (2003). Nine Characteristics of High Performing Schools. Olympia, WA: Office of Superintendent of Public Instruction.

test scores for the state's public schools by comparing their test scores to top-performing schools in their demographic group—schools with similar levels of poverty and mobility, proportion of English language learners, and other factors. Schools that beat the odds—that make the most of their "window of opportunity"—have four things in common:

- A caring and collaborative professional environment
- Strong leadership
- Focused, intentional instruction
- The use of assessment data to drive instruction

These four factors are explored in more depth in later chapters. Chapter 4 includes the necessity for engagement and involvement of staff in collaborative culture building and decision making. Chapter 12 focuses on instructional practice. Chapter 16 outlines characteristics needed for strong leadership. The bottom line is the importance of data—in this case, the up-close formative assessment data that teachers can use to make decisions about student learning and to plan instruction that meets their needs.

Data Work in High-Performing Schools

Over the last 20 years, through various official and unofficial roles and channels, I've been privileged to work with schools in over 30 states and several countries. Through 12 years of affiliation with the U.S. Department of Education's Blue Ribbon Schools program (prior to the version introduced by President George W. Bush and Secretary of Education Rod Paige), I was able to review the practices of award-winning schools and applaud the increasing use of data to describe their practices and their impact on student achievement. Figure 2.2 outlines the critical tasks that have differentiated the extraordinary from the ordinary within the scope of my personal observations.

Data—Essential, but Not Sufficient

This chapter has provided a glimpse into 30 years of research and 20 years of personal observation that underscore the importance of data to provide proof of effectiveness. Multiple authors and studies have repeatedly "discovered" the use of data in schools where achievement is high. But the data alone has not been sufficient. Each study has included other factors that describe how people work together, and many studies have captured the concept of passion as embodied in a clear mission and shared purpose.

These three powerful P's are captured in the strategic plan of the Association for Supervision and Curriculum Development (ASCD; www.ascd.org). Goal 4 of this plan states that the ASCD will develop educators' capacity to address complex problems, and continues,

Figure 2.2   What Do High-Performing Schools Do With Data?

- Create a culture of collective responsibility for all students
- Understand that assessment is an integral part of the instructional process
- Test their results against their espoused mission
- Make clear distinctions between inputs (by adults) and outcomes (for students)
- Use both objective and subjective (perceptual) data appropriately
- Focus on most critical priorities to conserve time, energy, and money
- Drill down for student- and skill-specific data in priority areas
- Plan forward as students rise—to respond to individual skill gaps
- Plan backward to fill gaps in the instructional program
- Look around at research, best practices, and exemplary schools
- Look within to analyze curriculum and instructional strategies
- Select proven strategies for implementation
- Identify and plan for student populations with specific needs
- Identify formative assessments to balance large-scale, high-stakes tests
- Monitor rates of progress over time—student and cohort
- Gather evidence of both implementation and impact of improvement strategies
- Consolidate multiple plans
- Take the initiative to tell "the rest of the story"

The 21st century educator will thrive in a work culture that stresses collaboration, knowledge creation, and a respect for diversity. No longer working in isolation, teachers and administrators will . . . examine ways to meet individual needs through the sophisticated and recurrent analysis of data. School communities will commit to long-term, ongoing, school-specific professional development that builds both individual and community capacity. Wisdom, after all, develops only when knowledge is viewed through the lenses of keen judgment, insight, interwoven relationships, and wide experiences.

The case has been made for the importance of proof. Why, then, is "the sophisticated and recurrent analysis of data" not the reality? Chapter 3 describes some of the barriers to use of data and begins a discussion of ways to cope, which continues in Chapter 4, on engaging the people, and Chapter 5, on arousing passion.

3

Coping With the Barriers to Data Use

The schools in Chapter 2 and School B in Chapter 1 make better use of data than typical schools—which doesn't mean they are staffed with better people. Most educators do acknowledge the need for proof of a school's effectiveness, but that doesn't mean they know how to go about providing it. While I was writing the first edition of this book, I facilitated a consortium of school districts using Goals 2000 funds to design and implement a collaborative school improvement model. Sixteen districts participated during the design year, and another 12 districts reviewed the model and joined the consortium for implementation. The districts ranged in size and included K–12 districts with 4–16 schools and one small district with only one K–8 building; in total, 93 schools participated.

During the first year of the consortium, focus groups were conducted in the districts to determine their status with regard to use of data and the degree to which data influenced their goals and those goals influenced school and classroom activity. Figure 3.1 reports the types of data most frequently mentioned in answer to the question, "What data about student achievement do you currently use?"

The most frequently mentioned types of data were results from the state assessments of reading at the third-grade level and the fourth-, eighth-, and tenth-grade knowledge and concepts tests. One of the 16 districts did not submit the focus group transcripts, which means that 2 of the 15 reporting districts did not even mention the state assessments during the conversation. It may be that they were simply assumed to be

Figure 3.1 Kinds of Data Used by Districts in Goals 2000 Consortium

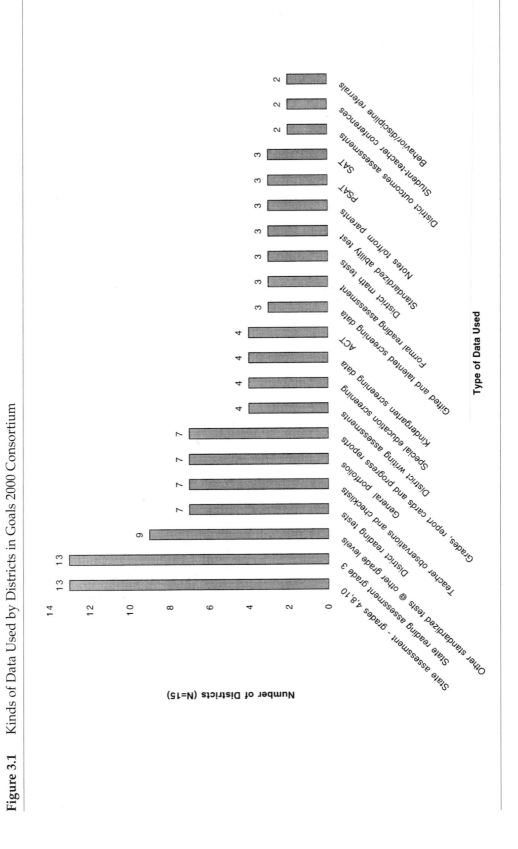

included automatically or—from comments I heard at other times—that the participants may still have been thinking, "This too shall pass," and didn't acknowledge them. Single-item responses that were not displayed in Figure 3.1 include other performance assessments, career portfolios, student self-evaluation, individual goal setting, timed tests, assignment books, class rank, number of graduates, pass-fail lists, Honor Roll, cumulative folders, health concerns lists, Advanced Placement tests, Armed Services Vocational Aptitude Battery (ASVAB), EXPLORE, and post-secondary follow-up data.

The pareto chart in Figure 3.2 displays information about how participants reported *using* the data. Wisconsin traditionally receives high ratings in state education comparisons, and these districts score in the mid-range of state rankings; they are not problem districts. Yet the use of data in these "good" districts in a progressive education state was primarily for sorting and selecting students into special programs and classes, such as applied English, study skills, and the "general education track." Reporting to parents—a legal mandate—came next in frequency. In less than half of the districts did a single participant comment on using data at the classroom level, and there was no mention at all of using data for schoolwide planning for improvement. Why might this be?

Reasons for Reluctance to Use Data

Based on my research, reading, personal conversations with school leaders, and observations in these districts, I have identified six reasons why data are little used and why it is so difficult to generate enough passion to get people engaged with the proof. The barriers to use of data include

- Lack of (proper) training
- Lack of time
- Feast or famine
- Fear of evaluation
- Fear of exposure
- Confusing a technical problem with a cultural problem

Each of these barriers is described in this chapter. Initial suggestions for coping with reluctance are provided, along with references to other chapters where additional strategies are outlined.

Lack of (Proper) Training

Improving schools requires two sets of skills that too few school leaders have had the opportunity to acquire in their graduate work or have seen modeled in their own experiences. The first of these is how to involve others in decision making. The second is how to use data in appropriate ways to guide the decision making.

Figure 3.2   Uses of Data by Districts in Goals 2000 Consortium

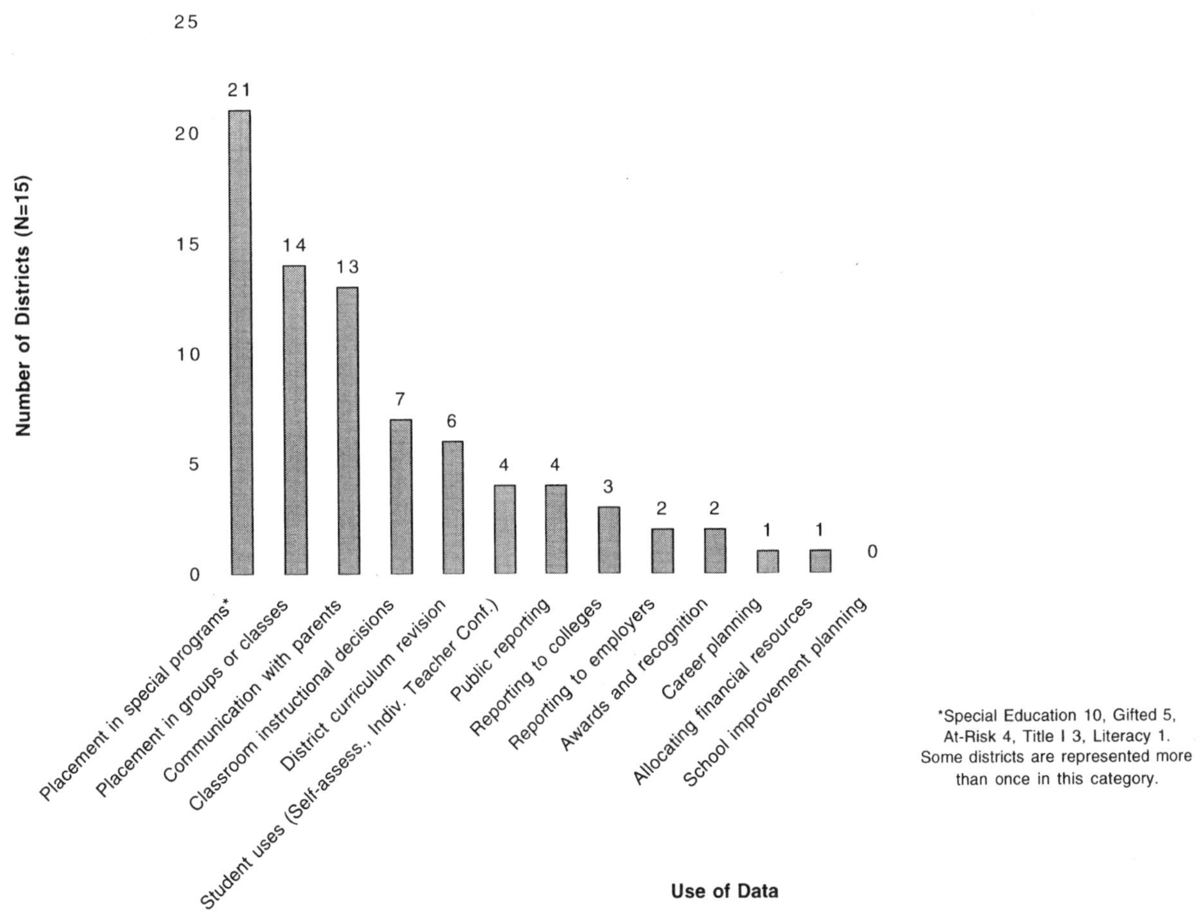

I first began trying to engage staff in collegial discussion of data about our school over 20 years ago. It was a real struggle, and I tried to figure out why. I wondered if it was a task I shouldn't have tackled with them, or if I was going about it all wrong, or if the staff members just weren't as qualified as I expected them to be. I even checked to see if I had as many teachers with master's degrees as the other schools did. Looking back, I realize that my facilitation skills were definitely underdeveloped and that data was a relatively new term in the practitioners' lexicon.

Unfortunately, not much has changed in the last 20 years. I believe even more strongly that collegial discussion of data is a task that must be undertaken. I'm just much more aware of the amount of professional development and support that is needed to have the task accepted.

This book isn't an analysis of graduate programs in education and educational administration. Many such evaluations have been done, with little impact. I verified that more than half of the teachers in the district had graduate degrees and had taken at least one course in tests and measurements or statistics. I have three graduate degrees myself and can recall no class discussion of what to do with assessment information in planning how to help the students do better. I have come to the conclusion that such courses are taught by researchers as though they are preparing researchers. As a result, the emphasis is on esoteric experimental design—which can't be replicated in a normal school setting—and use of empirical data unlike the types of data listed in Figure 3.1. Gerald Bracey (1997) agrees that many of the university professors who create and use statistics are more comfortable using them than they are teaching other human beings what they mean. And in all too many instances, statistics are taught in a theoretically rarefied atmosphere replete with hard-to-understand formulas and too few examples relevant to the daily life of education practitioners.

It *is* important to know whether a research study was conducted in such a way that it should be believed and its findings applied. It *is* important for students pursuing the terminal degree to conduct a rigorous study as a demonstration that they can properly apply the concepts of good research. However, a considerable number of doctoral degrees belong to practitioners who will need to use data in vastly different ways.

The uses of data suggested in this book would not meet the rigorous academic standards of a dissertation. That is not their purpose. Our purpose is to create readiness to try simple things, so we can experience success and see value in using data and then have the will to gain more sophisticated skills.

The unfortunate reality is that the data-related training teachers have had becomes a barrier rather than an asset. Most of us hated the courses, felt we barely passed, and learned just enough to think that any use of data we could fit into a regular school routine would be dismissed for lack of validity, reliability, statistical significance, or sophistication. It's not just what we have to learn that's the challenge—it's what we have to unlearn.

Unlike the list of statistical terms, definitions, and formulas we once stored in short-term memory until the exam, Michael Fullan (2003a) describes assessment literacy as the

- Ability to gather dependable student data
- Capacity to examine student data and make sense of it
- Ability to make changes in teaching and schools derived from those data
- Commitment to communicate effectively and engage in external assessment discussions

The ability, capacity, and commitment to use data cannot be developed through training in the traditional sense of courses and workshops. It is far more complex than individual knowledge and skill acquisition, and it must be embedded in the ongoing work of groups of professionals. The activities described throughout this book are designed to engage educators in doing—not learning about—the data work that will inform school and classroom practices.

Lack of Time

In recent months, I have had the privilege of working in various settings with a state principals' association, the professional development cadre of a state teachers' association, the administrative teams in several districts, and state and regional affiliates of the Association for Supervision and Curriculum Development (ASCD). To increase my effectiveness, I solicited the topics and questions they were hoping we would address. Every list included a collection of "How do we find time to . . . ?" questions.

The three examples in Chapter 5 (see Swapping Stories) all refer to the use of time. This is not the perennial plea for free time for individual planning and preparation, but time to work collaboratively. When we are overwhelmed with all the things we know we *should* do, we resort to completing the things we know we *can* do. It's the only way we can maintain the illusion that we are in control of our professional lives. Chapter 4 includes more specific discussion of structures and time to engage people in collaborative data work. The most powerful way to cope with both barriers of poor training and time is a serious evaluation and redesign of the current time and practices for meetings and staff development.

Feast or Famine

When a school begins its efforts to become more results oriented, there are two times when participants are likely to hit the panic button. The first is when we outline—as we do here in Chapter 6—the kinds of information we want to know and be able to use. About the time a tentative list has been drafted, the blood drains from the faces of the participants and they look at me in horror. "We don't have any data! Where are we going to *get* all of this?!" Then we begin to identify where each kind of data is now housed, who has access and will retrieve it, and so forth.

A month or so later, we get together again. Now they have boxes full of the desired data—and all the other information that has been uncovered in the meantime—and the faces are flushed with anxiety. "What are we going to *do* with all of this?!"

The increased demands of state accountability systems, most recently exacerbated by the No Child Left Behind Act, has caused the "famine" aspect of this barrier to pale in comparison with the "feast" aspect that has proliferated to the point of "force feeding."

To cope with this data overload, several strategies in Chapters 4, 5, and 6 emphasize careful selection of data elements that match current issues and interests of the staff.

Fear of Evaluation

The greatest conundrum encountered in my early attempts to help schools use data was the fear expressed in questions like, "How can I keep this from being used against me?" and "Why would I want to help create the hatchet they could use to 'give me the ax'?" This was particularly puzzling because no one could describe any example of a person dismissed from a teaching or administrative position based on performance of students.

Implementation of No Child Left Behind may change that, although much remains unclear as of this writing. Whether it becomes fully realized or not, the anxiety is much more well founded when the lack of "adequate yearly progress" by any group on a single measure of reading or mathematics could lead to loss of students, and thereby loss of resources, loss of staff and leadership, loss of involvement in decision making, and eventual closure or takeover of the school. Anne Wheelock (2002) identifies the hatchet-holders when she refers to

> politicians with an ax to grind who then use the data, often for purposes that serve neither schools nor their schools well. As a result, many educators have come to think of data—whether couched in terms of the numbers of students passing standardized tests or student survey information gathered to determine how students view their teachers and classrooms—as the stuff that bureaucrats in faraway offices use to beat up on schools. (p. xii)

The threats of evaluation with negative consequences are more real in the 21st century than they have been, but coping with the fear requires the same discipline of focusing on the goal and doing what is right for children for their own sakes, rather than seeking more politically expedient strategies.

Fear of Exposure

Among the informal leaders in the consortium districts, I encountered a more puzzling type of resistance that was less overtly expressed. Individuals who were recognized as "master teachers" would become enthused about using schoolwide data but shy away from discussions of individual students or classrooms. Several attempts to understand their ambivalence yielded this honest observation: "Everyone thinks I'm a great teacher. I'm three years from retirement. How would I ever recover if the data shows I'm not as good as all my friends think I am?"

The same fear of exposure surfaced in a conversation recently with a highly regarded teacher who is learning to be a peer coach. His initial training includes being intensely coached himself, which entails more rigorous self-reflection than many of us would be willing to risk. After the first few weeks of this experience, he stated, "I feel like a 'scammer.' I've been so unaware and unintentional in my teaching—it's almost like I'm a fraud." Fortunately, he has now come through the pain of that self-realization and reached a level where he is both more competent and more confident.

These revelations of fear point out two important concepts about people in change.

1. Every new challenge requires a different definition of ability based on the knowledge and skills needed in that specific endeavor. High performers with many talents and intense dedication can still feel—and be—less prepared and enthusiastic about new challenges in less familiar areas.

2. Leaders of change must be diligent about their own evaluations of others, or they may falsely interpret normal fear of failure as resistance and lack of commitment. Clarifying questions and needs assessments can help an organization identify and provide the human and technical supports that are needed. If we want people to move out of their comfort zones, the "new place" to which they will go must be seen and felt as safe and the "bridge to cross" must have a firm foundation and solid guardrails.

Confusing a Technical Problem With a Cultural Problem

When we ask teachers to look at evidence of their school's effectiveness, we are not just asking them to crunch numbers and plot graphs. That's the technical part. The reality is that we are challenging the existing culture.

Schools have been characterized by individualization and isolation, described as a set of individual enterprises bound together by a common parking lot. If there are "shopping mall" high schools, there are also "strip mall" elementary schools where independent entrepreneurs run "boutiques" connected only by common walls.

Collaborative work with data is essential to accepting collective responsibility for the learning of students during their total time at that school. The barriers that have to fall are not just those of fear and lack of training. Cultural norms, like "Let me close my classroom door and do my own thing," must be replaced by more systemic thinking. Chapters 4 and 5 describe the use of structures, activities, and time to create change in the culture of the school.

Assessing Data Readiness

Just as the master teacher would assess students before planning instruction, change agents need information about the knowledge, skills, and attitudes of members of the organization. Assessments of readiness can range from the informal and humorous to the very structured and formal.

Self- and Staff Rating

A light-hearted diagnosis can take place by asking staff members to give themselves a 1–10 rating, with the low of 1 described as "dataphobic" and the high of 10 describing your own school's "Data Dude" or "Data Diva." The humorous descriptions relieve stress, and the explanations they feel compelled to give for their rating reveal questions that need to be clarified, skills that need to be learned, and supports that need to be provided.

When participants in this informal exercise are administrators or members of a leadership team, they will rate their own reactions to the use of data and may not pause to consider whether they are typical of the entire staff. In this situation, it is advisable to do a second rating in response to this stem: "The average of the rest of our staff who aren't here would probably be . . . ." Sensitivity to the difference in comfort level between the leaders and the overall group is essential.

Data Awareness Questionnaire

More specific information about awareness of data as a factor in readiness can be gathered through use of a structured set of questions, such as those listed in Figure 3.3. The answers could be gathered in writing, but there are risks involved. Not everyone will participate and it will feel more "serious," potentially increasing the fear rather than alleviating it.

Another approach would be to give each individual the questions in a group setting, provide time for them to think about their responses, then share and compare their answers. A recorder in each group could capture the range of responses and compile them later in a less formal, more anonymous fashion.

Concerns-Based Adoption Model

Organizations are made up of human beings with vast prior experience and a wide range of personal needs and interests. Each individual makes personal decisions about how much to invest and risk, based on an analysis of why it is important, how much extra time it will take, whether others will join the effort, and so forth. The Concerns-Based Adoption Model (CBAM) is based on studies of how teachers react to new innovations (Hord, Rutherford, Huling-Austin, & Hall, 1987). One component of the CBAM model identifies a developmental sequence of seven stages of concern through which people move as they accept and adjust to change (Holloway, 2003; see Figure 3.4).

Figure 3.3   Data Awareness Questionnaire

1. _____ % of the students in our school were successful meeting standard on their most recent assessment of reading skill.

2. The aspect of reading that was problematic for the most students was

   _____.

3. _____ % of students in our school successfully met standard on their most recent writing assessment.

4. The most common area(s) of difficulty in writing tasks is/are

   _____.

5. _____ % of students in our school are taking and succeeding with the level of mathematics needed for the next stage in their future.

6. The area of most critical needs for increased achievement in mathematics is _____.

7. _____ % of students in our school enjoy being at school and feel their work is interesting and important.

8. The main subgroups in our student population are _____ and a comparison of their performance would show that _____.

9. To get the answers to these questions, I would

   _____.

10. I have discussions about questions like this with _____ (whom) at _____ (when, where).

Once individuals in the organization become aware of an impending or a developing change, their first concerns revolve around wanting to know more about it and how they will be affected personally. As these questions are answered and they become willing to adopt the new practice, their concerns relate to how they will manage logistics, such as time, materials, and record keeping. When these concerns of self and task are addressed, teachers become more interested in how their use of a new practice is affecting students. More advanced stages of concern relate to sharing their new efforts with colleagues and using their own ideas to modify and improve the new practice. The researchers also developed procedures for assessing the concerns of participants.

Stages of Concern Questionnaire. The Stages of Concern Questionnaire (SoCQ) is a survey instrument that includes 35 items and requires only 10 to 15 minutes to administer. It can be hand or machine scored. The result is a profile that shows the intensity of each concern for that respondent. Average scores for groups can be calculated and reported.

Figure 3.4 Stages of Concern

Tools For Schools February/March 2003

7 Stages of Concern

The Concerns-Based Adoption Model outlines seven Stages of Concern that offer a way to understand and then address educators' common concerns about change.

Stage 0: Awareness
Aware that an innovation is being introduced but not really interested or concerned with it.

- ☐ "I am not concerned about this innovation."
- ☐ "I don't really know what this innovation involves."

Stage 1: Informational
Interested in some information about the change.

- ☐ "I want to know more about this innovation."
- ☐ "There is a lot I don't know about this but I'm reading and asking questions."

Stage 2: Personal
Wants to know the personal impact of the change.

- ☐ "How is this going to affect me?"
- ☐ "I'm concerned about whether I can do this."
- ☐ "How much control will I have over the way I use this?"

Stage 3: Management
Concerned about how the change will be managed in practice.

- ☐ "I seem to be spending all of my time getting materials ready."
- ☐ "I'm concerned that we'll be spending more time in meetings."
- ☐ "Where will I find the time to plan my lessons or take care of the record keeping required to do this well?"

Stage 4: Consequence
Interested in the impact on students or the school.

- ☐ "How is using this going to affect students?"
- ☐ "I'm concerned about whether I can change this in order to ensure that students will learn better as a result of introducing this idea."

Stage 5: Collaboration
Interested in working with colleagues to make the change effective.

- ☐ "I'm concerned about relating what I'm doing to what other instructors are doing."
- ☐ "I want to see more cooperation among teachers as we work with this innovation."

Stage 6: Refocusing
Begins refining the innovation to improve student learning results.

- ☐ "I have some ideas about something that would work even better than this."

One-Legged Interviews. The SoCQ is the most formal method of identifying the concerns felt by participants in a change process. Hord, Rutherford, Huling-Austin, and Hall (1987) describes the use of face-to-face conversations in which the interviewer asks simple questions, such as "How do you feel about using data to make changes in our school?" This may be followed with one or more specific probes. This informal dialogue has been referred to as a *one-legged interview* because it should be so concise that it could be conducted "on one leg" and completed before losing one's balance.

Responding to Concerns

When change leaders gather data about individual and group concerns, they create an expectation that the concerns will be addressed. The credibility of the leader, and the perception of safety ahead, depends on timely, multiple responses aligned with the range of concerns expressed. Many good innovations have fallen by the wayside because a one-size-fits-all implementation plan addressed only a few of the actual concerns of the participants. Figure 3.5 outlines appropriate responses for each stage of concern (Holloway, 2003).

As districts, schools, and individuals tackle the important data work outlined in Chapter 2, a variety of concerns will arise from different sources in a bewildering chronology of times and events. Honoring them as natural and will lead to more successful responses than labeling them as resistance and lack of commitment. There are enough barriers in our way without erecting more built of anger and distrust.

Figure 3.5   Responding to Stages of Concern

Tools For Schools   February/March 2003

Address Individual Concerns

To help bring about change, you first must know an individual's concerns. Then those concerns must be addressed. While there are no set formulas, here are some suggestions for addressing the stages of concern.

Stage 0: Awareness concerns
- ☐ If possible, involve teachers in discussions and decisions about the innovation and its implementation.
- ☐ Share enough information to arouse interest, but not so much it overwhelms.
- ☐ Acknowledge that a lack of awareness is expected and reasonable and that there are no foolish questions.

Stage 1: Informational concerns
- ☐ Provide clear and accurate information about the innovation.
- ☐ Use several ways to share information — verbally, in writing, and through available media. Communicate with large and small groups and individuals.
- ☐ Help teachers see how the innovation relates to their current practices — the similarities and the differences.

Stage 2: Personal concerns
- ☐ Legitimize the existence and expression of personal concerns.
- ☐ Use personal notes and conversations to provide encouragement and reinforce personal adequacy.
- ☐ Connect these teachers with others whose personal concerns have diminished and who will be supportive.

Stage 3: Management concerns
- ☐ Clarify the steps and components of the innovation.
- ☐ Provide answers that address the small specific "how-to" issues.
- ☐ Demonstrate exact and practical solutions to the logistical problems that contribute to these concerns.

Stage 4: Consequence concerns
- ☐ Provide individuals with opportunities to visit other settings where the innovation is in use and to attend conferences on the topic.
- ☐ Make sure these teachers are not overlooked. Give positive feedback and needed support.
- ☐ Find opportunities for these teachers to share their skills with others.

Stage 5: Collaboration concerns
- ☐ Provide opportunities to develop skills for working collaboratively.
- ☐ Bring together, from inside and outside the school, those who are interested in working collaboratively.
- ☐ Use these teachers to assist others.

Stage 6: Refocusing concerns
- ☐ Respect and encourage the interest these individuals have for finding a better way.
- ☐ Help these teachers channel their ideas and energies productively.
- ☐ Help these teachers access the resources they need to refine their ideas and put them into practice.

Hord, S.M., Rutherford, W.L., Huling-Austin, L., & Hall, G.E. (1987). *Taking Charge of Change*. Alexandria, VA: Southwest Educational Development Laboratory.

4

Engaging the People

Publishers create book titles like newspapers create headlines—and the writers may not be quite sure their content is represented accurately. Getting *excited* about data might be a bit of an oversell. I'd actually settle for willing engagement with data as a starting point. The subtitle of this book, on the other hand, is 100% essential and can't be overstated. People, passion, and proof are critical ingredients in the powerful formula needed to increase student achievement.

The first two chapters focused on the third P—*proof*: its role in aligning plans and its presence as a factor in effective and exceptional schools. Chapter 3 began to focus more on *people*: how they feel about data, what they do (or don't do) with data and why, and how to help them get into it, get used to it, and end up valuing it—even if not getting *excited* about it.

The people we're talking about are the full range of interested parties frequently called *stakeholders*. The school improvement process should be open and participatory, involving teachers, administrators, support staff, students, parents, community representatives, and business partners in a variety of ways. For convenience, I use two inclusive terms. The word *staff* refers to all the adults who work in the school, whether they are licensed teachers, aides, clerical support, or administrators. The term *constituents* refers to the interested adult parties outside the school, including parents and community members. *Students* belong in a category by themselves. They are the most intimately involved with and aware of the school's needs and successes—at the same time that they are least integrated into analysis, decision making, and the planning processes.

Internal and External Engagement

Although the entire school improvement process should be participatory and decision making should be shared, teachers must be given special status in the actual gathering and analysis of data. Chapter 3 listed several reasons why this is new, unfamiliar, uncomfortable work. Leaders should be sensitive to these feelings and provide shelter for teachers—not to shield them from the data, but to provide a safe environment for their explorations. All constituents have a right of access to data, but teachers should have first chance to explore, analyze, and prepare to discuss the data with others. Later in this chapter, there are sections that describe roles of the data team, the leadership team, and the staff as a whole.

The need for a safe passage through change is not the only reason to focus on internal engagement. Too many schools and districts operate as though there should be a last, final box on the right hand side of Figure 1.1 called "Buy-in." A small team carries out the process in private, sets the goals, develops the plans, and "delivers" them in final form for the stamp of approval by the rest of the staff. Unfortunately, this approach carries the risk that the stamp will be by feet. That's why my phone may ring, and I hear the frustration that "no one is really doing the strategies we picked," and can I come and help them "get buy-in?"

Educators are not gullible consumers who will buy in to something if you just attach the right incentive or make the right "deal." What we should be seeking is ownership, not as something purchased, but as something grown, crafted, or invented. Ownership must be created along the way through involvement and communication at every step. Many of us are so mobile now that we no longer remember the term or the pride associated with *the family home*. For the past generation, the last payment on the house meant a major celebration of ownership, and friends and neighbors were invited to help "burn the mortgage." But the pride of ownership started with the earnest money that was put down years before as a first step toward purchase. Engagement of the people from the beginning is essential for success in a complex, collaborative endeavor.

Constituents outside the school also need a sense of pride and ownership. A section on Making It Public recurs in various chapters throughout the book to emphasize the importance of that external engagement. That section in Chapter 1 described a way to make the entire school improvement process transparent by displaying the components that are underway. However, direct, ongoing participation by parents and community members is difficult. My own research on implementation following training of school leadership teams verified that participation by community members seems to drop off after the mission is written and goals are set (Holcomb, 1995). The difficulty of maintaining consistent participation is exacerbated by the need to ensure that constituents represent the full range of parents and community members who are part of the school's clientele. As a result, I place less emphasis on representation of constituents through positions on standing committees and rely more on the combination of broad involvement at key decision points and use of *ad hoc* groups to accomplish specific tasks. Standing committees have a limited number of slots available for constituents and demand a long-range commitment. A series of *ad hoc* groups, each with a specific task and a defined time commitment, can provide opportunities for many more participants, can attract those with interest and expertise to apply to just one aspect of the process, and can make it easier to recruit busy people when they know they aren't signing on for life.

The Cultural Problem

One of the barriers to data use identified in Chapter 3 is the tendency to confuse a technical problem with a cultural problem. When we provide a review of statistical terms or have a technology workshop on how to make graphs, we are addressing the limited use of data as a technical problem. When we realize that people don't care about statistical terms or wish to show their graphs to anyone else, we realize that we have a cultural problem known as "give me my students, let me shut the door, and leave me alone until next June."

Many studies refer to the culture of individualization and isolation that is prevalent in our schools. I personally recall my typical day as a classroom teacher: get to the staff room early to make copies before the machine breaks down, runs out of paper, or the line gets too long; hurry to my classroom to make final preparations for the day and write things on the board (first black, then green, then white); meet students at the door, teach the large group and small groups, work with individuals, and keep some in for discipline or extra help at recess and at lunch time and after school; recoup from today and reorganize the classroom for tomorrow; and drag my book bags to the now-empty parking lot—all with no more than a passing nonverbal smile or gesture to another adult the entire day.

The system just wasn't set up for me to interact with my peers, except once a month at a "sit-n-get" faculty meeting. The idea of talking with other teachers about my practice or sharing the work of my struggling students would have been astounding. In fact, only perfect work was ever shared, because those bulletin boards outside the door had to compete with the others all down the hallway. That's how the principal wanted parents to be impressed.

We've come a long way, but we still have not created cultures of collective responsibility for the success of all students. We don't have a culture of collective responsibility for all students if the fourth-grade teachers are the only ones who look at the state test results, and many of them are trying to transfer to third or fifth grade so they won't have to deal with "the year of the test." We don't have a culture of collective responsibility for all students if the high school test results are divided up among department heads—you get the math scores, you get the writing scores, and the rest of you get home free. We don't have a culture of collective responsibility for all students when they complain that "Mr. X doesn't do anything about it" and Mr. X replies, "They're not my kids." Our data work will not result in overall increased student achievement unless it engages all of us and results in a culture of collective responsibility for all students.

Creating the Culture of Collective Responsibility

It was a balmy day in August and California Superintendent John Sugiyama had gathered the administrative team to review the district's priorities for the coming year and plan opening-day activities for staff. The superintendent's charge was to shift attention from adult issues to outcomes accomplished for students. He realized that this would require a transformation of the culture of schools, and stated at this meeting that "the key to changing a culture is to create structures, processes, and activities that cause people to think about different things in different ways with different people than they ordinarily would."

As I made note of his comment for future reference during my work with that administrative team, I realized that he had captured the real purpose of this book. The *processes* he referred to are those that lead to continuous school improvement to increase student achievement. The *structures* include the administrative team, the data team, the leadership team, and the staff as a whole. This book provides a set of *activities* to engage staff in looking at a different thing in different ways with different people. The "different thing" is data. The "different ways" are through planned, structured, facilitated, collaborative conversations that require careful preparation and skilled leadership. The "different people" are colleagues from other grade levels or departments other than those one would encounter in the normal course of things.

Figure 4.1 represents structures that may be in place in many schools but that do not change the culture because they don't engage the right people with the right things or in the right ways; in short, they don't break down the natural barriers built in to the system we call school.

Figure 4.1 represents a school as a large circle, divided into segments like a pie. For an elementary school, these segments are the grade levels. For a high school, they are usually subject area departments. Middle schools may define them in a variety of ways. They are the subdivisions that house people with a common assignment. If collaboration does occur, it is likely to be limited to members of the same segment or slice. Depending on the culture of the school, the walls between these segments may be permeable and could be replaced by dotted lines—or they might have to be more accurately represented by a triple-thick border. The architecture of some high schools erects very solid walls between segments when it places traditional subject area departments in separate wings with their own entrance and exit doors to their own parking areas.

Figure 4.1   Creating a Culture of Collective Responsibility

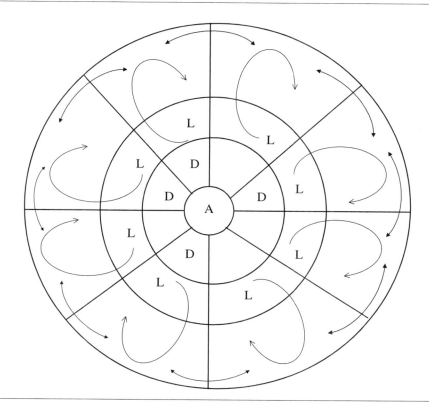

The concentric circles labeled with the letters *A*, *D*, and *L* refer to the administrative team, the leadership team, and the data team, which are explained in the following sections. The looping arrows represent the need for feedback loops, processes by which all members of teams ensure that they are sharing information and gathering input from all of those they represent. The two-way arrows around the perimeter of the circle illustrate the importance of engaging the whole staff in interaction that breaks down or bridges the natural walls of the school configuration.

The Administrative Team

At the center of the school, responsible for the performance of every segment, is the administrative team. At the elementary school, this is typically a single individual—experiencing even more isolation than a regular classroom teacher. At the secondary level, the administrative team may include assistant principals, dean(s) of students or counselors, and perhaps the activities/athletic director. Because the ultimate accountability for the school rests with the administrative team, the school improvement process and development of the achievement plan must be a primary focus for it.

Where there are multiple administrators, decisions about delegating responsibility must be carefully weighed in terms of the unspoken messages they convey. An assistant principal may lead the data team as a component of the work, but the head principal must be closely involved with the overall analysis and plan development. Assignment of the school improvement plan to an administrative intern weakens the impact on the culture. This signals to staff that the school improvement plan is just a short-term project owned by someone less qualified than the ultimate leader of the school.

The Leadership Team

In an era of collaboration and participatory decision making, most schools have a leadership team that works closely with the administrative team. This group should include representation from every segment of the school, as shown in Figure 4.1. Identification of members for this group should be carefully considered and not done using a *pro forma* approach, such as automatically tapping department heads or most senior staff members. A useful approach is to overview the work ahead, using material from Chapter 1 or Chapter 9, and to ask the full staff, "Knowing the tasks, who would you be most comfortable with as your representative?"

The leadership team should be given a different name if the school has had a representative group that dealt primarily with management details (e.g., textbook inventory) or resolving interpersonal conflicts among adults (e.g., whether the most senior teacher automatically gets the corner classroom with the better view). If such a history exists, this new team might be named the *achievement* or *instructional* team to clearly signal that its focus will be on increasing the success of students.

The leadership team does not make the decisions about how to improve the school; the decisions made by the team are about how and when to engage peers, students, and constituents in the decision-making *processes*. Team members prepare, plan, coordinate, orchestrate, and follow up on the work done with the full staff.

Creation of the culture of collective responsibility rests upon the diligence with which members of the leadership team maintain the feedback loops illustrated in Figure 4.1. Whenever the leadership team meets, information must be shared back to all other staff members in the segment that do not attend the meetings. Input should also be gathered for future discussions on ongoing issues still under deliberation. A simple protocol, such as the one illustrated in Figure 4.2, can facilitate this process.

The Data Team

The circle of *D*'s around the administrative team represents the data team. This group should be a subset of the leadership team, or have some members that belong to both groups, in order to communicate closely and inform each other's work. There is no letter *D* in some segments, which illustrates that the data team is a smaller group and may not include a member from every grade or department. There may, in fact, be members

Figure 4.2   Communication Protocol for Leadership Team Feedback Loops

Leadership Team Meeting Date: _____
Your representative: _____

Members Present:

_____
_____
_____
_____
_____
_____
_____
_____
_____

   Goals for this meeting:

   •
   •
   •
   •

I.   Issues Discussed (for each issue, use bullets for main points and asterisk the input you provided from your grade/department).

II.   Decisions Made (list each decision, who will be affected, when it will take effect).

III.   Tasks Accomplished (list project, process, or product completed and how it will be distributed and used).

IV.   Next Steps and Meeting Date:

   •
   •
   •
   •

V.   Input Needed (for each topic, include method for input and deadline).

of the data team who are not members of the leadership team but who possess the skills and interests needed.

The leadership team and data team work in tandem. For example, the leadership team (which includes the administrators) considers the data to be gathered; the data team determines *how* to collect it; delegates or distributes the collection tasks; and compiles the data.

The leadership team identifies data most significant for all staff to discuss; the data team prepares the graphics, materials, and so forth. Then the leadership team facilitates the group activities.

Members of the data team should be individuals who *do* get excited about data and are comfortable working with it. They may be the individuals characterized in Chapter 3 as the "data dudes" or "data divas." They may not have time or interest in the full set of responsibilities of the leadership team, but they can help identify, prepare, and interpret data in preparation for consideration by the leadership team or for sharing with the whole staff. They should, of course, be assessment literate as defined in Chapter 3, with particular expertise in determining whether data is dependable, making sense of it, and being able to display and discuss it. In addition to these technical skills, the members of the data team should also be individuals who have established strong relationships of trust with other staff members. If the school is in data overload, this team will help sort out the most significant data elements for first review, which gives them power to portray a picture that highlights their personal interests and issues. They must have the respect of staff and the reputation for being totally objective.

Shared as a Whole

The Concerns-Based Adoption Model (CBAM) was introduced in Chapter 3. The earliest stages of concern are awareness and information. Staff members have varying levels of interest and opportunity to be actively involved in the data work and achievement planning of the school, but all must be aware and fully informed. For example, every staff member should be able to answer the questions on the Data Awareness Questionnaire in Chapter 3. Conversations that occur in later chapters—such as examination of best practice and current practice in the school—need to be facilitated by the leadership team in ways that cross the grade-level or department segments of the school. An example is the Carousel Data Analysis discussed in Chapter 8.

The entire staff should also be involved in considerations of major changes in programs, practice, or structures that are part of selecting strategies to increase student achievement. A review of the differences between School A and School B in Chapter 1 makes this clear. This book recommends full engagement of all staff at these crucial points:

1. Developing and affirming the school's mission

2. Identifying significant, meaningful data to be compiled for the school portfolio

3. Interpreting the data, requesting more data, and identifying areas of concern

4. Focusing areas of concern to a few priorities and developing goals

5. Participating in study groups to further analyze data in priority areas and recommend validated strategies

6. Affirming the completed achievement plan

7. Participating in staff development to learn the use of new strategies and assessments

8. Discussing evidence of progress with implementation and impact on student achievement

Finding Time

One of the barriers to data use identified in Chapter 3 was lack of time, and the initial recommendation for coping with that barrier was to reexamine all existing available time and how it is used. New time almost always entails new money, a topic further explored in Chapter 14. The first step is to maximize the available resources, including staff meeting time and professional development opportunities. This book provides activities that range in time from 20 minutes to 2 hours. The short activities can be embedded in staff meetings, especially if there is a commitment to devote those meetings to productive professional development activities rather than announcements and housekeeping matters. One principal transformed staff meetings and increased use of new technology by transferring all "information dissemination" to the e-mail network and using meeting time entirely for adult learning.

Longer activities (such as those related to numbers 2–5 and 7 above) require provision of time through early release afternoons, late-start mornings, or inservice days built into the school calendar. One such window of opportunity per month is ideal, but staff engagement can occur successfully with one per quarter.

The leadership team needs to meet once a month to coordinate the professional development activities that result in decisions about student achievement. The most frequent practice has been to provide substitute teachers so this team can meet during school hours. In some cases, the scarcity of substitutes and the staff members' preference to be in class with their students has led to a different format. In these cases, leadership teams meet for two to three hours outside the school day and are compensated accordingly. Some schools have been creative in their scheduling, so that planning times of team members are coordinated and meetings can be held during the last hour of the day—partly on school time and partly as additional commitment.

Some members of the data team, or a key staff member who co-chairs the leadership team with the principal, may need additional time for such hands-on tasks as preparing data displays. In some schools, this key individual is provided additional time by having one less teaching preparation (secondary) or being relieved of supervisory duties (elementary lunchroom, recess, etc.). Creative scheduling can also make it possible for members of the data team to have a common planning period. The collective bargaining agreement in some districts provides for a stated number of hours for individually directed professional development. This makes it possible for team members to "pay themselves" by identifying their work with the data team or leadership team as their individual professional development—and it certainly qualifies as a learning opportunity!

Making It Public

Although constituents do not have a major hands-on role with the data work and development of the achievement plan, they do need to be regularly informed and to have an opportunity for input and reaction at the same key points listed above for all staff. In addition to the data team, some schools develop a Communication Cadre as a subset of the full leadership team. One of their roles is to communicate effectively with community members about assessment results and their implications for instruction.

If communication is a two-way street, then communicating about *data* is like a traffic pattern of multiple streets, some of which are two-way, some one-way, and some limited to specific kinds of vehicles or special purposes, such as car pools. Plans for communicating information about student performance must identify multiple audiences, the specific purpose for communication with each audience, and then the appropriate communicators and channels for each audience and purpose. Audiences for communication about data include the media; community groups, such as employers and taxpayers' organizations; teachers; students; and parents. The question of who is the appropriate communicator relates to credibility and trust of the audience. Another issue is the vocabulary and background knowledge of each audience. Communication decisions are further complicated by privacy issues related to confidentiality of student information. A focus on two simple principles can increase our effectiveness in this complex set of communications. Our closest constituents want to believe us, and we are miles ahead if we keep it short and simple.

Credibility Begins at Home

I wish I had a dollar for every hour that I used to spend trying to help people understand national and international comparisons and find ways to explain to their communities why it's like comparing apples and oranges to compare U.S. test scores with Japan's. We worked hard to summarize the technical concepts in everyday English, but it still sounded like a lot of defensive rationalization—and I discovered that most of the folks at home aren't all that worried about international comparisons. It matters a lot to journalists and politicians, but talk to everyday people at the local cafe where breakfast is $3.50 and the regulars have their own tables, and you'll discover they really aren't losing sleep over it. All they really want to know is that *their* kids are doing okay.

It was these essential ordinary people who pointed that out to me, but I should have known it already. I've been reading the Phi Delta Kappa (PDK)/Gallup poll of the Public's Attitudes Toward the Public Schools for at least 18 of its 35 annual iterations. It was only this past fall, as school districts struggled with the question, "How will we explain that our students look good on national percentiles but not so good on state proficiencies?" that the real implication of one of these findings hit home.

The pollsters repeatedly ask what grade (A, B, C, D, or F) the respondents, in a carefully structured sample of Americans, would give to public schools in the nation as a whole, what grade they would give to their local public schools, and what grade they would give to the public school their oldest child attends. The pattern varies only a little from year to year. For example, in the most recent poll, only 26% gave A's and B's to the U.S. national system, 48% gave A's and B's to their local schools, and 68% gave A's and B's to the school their own child was attending (Rose & Gallup, 2003). The public in general—and parents in particular—already have more faith in their local schools than in the national system of public education. This being the case, local school districts would be better off to save the time, energy, and resources they've invested in trying to respond to national and international statistics. The same time, energy, and resources would be better invested in communication that builds on an existing foundation of trust in local schools by local people.

That's why this book emphasizes the use of school-specific data and the involvement of parents and public at the individual school level. Strengthen existing relationships and develop key people as advocates and opinion leaders. Credibility begins at home.

The K-I-S-S Principle

Local communication does best when we work to *keep it short and simple*—the K-I-S-S principle. I remember watching for the signs of puberty and gathering pamphlets on how to communicate sensitive information to preadolescents. The advice I received seems so relevant to data communication:

- Anticipate what the questions might be.
- Be prepared with short, simple answers.
- Be as knowledgeable as possible, but don't try to share everything you know.
- Answer the questions they ask, but only the questions they ask.
- Keep the door open for more questions and more details as they become more comfortable and curious.

When the new state assessment was introduced in Wisconsin, several organizations worked on projects to help districts communicate with their constituents. At one extreme, the Department of Public Instruction prepared a 16-page "guidette." It didn't model the K-I-S-S principle of short and simple, and it didn't get used.

On the other hand, the Wisconsin Education Association Council (WEAC) worked with the state Parent Teacher Association (PTA) and developed a single-fold, four-page brochure for parents called *Understanding the New Proficiency Scores* (1997). District administrators and curriculum directors referred to the first two pages (seen in Figure 4.3) as the best resource they had, and this publication was the one that proved useful with constituents. One of our downfalls as educators is that we try to share all that we know instead of figuring out how much our constituents actually want to know, and then answering their questions. Like the title of this chapter, the key to the WEAC's successful publication was *engaging the people*. They asked the PTA what parents would want to know and answered those questions.

Figure 4.3   Understanding the New Proficiency Scores

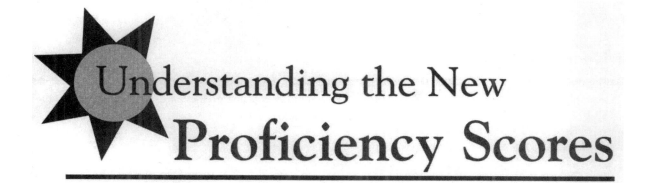

Understanding the New
Proficiency Scores

Parents learn how their children are doing in school in many ways, including teacher conferences, report cards, and graded student work that is brought home.

There is an additional source of valuable information – the scores your child receives on the standardized achievement tests administered each year by the Wisconsin Department of Public Instruction to 4th, 8th, and 10th grade students throughout the state. These tests are called the Wisconsin Student Assessment System Knowledge & Concepts Examinations. As you review the results, keep in mind that test scores are only one indicator of the knowledge and skills possessed by a student, or group of students. Testing experts warn against giving too much weight to the results of a single test because tests measure only a sample of what is taught in school.

The Department of Public Instruction reports student achievement in five content areas: Reading, Mathematics, Science, Social Studies, and Enhanced Language. The scores a student receives in Reading, Mathematics, Science, and Social Studies are based on answers to mostly multiple choice questions, with a few short answer questions. The Enhanced Language score is based on answers to multiple choice questions, short answer questions and the score received on a writing task (an "informative" composition in grades 4 and 8 and a "persuasive" essay in grade 10).

The state tests are called standardized achievement tests because everything, from the directions given to the time allowed to take the tests to scoring and reporting, is made uniform, or "standardized." These procedures ensure scores are as fair and reliable as possible.

What's new this year?

This year, for the first time, two kinds of scores are reported for your child. Norm-referenced scores (such as percentiles) compare your child with students throughout the country. These types of scores have been used in the past.

In addition to norm-referenced scores, this year, proficiency scores also are reported. Achievement for each child is reported in terms of four proficiency categories, or levels. These levels are Advanced, Proficient, Basic, and Minimal Performance.

(Continued)

Figure 4.3 (Continued)

What is a norm-referenced score?

Norm-referenced scores answer the question, "How does my child compare with others?" For example, if your child scored at the 63rd percentile in mathematics, he or she did better than 63% of the students in the comparison group (the national sample) who are in the same grade and who were tested at the same time of year.

What is a proficiency score?

A proficiency score answers the question, "How does the achievement of my child on this test compare with established high expectations for academic success?" A driver's test is an example of a test with two proficiency levels: pass or fail. Whether you pass or fail the test does not depend on how well others drive, but whether you achieve an acceptable level as determined by the driving examiner.

Students receiving a score of Advanced did exceptionally well by showing in-depth understanding of the content area. Likewise, Proficient represents a competent level of achievement. Students who score at the Basic level are achieving at a fairly solid level, although they have some weaknesses that should be addressed. Basic does not mean that your child is failing in the content area.

Children receiving Minimal Performance scores have limited achievement in the content area.

If you are concerned about the achievement of your child in any content area, you should meet with your child's teacher to determine what you as a parent, along with the teacher, can do to help your child do better in school.

The proficiency standards were established in 1997 by parents, educators, and people from business and government at workshops conducted by the Department of Public Instruction.

Why are proficiency scores included in the reports?

Proficiency standards have been established to set high expectations for all students. Comparative (norm-referenced) scores show that Wisconsin's students do better than students throughout the country on nearly all tests. However, a proficiency score judges performance in terms of high academic standards set by people in Wisconsin.

Reprinted With Permission From Templeton Middle School, Sussex, WI.

5

Arousing the Passion

Public demands for accountability are motivating increased awareness of the need to provide evidence of a school's effectiveness. School boards are requiring schools to demonstrate how they use data to guide decision making and plan their improvement efforts. Even accreditation requirements are moving from an input model of verifying factors like adequate resources and qualified staff to an output model focused on evidence of student success. Reauthorization of federal funds has emphasized the need to use proven programs and approaches and to document improvements in student achievement. Public school choice is a reality in an increasing number of states, and some states are already funneling tax funds into vouchers for students to attend private schools. Public education is a service industry that must be user friendly or lose its market share to vouchers, private schools, and for-profit enterprises.

These factors create an undeniable need for schools and districts to demonstrate the results they achieve for their students and constituents. They also represent an increased level of outside threat to educators. Mandates and competition don't kindle enough enthusiasm and energy to learn the new skills needed for these unfamiliar tasks and to complete the extra work. A more personal meaning must be created to motivate complicated work with data and to address complex problems of student achievement. The activities in this chapter have been successfully used to help people generate the passion needed to produce the proof.

The Motivation Continuum

Educators are familiar with the terminology of *intrinsic* (or internal) motivation and *extrinsic* (or external) motivation. Most would agree that

Figure 5.1   The Motivation Continuum

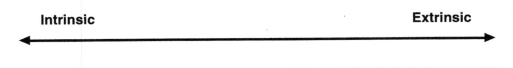

intrinsic motivation is the more powerful force for change. The Motivation Continuum activity allows participants to choose factors that create meaning and motivation for each of them as individuals. There are two versions of this activity that can be further adapted depending on the group.

The Reflective Continuum

The first version of the Motivation Continuum activity is best suited for occasions when the audience can work in small groups and is open to reflection and serious discussion with peers. It takes about 15 to 20 minutes to complete. Each group of three to five participants needs a blank form like that presented in Figure 5.1. This form may be produced on 8½" × 11" paper for each participant, or each group can use large chart paper and markers to create a joint product. A supply of stick-on notes may also come in handy.

First, ask individual participants to think about the question, "Why is it important to be able to produce evidence of what the school achieves for its students?" If they are using individual worksheets, they may write directly on them. Or, each participant can have a supply of stick-on notes and write one of the factors he or she identifies on each note.

After generating reasons why the use of data is increasingly important, have participants arrange the factors they identified along their own worksheet or on the large chart. They should discuss the degree to which each factor is driven by outside forces or arises from internally perceived needs and desires. Figure 5.2 shows the factors identified by a group in a recent workshop.

After time has been allowed for discussion, ask participants whether any of these factors seem inappropriate or unfair. Acknowledge that it's perfectly all right to feel this way, and tell them to cross out the reasons that feel *demotivating* to them as individuals. Participants then circle or star the factors on their own continuum that they find most meaningful. These are the sources that will provide motivation for their ongoing exploration of data.

Conclude the activity by asking each participant to make a one-sentence response to a prompt, such as, "I can be motivated to work with our data if I remember that. . . ." These statements are the first level of commitment to get engaged with data.

Figure 5.2   The Motivation Continuum: A Completed Example

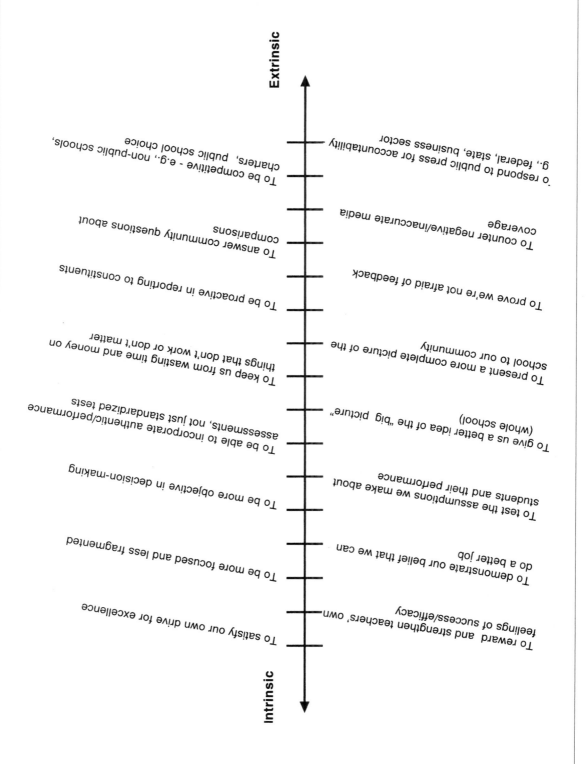

The "Live" Continuum

To be successful with the first version of the Motivation Continuum, the facilitator needs to be confident of the group's willingness to be reflective. Sometimes the facilitator is not that familiar with the group or the group is simply too large for that approach. The "live" Motivation Continuum is a variation that takes about 20 minutes and has been used successfully with as many as 200 teachers in an auditorium setting. It even worked with a group of 85 high school teachers on the Friday afternoon before Christmas vacation!

Instead of having participants work in small groups to generate the reasons to get engaged with data, this variation starts with factors previously identified in other groups, such as those in Figure 5.2. In preparation, print these factors in bold colors on strips of chart paper. Also prepare two signs, one saying *Extrinsic* and one saying *Intrinsic*.

Tell the audience that you have been working with teachers in other schools and have brought their ideas about using data to get this group's reaction. Describe this as an audience participation game show, where audience members will need to be active, loud, and demanding in order to succeed.

Recruit two volunteers to hold the *Extrinsic* and *Intrinsic* signs and ask them to stand at opposite ends of the front of the room. Briefly review the two terms as they relate to motivation, and then identify participants to hold the strips of paper on which you printed the factors from Figure 5.2. The responsibility of the audience is to scream, yell, and gesture at their colleagues to tell them where to stand so the factors they represent are in order across the room based on their extrinsic or intrinsic value.

Most audiences relish the rare permission to be rowdy at an inservice and participate readily in the true spirit of *The Price Is Right*. If people hesitate, humor them with comments like, "Isn't there someone up there you always wanted to tell where to go? Now's your chance." Or goad them a little with, "Don't tell me you just want to 'sit-n-get'?!"

After the audience members have arranged their colleagues along the live continuum, use another old game show adaptation called the Applause-o-Meter. At least a few in the group will remember winners being chosen by the length and volume of the applause. Tell the audience that it will now rate the motivational power of these factors. Participants can be silent or boo and hiss at factors they reject, and clap and whistle for those they accept as meaningful reasons to get more engaged with data. As you move along the continuum, have the people representing factors that are validated step forward.

Conclude by briefly commenting on the importance of each of the factors the group validated as meaningful. Ask the group members to get a mental picture of their colleagues holding these words and remember that these are the real reasons they will be working more with data in the days to come. On one district's Data Day (see Chapter 9), photos were taken for a district publication, and the "lineup" of reasons to use data became a matter of record for future reference during school improvement activities.

Please, Don't Skip to the List

Every time I have used this activity with a group, someone has requested a copy of the list of factors to take home and distribute. Distributing the list—or displaying it on a transparency—is not a successful variation of the Motivation Continuum. Intrinsic motivation must be nurtured. It can't be delivered on a handout.

Swapping Stories

Among the items in Figure 5.2 are "to present a more complete picture of the school to our community" and "to give us a better idea of the 'big picture' of the whole school." Another phrasing would be "so we can tell our own story."

These activities help build motivation by providing examples of the kind of stories most schools would like to report. Gather examples from case studies and books you have read that describe school improvement efforts with documented results. One excellent source is Mike Schmoker's book *Results: The Key to Continuous Improvement* (1996), in which he reports many success stories, such as the following examples:

The bright side of collegiality can be found at Northview Elementary School in Manhattan, Kansas. Students realized huge gains . . . when teachers began to collaborate. In reading, fourth and sixth grade scores on district achievement tests rose from 59 to 100 percent, and from 41 to 97 percent, respectively. In math, fourth grade scores rose from 70 to 100 percent; sixth grade scores, from 31 to 97 percent. How? Principal Dan Yunk began to arrange for teams of teachers to meet routinely to analyze scores, identify strengths and weaknesses, and develop ways to effectively address them (pp. 14–15)

At Adlai E. Stevenson High School in Lincolnshire, Illinois, teacher teams meet once a month to collaborate, and analyze results at least four times a year. . . . Before the process was introduced, the school did not rank at all in the top 50 schools in the 13-state Midwest region. . . . When goals were established and collaborative time was instituted, the school ranked first in the region, and . . . it was among the top 20 schools in the world. . . . Last year, the school established new records in every traditional indicator of student achievement, including grade distributions, failure rates, average ACT scores, average SAT scores, percentage of honor grades on Advanced Placement examinations, and average scores in each of the five areas of the state achievement tests. (pp. 15–16)

A middle school in Richmond County, Georgia, had instituted measures to help at-risk students: lower class size, special programs, and counseling. Nothing happened. It was not until teachers began to meet in study groups to help each other implement more effective teaching strategies that results came. In one year, the average student went from making 6 months' progress to making 10 months' progress. The promotion rate increased from 30 to 70 percent. The following year, it increased again—to 95 percent. (p. 21)

Prepare several of these excerpts in a large font on separate sheets of paper. Identify "news reporters" to read these success stories and—if your room setup allows—have them sit on stools behind a table or podium to give the impression of a news broadcast. One way to follow each story is to ask the audience, "What role did data play in being able to report this news?" Other questions may be

- "Would you like to be able to report this news about your school?"
- "What were the key factors that made these gains possible?"
- "How would it sound if the story were of your school?" Have the reporters read the story again, substituting the name of their school in the text.
- "What success story do you want to be able to tell about your school?" Ask each participant do a Quick-Write (Holcomb, 2001, pp. 117–118) of three to five sentences, but call it a sound bite they wish they'd hear on their local station. A few of these can be read aloud to the group. These "desired stories" can also be saved for future use. A collage of them can be created on a bulletin board in the teachers' lounge. They can serve as starting points if the school has work to do on its mission. One or two of them can be read as warm-ups at each faculty meeting or work session that involves data and school improvement.

Language, Humor, and Music

Application of the brain research to our instructional approaches is increasing and making us more effective with students (Sylwester, 1995). The power of the limbic system to override both rational thought and basic bodily functions is awesome. As the emotional center of our brain, the limbic system relays stimuli to the neocortex, where reasoning and planning take place. Because the limbic system influences what we pay attention to, consider important, and remember, we must ease anxiety and reduce stress when we challenge people to get engaged with data. Facilitators of cultural change need to be skillful users of language, stories, humor, and music as ways to soothe anxiety and encourage risk taking. The next three activities are designed to achieve that goal.

Matching Our Language

Many years ago, in what seems another lifetime in another world, I taught first graders. One of the ways we learned to use language was by making individual word booklets that were called *My Own Dictionary*. That's probably where I got the idea that groups who work together need *Our Own Thesaurus*.

To communicate and reduce conflict, we need to agree on what we will call the things that we do. We have often helped create our own Frankenstein monster in the form of the "last year's new thing—this year's new thing—next year's new thing" phenomenon. We bring in an additional component to strengthen an existing process, but we also transport a whole set of terms for it that make it sound like something entirely foreign. Then our colleagues wonder what happened to the other model, because it had its own separate language. *Our Own Thesaurus* can be used at the beginning of a new program or process to help everyone acquire a common vocabulary and create a consistency of language that provides continuity and reduces miscommunication.

In preparation, list terms that are part of the new approach on a flip chart, leaving plenty of space between them. The first step is to go through the list with the group, asking participants to name as many adjectives as they can for each term. Repeat each word and record it. It's helpful to ask someone else to serve as recorder, so you can observe nonverbal signals during this part of the process. You will note some interesting reactions to words that some people assume mean the same thing and other participants don't think are the same thing at all.

After the thesaurus has been generated, go back through each term and ask the group to discuss language that has been used in the past. Encourage participants to focus also on the connotations that have become attached to certain words. Sometimes people will realize they've thought they disagreed for years when they simply had different definitions for terms they were both using.

Complete the activity by asking group members to select those terms that sound familiar and have positive connotations in their setting and agree to use them consistently. Figure 5.3 shows the product of this activity when the group was blending the vocabulary of its strategic planning process with the terminology of accreditation by the North Central Association of Colleges and Schools. The result was agreement on a single term for each of five components, with an intentional decision to use *many* words for assessment so participants would expand their horizons beyond the automatic association with "tests." Some words were crossed out; they had appeared in more than one place and the group decided to avoid them because they could cause confusion.

The Magic of Metaphor

At the start of workshops that relate to data or work on the school portfolio, I ask people to introduce themselves with the usual name, position, and school, and then to complete this sentence:

When I think about data and graphs, I feel (like a/an) _____ because _____.

Figure 5.3   Our Own Thesaurus

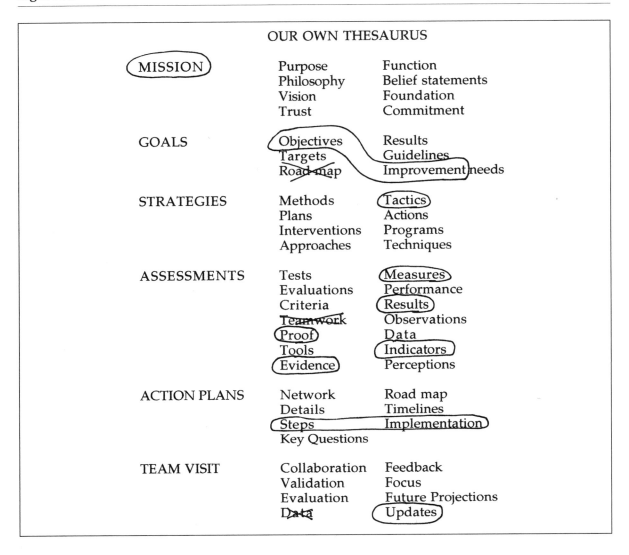

Here is a sample of typical responses:

- "I feel helpless because what we have is not very good."
- "I feel excited because this will strengthen what we have."
- "I feel like an owl because I'm wondering 'who-who-who' is gonna do this."
- "I feel like I'm in a stats course and wonder if I'm supposed to make the numbers lie for our benefit."
- "I feel like a computer because this will be dehumanizing people."
- "I feel like I'm in the wrong room because I noticed the accountants are meeting next door."
- "I feel like I'm on *The Price Is Right* because something's hidden behind every door."
- "I feel like a deer in the headlights because I don't know which way to run."

- "I feel like I'm at the edge of a minefield with a long stick because there's so much negative reaction and doesn't seem to be much appreciation of what we do well and how hard we work."
- "I feel like a professional because I can finally use the math skills I teach to help my whole school."
- "I finally feel like I belong because I hate touchy-feely workshops and it looks like we're going to do real work here."

During the introductions, capture some of these on the flip chart. If the room setup allows, it's even more effective to jot some of them down on a notepad as you walk around the room. This allows you to observe non-verbal signals and chuckle to yourself at the shocked looks on many faces when someone says he or she *likes* working with data.

After the introductions, respond to some of these sentences. For example, you can reassure the "data-phobics" that we will be doing nothing more complicated than counting, figuring percentages, and simple graphing so if they have fifth-grade math skills, they will be fine. You will also have a chance to diagnose the levels of readiness of the group and adjust accordingly throughout the day. Because participants usually attend as members of a team from a school, I also use this activity to check the composition of the group. If there is just one excited person at each table, I can be fairly sure the day will go smoothly. When all the members of a team express anxiety, I ask them if they know someone back at their school who would probably answer the prompt with enthusiasm. Usually they do, and I suggest that they recruit that person to help with this part of their school improvement process.

Cheers and Jeers

Cheers and Jeers is an activity that provides an opportunity to use music and humor to relax and release tension. Ask participants to work in groups of three or four or as table groups, depending on the room setup. Their job is to create a cheer or jeer (depending on how they feel about using data). These can be performed all at once, or you can call on one table at a time throughout a full-day workshop when the group needs an energizer. People will actually work through breaks and lunch on their cheer or jeer, which raises the level of energy throughout the room. Here are some cheers and jeers I've enjoyed!

As a rap, while snapping fingers:

Data, data, data

Things were gettin' badda.

Data, data, data

Told us whatza matta.

Data, data, data

Now it's goin' up the ladda.

As a cheer, with motions:

Data, data, data's

Just yadda, yadda, yadda [thumbs to fingers like lips flapping]

Be a clown! [any funny pose]

Turn it around! [twirl]

Engage them all! [point around room]

Have a ball! [arms form circle above head]

As a song, to the tune of *Row, Row, Row Your Boat*:

C'lect, count, graph your data

So you'll know your school.

If you don't have proof to show

You'll look like a fool.

Monitoring Our Mission

The Motivation Continuum engaged people to identify intrinsic reasons why they would engage in work with data. Organizations often use the more formal process of writing a mission statement for the same purpose. So when I ask a group, "How many of your schools have a mission statement?" almost all of the hands go up. But when I ask, "Who will tell us what your mission statement says?" no hands go up and eyes drop to the table. When I follow up with, "If you don't know what it says, how do you know you have one?" the answers are usually,

"We did one in an inservice once."

"The Board went on a retreat and did one for the district."

"It's on the bottom of our letterhead."

Saying we have a mission statement but don't know what it says is like trying to convince the highway patrol that I'm a good, careful, safe driver—but just don't exactly know what the speed limit is.

If so many mission statements are lying around on letterheads without making a difference, why devote this section to it? Because a mission statement is one of the ways we can articulate the common core values of an organization, and it has the *potential* to make a radical difference. In his study *Peak Performers* (1987), Charles Garfield noted the passion that some individuals have for their endeavor. He described their sense of mission as "an image of a desired state of affairs that inspires action, determines behavior, and fuels motivation." That's how you know if your school really has a mission statement: Does it inspire action? Does it determine behavior? Does it fuel motivation?

In *Asking the Right Questions* (Holcomb, 2001), I described an affinity process for developing a mission statement that has been used by schools that don't have one or believe they need to try again. In Chapter 1 of this book, I pointed out the need for alignment between our mission statement and our school portfolio—what we say we're all about and the evidence of what we really do. Colloquially, it's expressed as "putting our money where our mouth is."

The activities in this chapter are meant to engage people's passion so we'll want to deliver the proof. I believe that almost all teachers chose their careers based on a sense of mission. I also believe that at least an ember of that passion still smolders somewhere deep inside even the most burned-out veteran in the profession. I've discovered, somewhat to my surprise, that getting engaged with data can help rekindle that passion. Here's one way.

Some mission statements just float out there with nothing to grab on to. Some data just sit and stagnate because they don't seem to connect with anything meaningful. The simple form in Figure 5.4 can help people make those connections. Before using the Monitoring Our Mission activity, verify that the school has a mission statement and have it ready on a transparency. If you are working with a group of people from various schools, have a sample mission statement (see below) that participants can use for practice if they don't have one or can't remember it.

Ask the participants how many of them know they have a mission statement for their school or district.[1] Give them a few minutes to find it in something they brought or work together to write it down as accurately as they can recall it. Offer the example you brought for practice or show them the transparency of their own mission statement as an "answer key" to see how well they did.

Next, call attention to the first column of Figure 5.4. Our mission is what we say we will do as a school. It's a set of commitments. Ask the participants to look at their mission statement and circle the words or phrases that represent key components or commitments. Here's an example:

The mission of Our Town School is to provide a safe, orderly environment where students master their academic skills and become productive citizens and lifelong learners.

The key components of this mission statement are

- Safe, orderly environment
- Mastery of academic skills
- Productive citizens
- Lifelong learners

Have the participants write these words or phrases in the boxes in the first column, because they are **What We Say** we will do.

Figure 5.4   Monitoring Our Mission

What We Say	Evidence We Have	Evidence We Need

Next, tell them you assume that considerable time and energy probably went into development of this mission statement and that there was strong support that their school should accomplish these things. If so, we need to provide evidence that the mission is being fulfilled.

The second column is titled *Evidence We Have*. The task now is to consider the types of data already available somewhere in the district and school that are relevant to that aspect of the mission. When I first began using this activity, I left it at that and was quite surprised at how stuck some groups would be. The lack of awareness of data that are regularly collected and probably communicated annually to all patrons is alarming. Now, I keep a list of available data handy on a transparency and almost always discover it's needed to help groups get started. (See Chapter 6 for ideas.)

As the participants identify indicators for the components of the mission statement, there will be comments like, "We should be keeping track of that" or "We don't have any way of knowing" or "That can't be measured." These ideas go in the third column, where participants record types of data that will be needed. For example, many classroom teachers keep track of student behaviors that are related to employability skills—for example, tardiness, materials ready to work, and homework completion. This data may never have aggregated compiled on a schoolwide basis, but it could be. We'll discuss the values that can't be measured later in this chapter.

After the groups have worked a while, ask them to take a look at the *Evidence We Have* column, and put a letter S by the items they've listed there that are student results and an A by those that are adult activities. The significance of the coding is to remind us that the evidence we need to produce is that something more or better is occurring for children. Traditionally, we have reported such things as "We have DARE and peer mediation and conflict resolution" as evidence that we provide a safe, orderly environment. They are *programs* we offer—which is not the same as *results* we achieve. If the participants have listed types of data that are all adult activities, programs, and practices, encourage them to be sure that the *Evidence We Need* column will eventually provide indicators of results for students.

The completed products fulfill several purposes. First, the process of filling out this form reconnects people to their mission statement. Sometimes it makes them decide to revise their mission or start over completely. Second, connections are made between the passion and the proof—what we believe is important to do and how we will know we're doing it. Third, the *Evidence We Have* column is the directory of items to include in the initial baseline version of the school portfolio (see Chapter 6). These types of data meet the criteria of being available and being of importance to the school. Fourth, the *Evidence We Need* column generates awareness of information that should be added as the school portfolio is continually updated.

Including the Unmeasurables

Sometimes, people tell me that they've been told not to put anything in a mission statement or school improvement goal that isn't measurable. So, they shy away from things like character education and creativity. In the example above, "productive citizen" and "lifelong learning" might be considered unmeasurable if we think only of paper-and-pencil tests and numerical scores. But there *is* much more to what we accomplish as a school than just content and skills, and sometimes those are the things that inspire us most. If they arouse our passion, we should keep them in the language of our mission and goals. We just need to stretch our vocabulary from *measurable* to *observable*. Here's one way to approach a seeming unmeasurable.

Challenge the participants to reflect silently and identify a person they know and regard as a lifelong learner. Ask them to jot down the things they see that person do or hear that person say that add up to their impression that this person is a lifelong learner. Then, record a general list from the group. Prompt as needed to be sure the factors are all observable. For example, "He's a risk taker" needs the clarification of "What do you *see* him do that you call taking risks?" A typical list includes items like the following:

- Gets interested in something and wants to know more
- Goes to the library to gets books and gets on the Internet
- Reads a lot
- Shares new ideas and knowledge
- Tries to get other people interested
- Takes courses and workshops that aren't required
- Likes to figure out his or her own way to do things
- Sets goals for him- or herself

These are indicators of lifelong learning in an adult. We work with children to develop these characteristics. Now, ask participants to link up with two or three others who teach (or parent) students of about the same age. Their task is to take this list and discuss, "What does each of these behaviors look like at age 17? At age 11? At age 7?"

Two observations usually emerge when groups report out. One is the conclusion that most of those behaviors look pretty much the same at any age and could be observed in the school setting. The second is a realization that many of the school's own practices limit the opportunity to observe these characteristics and may thus be inhibiting rather than nurturing their development.

Figure 5.5 provides an example of the Monitoring Our Mission activity completed for both the measurable academic skills and the observable characteristics of citizenship and lifelong learning.

Mission in Action, or Missing in Action?

There is power in language. If there weren't, we would be unmoved by Lincoln's Gettysburg Address or Martin Luther King, Jr.'s "I Have a Dream" speech. There is also power in the process of collectively articulating what is important, what is nonnegotiable, what is essential to our professional spirit. There is even greater power when the result of that collaborative product is actually used in daily life.

Just as we need people who are by nature "number crunchers" to play a vital role in our work with data, we need people who are by nature "cheerleaders" and "zealots" to keep our mission alive. Conscious planning should go into ways of referencing the mission frequently during faculty meetings and other events. Here are a few ideas I've learned from school "mission"-aries:

- When new staff members are hired, be sure that a presentation on the mission of the school is part of their orientation.
- When a tough decision is being made, ask the staff to complete such statements as, "This fits our mission because . . ." or "This does not fit our mission because . . ."
- Keep a Mission Box (a version of a Suggestion Box) in the office. Students, teachers, and parents can drop notes in it to report actions they have seen that exemplify the mission. Some of these can be read with the announcements or shared in newsletters.

Figure 5.5   Monitoring Our Mission: A Completed Example

What We Say	Evidence We Have	Evidence We Need
Safe, orderly environment	• Discipline referrals • Expulsion/suspensions • Vandalism	
Mastery of academic skills	• Scores on state assessments • Percentage of students passing district criterion-referenced tests • Degrees of Reading Power test • ACT scores	• Desktop access to individual student records of mastery • Performance assessments (portfolios, exhibitions)
Productive citizens	• Attendance/truancy • Tardiness • Homework completion • Percentage of students in leadership roles (clubs, council, peer mediators, etc.) • Number participating in co-op work experiences • Graduation/dropout rate	• Participation in community service activities (church, Scouts, food drives, etc.)
Lifelong learners	• Number and quality of independent projects completed • Co-/extracurricular participation • ACT participation • Feedback from local business partners	• Interview mature adults in community about what contributed to their lifelong learning habits • Survey students about learning opportunities they pursue outside of school (piano, etc.)

- Short scenarios of problem situations can be presented to the staff. Ask small groups to prepare or role-play responses that are consistent with the mission statement.
- Have elementary students learn the vocabulary of the mission statement and draw what they think it means.
- Have students of all ages identify what their roles are in contributing to the mission of the school.

Figure 1.1 showed *Mission* in the upper left-hand corner, illustrating that our use of data and our focus on student achievement must come first and foremost from the core values that drive us personally and bring us together professionally. However, the statement and sense of mission in the school remains under construction. Imagine a dotted arrow on Figure 1.1 going around the entire figure, and from each component back to *Mission*. As we learn more about our students, we reexamine our beliefs. As we engage in deep reflection about our practices, we clarify our understanding and expectations of ourselves. Moreover, as we courageously assess the results of our common efforts, we build the culture of collective responsibility for the success of all students. As Fullan and Hargreaves (1991) reminded us, "In collaborative cultures, the examination of values and purposes is not a one-time event . . . but a continuous process that pervades the whole school."

Note

1. The question of relationship between district mission statements and school mission statements arises occasionally. In my experience, district mission statements tend to include more components that address resources, facilities, and long-range planning, whereas school mission statements are more focused on teaching, learning, and the school environment or climate. If there is a district mission statement that was generated with lots of involvement and seems well accepted at the building level, it may work as the school mission statement as well. If the district administration or board is adamant that there be only one mission for every school in the district, the lack of "home ownership" would concern me, but there's no point in a school going through the time and effort to develop a mission statement if it won't be honored by the district and can't be used to guide decision making. If the district mission is old or was developed without extensive involvement of teachers, then the principal needs to verify that it's permissible to have a separate school mission, as long as it does not contradict the district mission. This is usually acceptable at the district level and poses no problem at the building level because value systems are rarely that different.

6

Starting With the Significant

A colleague of mine from the University of Wisconsin uses the expression, "Schools are data rich and information poor." This is another way of stating the problem I called *feast or famine* in Chapter 3. What he meant was that there are all kinds of data available in school districts, but very little is actually used to *inform* people and their decisions and actions. Those who worry about "where will we get any data" are forgetting—or aren't aware of—the multitude of grants, projects, and other funding sources that all have strings attached in the form of reporting requirements. Public schools also have accountability to state departments of education, who usually receive their mandates from federal and state legislatures, all of whom demand information on a frequent basis. The problem is that almost no one has a complete picture of all the data in a system—and who has it, and how to get it.

The development of a school portfolio is the first step toward converting existing data into meaningful information. This chapter begins with a reminder that our definition of the word *data* encompasses far more than the test scores that immediately come to mind. It goes on to acknowledge the many mandates for data collection and reporting that are part of state and federal requirements.

The pre-No Child Left Behind version of Blue Ribbon Schools provides a comprehensive outline of data that exists in most schools, but is only compiled, analyzed, and used for decision making in exceptional settings. A simpler way of organizing the school portfolio is outlined here with four questions that relate to students, staff, parents, and community. After a reminder of the importance of analyzing data, over time, five questions are offered as ways for the leadership team to focus the spotlight on the types of data that are of interest and significance to the school. This initial exposure to meaningful data will generate additional questions and issues that snowball to create an increased awareness of the realities of the school.

Data > Test Scores

For those who equate *data* with *test scores*, phrases like "data-driven decision making" create instant anxiety. Figure 6.1 provides a reminder that data (the plural form of the Latin word *datum*) are just pieces of information, and we gather information from a range of sources on a variety of topics.

For those who sincerely—and rightly—remind us to think of the whole child, this overview of the multiple sources and kinds of data available provides reassurance and also piques their interest in some of the other indicators. Their perspective and participation is important to help balance our attention to both the cognitive and the affective domains of our work.

This list can be the starting point for a school portfolio. It certainly identifies data available in every district. However, there are several important distinctions between a state performance report like this and a school portfolio. The most obvious one is the difference between a mandated list and a collection of data chosen by the school as having significance for staff and constituents. A second is that states are interested in district information whereas the school portfolio is focused on the individual building. If a district is large enough to have more than one school at any level (elementary, middle, or high school), the district's data will need to be broken down by building.

The third difference is that state reports are primarily quantitative, whereas school portfolios should include a balance of quantitative and qualitative data to reflect perceptions of staff, students, and constituents. Perhaps the most important contrast is the type of comparisons made. State reports are used to compare districts throughout the state. A school portfolio would include two different types of comparisons. One is a comparison of the school's own performance over time. The other would be a comparison to schools that are similar in nature and have achieved desired results.

This is *benchmarking*, as the term is used in the business sector. A business asks, "Who's in the same kind of business we are with the same kind of product trying to reach the same market—and doing it best?" A school might ask, "Who works with a similar student population in a similar context and has high achievement?" These comparisons help identify models for further study and can lead to networking with other schools.

The No Child Left Behind Act of 2002 added to the range of mandates for public data reporting. The number of assessments has been increased from three (one elementary, one middle, and one high school) to fourteen—reading and math at Grades 3–8 and a high school grade. Disaggregating data is no longer a mainly urban practice, but is universally required by

Figure 6.1   Sources of Data

- College Entrance Tests
  - SAT
  - ACT
  - Other

- National Norm-Referenced Achievement Tests
  - Iowa Tests of Basic Skills
  - California Achievement Tests
  - Other

- Criterion-Referenced (Standards-Based) Tests
  - State
  - Local
  - National Assessment of Educational Progress

- Beginning- and End-of-Year Tests

- Midterm, Semester, and Course Exams

- Local Unit Tests

- Grades and GPA

- Graduation Rates

- Status of Graduates
  - 2 years out
  - 5 years out

- Local Unit Tests

- Team Projects/Exhibitions

- Performance Checklists

- Individual Student Work

- Homework Monitoring

- Student Attendance Data

- Student Participation Data
  - Extracurricular activities
  - Community service

- Student Behavior Data

- Student Demographics
  - Gender
  - Racial/ethnic group
  - Home language
  - Socioeconomic status
  - Mobility

- Climate/Perception Surveys
  - Staff
  - Students
  - Parents
  - Community

- Career Interest Surveys

- Questionnaires

- Focus Groups

- Interviews
  - Staff
  - Students
  - Parents
  - Community

- Checklists, Rating Scales, and Inventories

- Observation Logs

- Journal Entries, Anecdotes
  - Staff
  - Students

- Staff Attendance

- Staff Qualifications
  - Teaching in area of major
  - Graduate degrees
  - Years experience
  - Students

- Professional Development Participation

- Parent Involvement Data
  - Conference attendance
  - Volunteer participation

gender, socioeconomic status, race, ethnicity, English language ability, and special education disability. Each group must make "adequate yearly progress" in both content areas every year until the ultimate goal of 100% meeting standards is met by 2014.

In Washington State, a grid of tests across the top and reporting factors down the side contains 37 cells, referred to in the media as "37 ways to fail." Based on the cut scores currently in use on a rigorous state assessment, and the way the No Child Left Behind Act was being interpreted as of January 2003, 97% of the elementary schools in Washington State would be considered failures (Harvey, 2003). The impact of this designation, coupled with the reality of even further diminished resources as students may be lost through public school choice, charter schools, and vouchers, has a devastating effect on the morale of leadership and staff.

The ultimate threat of school takeover or closure exacerbates the anxiety as schools continue to be expected to do more with less. In such a context, the emphasis on engaging people and keeping them grounded in their passion (see Chapters 4 and 5) is even more critical. Later in this chapter, the importance of selecting[1] data that is of internal interest is stressed as a way to balance or cope with the increased external pressure.

State and Federal Mandates

In the time before No Child Left Behind, there was an earlier reauthorization of the Elementary and Secondary Education Act that required states to have rigorous academic standards and give at least one major assessment in an elementary grade, in a middle grade, and in high school. Even before that, there were state laws requiring that specific information be reported to all patrons of the school district. For example, Wisconsin's mandated reporting included

- Scores on Wisconsin Reading Comprehension Test (Grade 3)
- Scores on Wisconsin Student Assessment System—Knowledge and Concepts examinations (Grades 4, 8, and 10)
- ACT results
- Advanced Placement testing
- Advanced course work
- Graduation requirements
- Graduation rates
- Postgraduation follow-up information
- Extracurricular and/or co-curricular activities
- Attendance
- Out-of-school suspensions
- Expulsions
- Retentions
- Dropouts
- Habitual truants

- Staffing ratios
- Revenues and expenditures

The Blue Ribbon Approach

The U.S. Department of Education's program for the recognition of exemplary schools was known first as National Schools of Excellence and then as Blue Ribbon Schools. I have been honored to participate in this process in various capacities from 1991 until its revision by President George W. Bush and Secretary Rod Paige in 2002. I have promoted and taken pride in its increasing emphasis on assessment and documentation of results in student learning. Award-winning high schools have provided the following kinds of data.

Demographic Data:

- Enrollment by grade level
- Per-pupil expenditure
- Racial/ethnic composition
- Student mobility rate
- Percentage of limited-English-proficient students
- Percentage of students qualifying for free or reduced-price lunches
- Percentage of students receiving special education services

Student Data:

- Student participation rates in nonacademic services and programs
- Student participation in co-curricular activities and the degree to which it is representative of the overall composition of the student body
- Percentage of students who exceed graduation requirements

Data on Teaching and Learning:

- Usage data from library, information, and media services
- Number of students moving among ability groups, especially into groups with more challenging course work
- Participation in professional development and evidence of impact on improved teaching
- Evidence of how analysis of data at the school level has resulted in specific improvements
- Evidence of how technology has contributed to increased use of data for decision making

Data on School, Family, and Community Partnerships:

- Data on family involvement in school activities and the degree to which the families involved are representative of the overall student body

Indicators of Success:

- Results of standardized tests for each of the last five years, disaggregated according to the largest and most significant subgroups in the school
- Results of nonstandardized, or alternative, assessments developed at the school level
- Results of college entrance examinations (PSAT, SAT, and ACT) and percentage of students tested
- Percentages of students in various educational and employment categories a year following graduation
- Daily student attendance
- Student dropout rate
- Daily teacher attendance
- Teacher turnover rate
- Results of climate surveys
- Percentages of students involved in various types of safety, discipline, and drug issues

Through the data included in the nomination form, schools were required to demonstrate that student outcome results were consistently outstanding or that significant improvement had been achieved *over a span of the past five years*.

It is true that nomination packets were lengthy and described the program offerings in some detail, to be rated through the use of a rubric. There were two benefits to this approach: (1) the rubric represented and disseminated findings of research on most effective practices, and (2) the program descriptions provided guidance to schools that needed real-life examples of how to improve.

In the current version of Blue Ribbon Schools, schools that fall within the top 10% in performance in the state *or* that have at least 40% of students from "disadvantaged backgrounds" and showed "dramatic improvement" are identified by the State Department of Education and offered the opportunity to apply for recognition.[2] The application form is much easier. The descriptions are just a half-page in length each on use of assessment data, communication about student performance, plans to assist other schools, the literacy approach in use, one other curriculum area, instructional methods, and professional development and its impact and one page on the school's overall curriculum of significant content and high standards.

Pity the excellent and improving school that has "only 39%" of students from disadvantaged backgrounds and has shown dramatic improvement but is still "only" in the top 15% in the state. Pity the schools that are looking for specific guidance about how to replicate the success of other schools. And pity the schools that are judged on a state assessment system where meeting standard equates roughly to the 70th percentile on a national norm-referenced test, when the U.S. Department of Education defines "high levels" by referencing the 55th percentile.

Figure 6.2   Data to Answer Questions of Local Significance

Are students learning?

- State assessment data
- Districtwide assessments
- Curriculum-based classroom assessments
- Collaborative analysis of student work

Are students connected and engaged?

- Disciplinary actions
- Attendance
- Truancy
- Graduation/dropout rates
- Co-curricular participation
- Survey results

Are teachers/staff engaged and productive?

- Teacher attendance
- Professional development participation
- Survey results

Are parents and community confident and supportive?

- Parent-teacher conference participation
- Survey results

Regardless of whether the new and shorter version of the Blue Ribbon Schools program is an improvement, the types of data generated in the previous iteration remain an excellent resource for ideas about data that can provide valuable insights for instructional decision making.

Of Local Significance

Whether the school portfolio is housed in file folders or a three-ring binder, on the hard drive, or on a CD, the many kinds of available data must be organized under some major headings. In the Blue Ribbon approach, these were labeled

- Demographic Data
- Student Data
- Data on Teaching and Learning
- Data on School, Family, and Community Partnerships
- Indicators of Success

Another method of organizing the data is to address four questions that are of local interest and significance. Figure 6.2 lists these questions, with examples of pertinent data.

Community needs assessments and climate surveys are sometimes used to provide insights on the unique nature of the local context for schooling. Information on former students can include typical graduate follow-up studies, focus groups and interviews with students who have moved from elementary to middle school or middle school to high school, and feedback from dropouts. Sometimes, feedback from universities and employers can also be obtained. The school district's success or struggles to gain voter approval for operating levies and capital projects is another indicator of community confidence.

No Snapshots, Please

Between 1990 and 2000, the Blue Ribbon Schools program had become more rigorous by expanding its requirements for student performance data first from one year to three years, and then from three years to five years. Achieving sustained improvement over time is far more complex than short-term early gains. Small gains that are loudly touted may not even outdistance the standard error of the assessment, so they are just as likely to descend to the same point or even lower the next year. Chapter 7 provides the example of a school profile that provides a rolling three-year trend, always displaying current results in reference to the previous two years. "Bragging rights" should not be extended on the basis of a single "snapshot" of student performance—and neither should blame.

Finding the Starting Point

The multiple sources of data outlined in the preceding sections of this chapter illustrate the feast aspect of the feast-or-famine problem described in Chapter 3. The administrative team and data team (see Chapter 4) need to have a working familiarity with all of this data, but the staff as a whole won't be able to swallow it all. To get from this glut of information to the *hors d'oeuvres* that will whet people's appetites, the leadership team needs to select data that will match perceived needs and interests of the staff and stakeholders. Here and in Figure 6.3 are five questions—any of which may highlight the first data staff might attempt to digest.

1. What Evidence Would Demonstrate That We Are Fulfilling the Commitments Embedded in Our Mission Statement?

The Monitoring Our Mission activity in Chapter 5 was provided as a way to "arouse the passion" by adding greater meaning to both the mission statement and the types of data that would show progress or accomplishment. For schools with recent and lively work and dialogue articulating core values, this is a good starting point. For schools with staff that reject or resist the whole idea, there are four other suggestions.

Figure 6.3   Key Questions for Meaningful Data Selection

1. What evidence would demonstrate that we are fulfilling the commitments embedded in our mission statement?

2. Do we have any existing, ongoing goals that lack baseline data from which to measure progress?

3. Is there more than one source of evidence for this decision or more than one indicator of need for this goal?

4. What are the assumptions we make about students and their learning? What do we need to do to verify them?

5. What data might help resolve smoldering issues in our school?

Questions such as #4 above about assumptions and aspects of the study phase (see Figure 1.1 and Chapters 11 and 12) will surface the real operating principles of the school and provide leverage for further exploration of prevailing beliefs in the school culture.

2. Do We Have Any Existing, Ongoing Goals That Lack Baseline Data From Which to Measure Progress?

In Chapter 1, we discussed the importance of identifying improvement goals based on data. That's the ideal and should apply to any future goal setting. The reality that I encounter is that few schools can actually start their school improvement process with a clean slate. Most schools have something they are already working on, whether it was determined at the school level or imposed through some other process, such as a district strategic plan or a state initiative. Whether existing goals came from internal or external sources, most were developed solely on the basis of participants' perceptions. Working on the initial school portfolio provides an opportunity to backtrack and decide what evidence is needed to establish a baseline from which to measure progress.

On the day of this writing, a workshop participant showed me a goal aimed at improving parent participation in conferences. She said

> You know, we were frustrated because we feel we don't get enough support from parents. But I'll bet if we checked how many report cards had to be mailed home, we would discover that most parents

do come to conferences. What we really want is something beyond that. So, we need to check the data. If it's low, we should keep the goal. If it's not, we need more discussion of what we're really after. And maybe we should include parents in the discussion.

Right!

3. Is There More Than One Source of Evidence for This Decision or More Than One Indicator of Need for This Goal?

The question of evidence for and indicators of need applies both to existing goals, such as the parent conference example, and to pending decisions and future goals. A basic principle from research is the concept of *triangulation*. Long before global positioning satellites, the term described navigation at sea using charts, instruments, and a few bright stars to plot current location and direction. Its application to decision making for school improvement is the need it implies to have multiple indicators that confirm where we are and where we should be going.

In discussing question #2, above, I implied reservations about goals set solely on the basis of participants' perceptions. That is not to discount the importance of perceptual data, but such data are usually not sufficient. Perception that is confirmed by objective indicators is far more valid for decision making. In the absence of so-called hard data, perceptions that are shared by more than one group provide a better basis for action. Here are examples of both kinds of triangulation as support data for school improvement goals.

Elementary School A's goal is that "all students will increase their application of math computation, concept, and problem-solving skills in all curricular areas." Three indicators—two objective and one subjective—of the need to address student achievement in math are as follows:

- Standardized test scores below the state average for math problem solving
- Only 60% of the students mastering the district's math outcomes based on locally developed criterion-referenced tests
- Former students of Elementary School A, who have completed 6th grade at Middle School B, stated in focus groups that they were not prepared for the challenges of math at that level.

High School C's goal is, "All students will increase their application of computer skills across the curriculum." Support data presented for this goal include

- Student survey results requesting more chances to use computers
- The SCANS (Secretary's Commission on Achieving Necessary Skills) report emphasizing computer literacy as an essential employability skill
- Community interest expressed through a $1.2-million referendum for technology

STARTING WITH THE SIGNIFICANT **79**

All of these indicators used by High School C could be referred to as subjective or opinion-based, but in combination they provide a powerful case for this goal. Certainly the community has spoken through the ballot box, and the school must respond with clear focus, a comprehensive plan to use these resources well, and evidence that the taxpayers' money was well spent and is making a difference for students.

4. What Are the Assumptions We Make About Students and Their Learning? What Do We Need to Do to Verify Them?

The increased emphasis on high-stakes accountability mentioned in Chapter 2 has also escalated the level of "blaming the victim" I observe in school conversations. "Our test scores would be better if they didn't make us test learning disabled kids." Or, "We'd be doing fine if we only had to count 'our own' students and not the ones who are moving in and out all the time." Regardless of the mandates of No Child Left Behind, these comments provide clues to factors that should be used to disaggregate test data. Disaggregated data help us separate the "whys" from the "whines."

Disaggregation is *dis*mantling the *aggregate* information that is typically reported to us as a mean or average number. These measures of central tendency are relatively useless for understanding our students. Bracey (1997) states this concept as a law: "No measure of central tendency without a measure of variation." After all, how many "mean" students do you have in your school? Returning to data that is raw enough to show us range and distribution will help us understand the patterns of success and failure in our student population much better. We must always be asking, "Does this tell us about our whole school? About which kids in particular does it tell us something? Who are we seeing reflected here and who are we missing? Who may be falling through the cracks because we've rolled them all up into one big average?"

Demystifying Disaggregation. If the term or concept of disaggregation is unfamiliar to your group, try one of these two quick illustrations. Because I am "vertically challenged," I ask the audience to identify two other people who are about 5 feet tall to stand with me. Then I ask for three volunteers to stand who would describe themselves as 6 feet tall. Looking at six people like this, I ask the group what our mean height is. Then, I pause and ask, "And how many of this group are 5 feet 6 inches tall?" I continue by asking what would be the easiest way to increase the mean height of the group standing. The answer is to send a short person home. The discussion can be further pursued by pretending that we are going to select a basketball team. What assumptions might we make? Yes, take the tallest. What else might we need to know? Yes, who can shoot. Disaggregating data about student achievement is like analyzing the field-goal and free-throw percentages of all the students to check our assumptions about height and basketball ability.

Another example that works well uses weight—so, don't ask for volunteers for this one! Tell the group to imagine that you weighed each person as he or she entered the room, calculated the mean, and posted a sign on the door that says, "The average weight of people in this room is 195 pounds." What would a passerby think about that information? Would they know if it was good news or bad news? Would they think this is a weight-loss group or a steroid-users support group? After some humorous speculation, people will indicate that it depends on other information about the group, such as how many of each gender are in the audience and what their age and height are. When we report information on student learning as a mean, it tells us about as much as the weight sign on the door.

Figure 6.4 provides a response to the earlier comment about including students with learning disabilities in the state assessment testing. Instead of a single number representing the mean, this stacked bar graph shows the percentage of students achieving in each quartile. In a normal distribution, 25% of the students would score in each quartile; in Figure 6.4, the scores of Exceptional Educational Needs (EEN) students have been disaggregated and the distribution of scores without them is compared to the distribution of achievement for the total school population. Even when special education students were included, 75% of the fourth graders, 79% of the eighth graders, and nearly 83% of the tenth graders scored above the 50th percentile. Teachers in the district were amazed at how similar the two bars looked when the scores of EEN students were removed from the results for the overall population at each grade level.

Figure 6.5 shows how a school disaggregated data to test assumptions about increased mobility in the district. This simple 2 × 2 grid was constructed based on criteria the school chose. When asked to identify a cut score that would determine adequate achievement, the school chose the 40th percentile because of its link to Chapter 1 funding (this was before the 1994 reauthorization that returned to the Title I nomenclature). The school was also asked how long a student would have to be in the district before it would accept responsibility for the student's learning. The school chose two years. The perception that the mobile students were failing at a far greater rate than the stable population had to be abandoned in the face of this data to the contrary.

Does this mean that teachers' perceptions about students are always false? Of course not. Sometimes, our worst fears are confirmed. However, the willingness to question our assumptions is a major step away from the conscious and unconscious ways we convey low expectations for some students and a major step toward building a collaborative culture in a school. When our assumptions are confirmed, we have valuable information that will help us select the most effective strategies to use with a targeted population.

Focusing on the Standard. Since the first edition of *Getting Excited About Data,* increased attention has focused on the achievement gap between the overall performance of the whole student population and various subgroups, or between the performance of white students and students of color. I strongly believe that Ruth Johnson's (2002) advice is accurate and fair, constructive and wise: We should look at outcome data relative to what the expectations are for all students. If all students are expected to achieve at grade level or above or are expected to be eligible for college

Figure 6.4 Scores on State Math Assessment: Distribution by Quartile With and Without Score of Exceptional Education Needs (EEN) Students

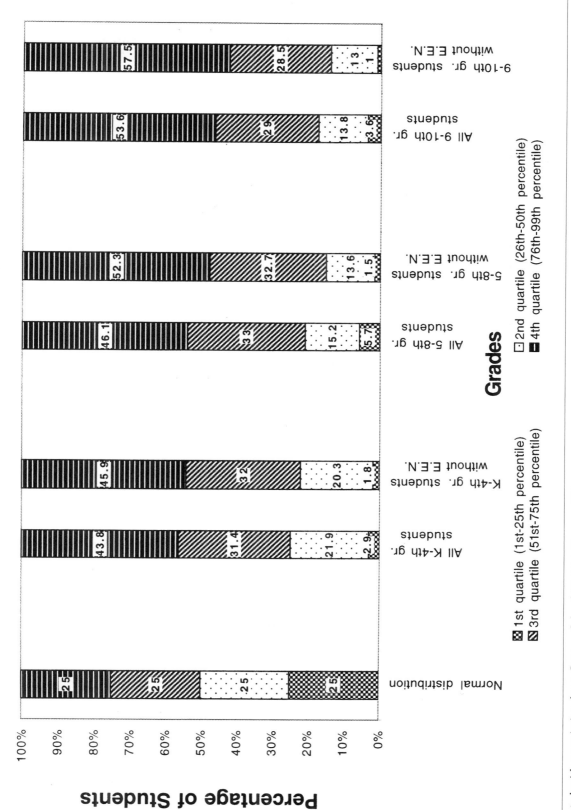

Reprinted with permission from Oregon School District, Oregon, WI.

Figure 6.5   Reading Achievement Scores Disaggregated by Mobility

	In district less than 2 years	In district 2 years or more
40th percentile or above	93% (n = 28)	92% (n = 72)
39th percentile or below	7% (n = 2)	8% (n = 6)

enrollment, the gaps or lack of gaps in achievement need to be noted for each group against that measure. The next step is to measure how far from the standard each group is. Simply measuring gap information from group to group can shortchange students. I have seen instances in which every group was below the standard. Although some groups were closer to the standard than others, there was an achievement gap for every group relative to the achievement expectation. Schools most often measure achievement gaps from group to group and not against the standard they want all children to achieve. This can be shortsighted if the highest group is achieving at a below-standard level.

The Bottom Fourth. Sometimes our assumption is that there *are* no subgroups in our student population because it appears so homogeneous. There may be no obvious racial differences and socioeconomic status may seem fairly level, with most of the students' parents engaged in the same few occupations with similar incomes. In these situations, preselecting a variable as the basis for disaggregation may seem like an exercise in futility. The alternative is to identify the bottom fourth of the students on any important measure. For example, look at grade distributions and select the bottom fourth of the students. Or look at attendance and select 25% of the students with the most days absent. Discuss these students by name and see if they have any common characteristics that may have been overlooked in the assumption of homogeneity.

5. What Data Might Help Resolve Smoldering Issues in Our School?

Many schools are plagued by conflicts that just won't go away because people are divided into camps based on philosophy or preference. The development of a school portfolio can be a window of opportunity to gather data that may resolve these dilemmas or, at least, create better understanding of the situation.

At School D, the issue of whether to have an open or closed campus had been bantered about for months. Arguments raged about rights of students versus risks of driving, nutritious lunch menus versus drive-through junk food, and supervision versus duty-free noons. The question of impact on learning had never surfaced. When the school improvement team began to compile data, the members asked themselves whether there was any information that could shed light on this issue. That's when attendance data became meaningful— not as an aggregated percentage of all students for the whole year, but analyzed by period of the day. Figure 6.6 shows the pattern of student absences the team discovered. Based on this data, the staff voted for closed campus. By serendipity, the staff also noted the increased absences during last hour and began to explore possible explanations, including scheduling of study halls and implications of student employment.

At Brooklyn Elementary School in Brooklyn, Wisconsin, frustration was high among the staff because the lunch personnel seemed to take too long to serve the children and this reduced their lunchtime. The teachers thought the answer was hiring more kitchen staff to serve the children. Based on the menus, teachers predicted how long it would take to complete serving. The staff then monitored the lunch line for 10 days to verify the actual time it took students to be served. Each teacher recorded arrival time, time the first student was served, and time the last child was served.

Figure 6.7 shows that the effects were much less than teachers expected. On 8 of 10 days, the variation in serving time for the whole school was 4 minutes or less. On every one of the 10 days monitored, the actual serving time was from 2 to 12 minutes less than predicted. Ruffled feathers were smoothed, and time and energy that might have been expended on a staffing issue could be conserved for other purposes. This type of data, gathered to resolve a specific problem, might be included in the school portfolio or might simply be compiled and analyzed to better understand a situation.

Making It Public

This chapter has moved from the general to the specific, first outlining a wide range of kinds and sources of data, then urging leadership teams to help the data team identify a smaller and more meaningful subset of the data for early exploration by a staff unaccustomed to this self-reflection. Of course, a hard look at the large scale assessment data for public accountability—comfortable or not—cannot be delayed for very long. The constituents will be asking questions, and one of the best ways to prepare them for the answers is to give them a "test drive" with the assessments.

Figure 6.6 Absences by Class Period: Grading Period 3

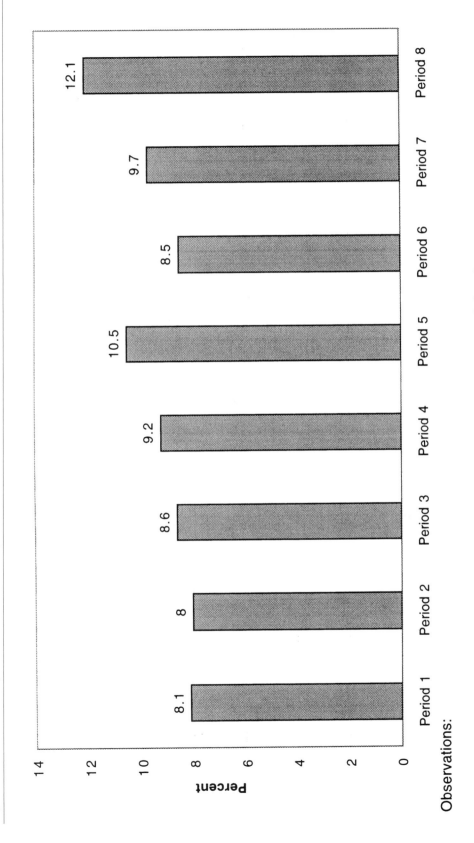

Observations:

1. The highest percentage of absentees occurs in the final class period of the day.

2. There is a higher percentage of absentees in periods that are part of the lunch cycle than in the morning class periods.

3. Overall, more students are absent in the afternoon than in the morning.

Figure 6.7   Time of Last Student Through Lunch Line

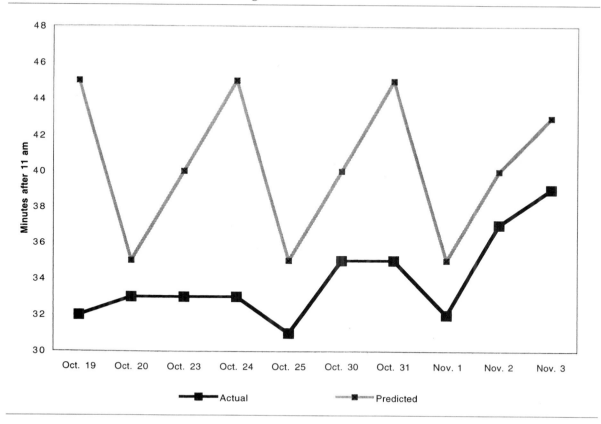

Test Drive the Test

Janesville, Wisconsin, is the home of Parker Pen, and General Motors makes cars there. These companies represent the major employers of the students who don't go away to two- or four-year colleges. So they judge the school district on the basis of the lowest 30%.

Over the past few years, administrators in this school district have made a concerted effort to build relationships with Wisconsin Manufacturers and Commerce. Their mutual goal is to allow teachers, administrators, school board members, parents, and community and business leaders to work together to continue to improve student performance in each local school district.

As part of this effort, the district developed a "WSAS SWAT team." This group guides all information sharing that relates to the Wisconsin Student Assessment System (WSAS). The team includes the superintendent, the district's public relations coordinator, central office directors, and supervisors. The SWAT team identified the following audiences:

- Central office staff
- Principals and assistant principals
- Clerical staff
- Custodial and maintenance staff
- Food service personnel
- CEOs of local companies

Meetings were held for all classifications of district employees, on contract time, to be sure that key messages were heard and understood by all. An official lesson plan was developed for all of these meetings. It included explanations of norm-referenced and criterion-referenced tests, district comparisons, and a sample of the kinds of test items students must answer. The messages were that

- Results will look different this year.
- The state of Wisconsin and Janesville district schools are expecting more from our students than other states and districts do.
- We will continue to improve.
- We will work together.

"We" was intentionally and overtly defined as district staff, students, parents, community, and the Chamber of Commerce.

For the last audience (CEOs), a special session was planned. These employers were invited to come in and take a "test ride"—that is, sit down in desks with the test booklets and a time limit and "experience the ride." Familiar with high-risk situations, these executives allowed themselves to be videotaped and commented on the nature of the test and their commitment to work with the district. This video was aired repeatedly on the local cable channel. It was a very visual demonstration of the concept of "we." It also illustrates the earlier comment about choosing who the communicators should be. Even if the words are the same, it's a different message when the company president says, "It's a hard test that isn't like the ones we used to take in school."

The Janesville district has addressed one more audience, a group that's most intimately affected by assessment but almost universally overlooked when it comes to communicating the results: *students*. Janesville has two high schools, and the tendency of the media to make comparisons between them has been a concern of teachers and parents. It's a problem that students tackled themselves. Students wrote their own article for the media, explaining the test scores and pointing out the absence of any statistically significant difference between the two schools.

Districts in Wisconsin's Big Foot Consortium have also involved students through an innovative project in a media class. With a budget of $500 and some clips from a Department of Public Instruction videotape, students produced a documentary about the state assessments that airs repeatedly on their public access channel.

Prime New Parents

These public communication efforts were initiated in the early days of state accountability systems, and some districts have since reduced efforts to develop familiarity with the high-stakes assessments used to evaluate schools (and students). This diminished effort may be based on a sense that everyone knows about the tests by now. However, new information tends to slide in, through, and out of short-term memory if there's no immediate hook to hold it there. As a result, young parents with their first school-age children now have a need to know, and mobile families moving from state to state need to understand the different assessments their children will encounter. Communications such as the following principal's recent newsletter message (and the insert shown in Figure 6.8) continue to be relevant and significant for parents (Adams, 2003).

Dear Parents,

   This is the time of the year that we hear a great deal about the state WASL (Washington Assessment of Student Learning) test for fourth, seventh, and tenth graders. While this assessment is very difficult, it does provide us with valuable information about how our students are achieving. However, we need to remember that it is only one of many indicators that we use to monitor student growth. In third grade, students take the ITBS (Iowa Test of Basic Skills) as well as a district writing assessment. In addition, every primary teacher evaluates the reading progress of their students by giving them Running Reading Records on a regular basis. We also give specific reading tests to all elementary students three times a year. Along with these state and district tests, each classroom teacher assesses the progress of their students using a variety of curriculum tests, projects, or activities. All of the information from this broad range of testing is then used to address specific student needs while at the same time helping us to identify areas of our curriculum that might need to be revised. If you have any questions about how your child has done on a test or is doing at school, feel free to contact your child's teacher. They will be more than happy to assist you.

The Snowball Approach

Whether schools begin with survey data that piques their interest or go straight to the technical specifications of the state-mandated assessment, the initial exploration will generate questions from both skeptics and enthusiasts. The reflective questions posed during the Carousel Data Analysis (see Chapter 8) include, "What do these data *not* tell us?" and "What else would we need to know?" Beginning to work with data is like starting a snowball at the top of a hill. It gains size, speed, and momentum as it goes.

   The key to getting people engaged with data is *start somewhere—* and that somewhere is wherever they are now in terms of readiness and interest.

Figure 6.8   What Does the WASL Look Like?

WHAT DOES THE WASL LOOK LIKE?

This month, our 4th grade students will be taking the WASL.

Wouldn't you like to be back in 4th grade?
How would you do on the Washington Assessment of Student Learning test?
Try your skills on these sample WASL problems!

Directions: Use these selections to answer the questions that follow. This table of contents is found at the beginning of a book called *Keeping Time* by Franklyn M. Branley.

Contents

This is part of the index found at the back of the book *Keeping Time.*

Index

1. From the table of contents you can tell what the book *Keeping Time* is about. Which sentence best summarizes what the book is about?

   ◯ A. It is about how clocks are made.

   ◯ B. It is about how people measure time.

   ◯ C. It is about how to travel through time.

2. Use the table of contents to find out which chapter of this book would tell you how long a day is on the planet Mercury.

   ◯ A. Chapter 14

   ◯ B. Chapter 16

   ◯ C. Chapter 17

3. Use the index to find out which pages of this book would tell you how long a day is on the planet Mercury.

   ◯ A. Pages 68-69

   ◯ B. Pages 96-97

   ◯ C. Pages 98-99

4. You can use the index in *Keeping Time* to find out how days of the week got their names. Look at the part of the index that is shown. Write two topics you would look up. Also give page numbers you would look up.

   _____

5. When should you use an index rather than a table of contents of a book?

   ◯ A. When you want to know which page gives information about a particular word or phrase

   ◯ B. When you want to know what important topics are covered in the book

   ◯ C. When you want to know the names of other books on a particular subject

6. The United States has several time zones, including Eastern Standard Time, Central Standard Time, Mountain Standard Time and Pacific Standard Time. Tell what parts of the table of contents and index in *Keeping Time* would help you find out more about these time zones.

   Table of contents:

   _____

   Index:

   _____

WASL puzzles....

Your class project is to build a bird feeder.

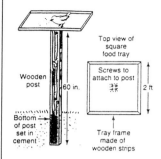

Item	Cost per Unit
wooden post	$2.50 per foot
wooden strips for tray frame	$1.00 per foot
tray bottom	$6.00
tools, screws, nails, wood glue, and cement mix	Loaned or donated by parents

Explain how you could use the information
Given to find the total cost of materials.
Use words, numbers, or pictures.

A refreshment stand buys hot dogs in packages of 10. Hot dog buns come in packages of 12. What is the **least** number of hot dogs and buns that must be bought to have an equal number of each?

- ○ **A.** 120 hot dogs and 120 buns
- ○ **B.** 60 hot dogs and 60 buns (correct)
- ○ **C.** 30 hot dogs and 30 buns

Mr. Kumar pays Tim and Dana a total of $30 for mowing his lawn.

Tell how Tim and Dana should divide the money fairly, based on the work they have done. Show your work.

Explain your thinking using words, numbers, or pictures.

Directions: Read the selection and answer the questions.

April Rain Song
by Langston Hughes

Let the rain kiss you.
Let the rain beat upon your head with silver liquid drops.
Let the rain sing you a lullaby.

The rain makes still pools on the sidewalk.
The rain makes running pools in the gutter.
The rain plays a little sleep-song on our roof at night —

And I love the rain.

1. These words might all be used to describe the rain in "April Rain Song." Circle the word you think best describes the rain in this poem.'

    Musical   Soft   Gentle

Tell what it is in the poem that made you choose this word.

_____

_____

_____

_____

_____

_____

2. What words in the poem are used to mean lullaby?
    - ○ A. Liquid drops
    - ○ B. Sleep-song
    - ○ C. Still pools

3. To which senses does the description in the poem appeal?
    - ○ A. Sight, hearing, touch
    - ○ B. Hearing, taste, touch
    - ○ C. Touch, sight, smell

Reprinted With Permission From Bellingham School District, Bellingham, WA.

Notes

1. Whenever I use the words *select* or *selective* in relationship to the school portfolio, I am referring to size, not bias. The school portfolio shouldn't be a public relations product that reports only the good news, nor should it be a deficiency document of only concerns. It should be accurate, but intentionally focused to avoid creating information overload in addition to all the other challenges of work with data.

2. This information was derived from the U.S. Department of Education Web site (http://www.ed.gov/offices/OIIA/Recognition/nclb-brs/) as of March 2003.

7

Displaying
the Data

Chapter 6 described approaches to *selecting* data that will be considered meaningful, relevant, and useful to a school's staff, students, and constituents. This chapter focuses on *displaying* the data so it is clear, accurate, and user friendly. How the data looks does matter. Realtors use the term *curb appeal* to refer to the first impression that clients have as they approach and drive by a property. A house could have a beautiful interior and an attractive price, but if it's not visually appealing, the sale will be difficult. In the same sense, if a school portfolio isn't visually appealing, the task of engaging people in discussion of the data and its implications for planning and decision making will be that much more difficult.

Size

A first consideration is size. In Chapter 6, we stressed the need to be selective about how much of all the available data to compile in a document that will be reviewed and discussed by all. Many principals have at least one 4-inch three-ring binder of data about their school and students. The administrative team, leadership team, and data team have a working knowledge of all the data. It's available to anyone else who wants to review it. They also have a mini-version: a small ½-inch binder or packet of data that is used for discussion and decision making. All staff should be familiar with this collection.

User-Friendly Data Displays

The second consideration is how to display the data. Figure 7.1 illustrates three major parts of a data display: the introduction or explanation, the graph, and the summary statements or findings. The title is clear and long enough to let the reader know whether this is the information being sought.

The Introduction

A short paragraph should be included with the data display to explain what test was used, who and how many were tested, when the test was given, and how it was analyzed. Because Figure 7.1 is an illustrative example, the name of a specific test is not given. Schools should name the actual test and the form or level that is administered. The introductory paragraph should spell out any acronyms used on the page and define terminology, such as *socioeconomic status* (SES) and *percentile*. The need to include an introduction is an important lesson I learned the hard way—through an embarrassing discussion with a community member who had misread SES as SEX and proceeded from there to an irate protest against gathering data on who's high, middle, and low in that function. It's humorous now, but wasn't at the time.

The Graph

Each axis of your graph should be clearly labeled, and any unfamiliar terminology should be explained in the paragraph at the top. If scores are in percentiles, the percentage sign (%) should *not* be used. Percentiles should be shown as simply the number, with the word *percentile* along the side. Alternatively, the *-ile* suffix should be added to the number (79%-ile) or the number should be printed as *79th* or *63rd* or *82nd*. This is an important distinction, because many readers who see "79%" will believe that students answered 79% of the items correctly. This error occurred in a community forum of school board candidates when a candidate stated, "The district's test scores are in the 70s and when I was in school, 70s meant a D. Our schools are performing only at the D level." Most districts would be proud of scores at the 79th percentile nationally.

It's also important to be careful about how the range is shown, especially on the vertical axis. If the data is in percentiles, the full range from 0 to 100 should be shown. If the school's scores are all below the 70th percentile, the graph should not be cut off at the 70th just to save space, because readers may say the axis went up only to 70th to make the scores look higher than they really are.

In *Asking the Right Questions* (Holcomb, 2001), Chapter 3 was devoted to data that helps answer the "Where are we now?" question. Pages 15 to 32 provide suggestions and examples of the use of histograms, pie charts, run charts, and pareto charts as ways of displaying data.

Figure 7.1   Scores on Standardized Test of Elementary Math Disaggregated by Socioeconomic Status (SES)

All students in grades 2-5 take the standardized test every October. These are the results for this year's students in each grade. Qualification for free or reduced price lunches is used to identify students as having lower socioeconomic status (SES). The percentile rank indicates that our students scored higher than such a percentage of students taking the test nationwide.

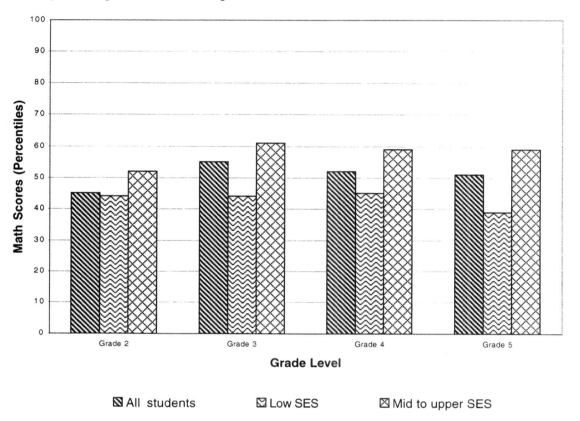

Strengths:
1. The means of math scores for all students in grades 3, 4 and 5 are above the 50th percentile.
2. The mean math scores for middle and upper SES students are above the 50th percentile at all grade levels.

Concerns:
1. The mean for all second grade students is below the 50th percentile.
2. At all grade levels, lower SES students score below middle and upper SES students. The discrepancy ranges from 7 percentiles on the second grade test to 20 percentiles on the fifth grade test.
3. It appears from this data that lower SES students fall further behind in math as they progress through the grades.

Beware of the color trap. With newer software and color printers, it's quite simple to create beautiful, multicolored graphs. These are appealing to the eye and easy to read—if you have an original copy and not a black-and-white reproduction. However, school portfolios are frequently copied for reference or distribution. If you are going to use color, be sure that you invest the extra expense of multiple copies in color. Otherwise, stick to various patterns of black and white so the codes used for bars, lines, and segments of a pie chart aren't lost in reproduction. (This point is well illustrated by the difficulty of describing *color coding* later in this black-and-white book.)

The Summary

Figure 7.1 summarizes the data with two statements of strength and three statements of concern. The next chapter describes a professional development activity that engages teachers as the interpreters of data, so the statement of strengths/concerns would not be developed by an individual or small group charged with constructing the graphs. Rather, it would be added later based on the interpretations done by staff. These statements must be factual observations, not evaluative judgments. For example, we state that the mean for all second grade students is below the 50th percentile. We do not say that second graders have the poorest performance or that we must improve performance of second graders. The latter would be a rush to judgment on what should be the school's improvement goal. Chapter 10 provides further cautions about premature goal setting.

Some schools prefer to write one paragraph or make one general set of summary statements rather than to separate strengths from concerns, as in Figure 7.1. This is a local decision. It may be less threatening to avoid the headings, but the disadvantage is that items needing improvement are easier to ignore and the thrill of celebrating successes is often missed as well. The choice of *concerns* as a heading, rather than using *weaknesses* as the antonym of *strengths*, is very deliberate.

A Self-Test

When the school portfolio—or each individual data display—is considered finished, two self-tests should be imposed. The first is to ask one or more persons not involved in any way to look at the portfolio or display and see what questions they raise or if they are able to answer a few key questions you ask about it. The second is to fold the page in half to see if each half—the visual and the textual—can stand alone. In other words, would a person who is strongly visual or spatial and who may look only at the graph get exactly the same message that a person who is strongly verbal or linguistic would get from reading the narrative only?

Displaying Longitudinal Data

The purpose of this book is to engage schools in the greater use of data as a step toward the essential mission of schools, which includes improving student performance. Chapters 5 and 6 focused on selecting the data to be gathered and displayed as baseline information in an initial school portfolio. However, the school portfolio is a *continuous work in process*. (Take another look at the shaded arrows in Figure 1.2.) Your school portfolio will be updated at least once a year as another round of test scores are received and another state report is submitted. For the school to see evidence of improvement, data must also be displayed over time. Figure 6.7 showed a run chart, or line graph, of lunch line times during a 10-day experimental period. I have seen line graphs used in many other ways, but it's technically correct to use a line graph only if the line represents the same variable over several points in time.

Different Students

A series of bar graphs can be constructed so that they compare performance of different students at the same point in their schooling. Figure 7.2 presents four years of math scores from Templeton Middle School in Sussex, Wisconsin, on the California Achievement Test (CAT). This improvement over time was accomplished simply by placing emphasis on the test as an important event in the school year. Teachers explained why the test was important and how the results would be used to help determine their individual goals for seventh and eighth grade. Students were given the practice test from the publisher, and announcements to parents emphasized attendance, proper rest, and encouragement for the students to do their best but not worry about the outcomes.

The data in Figure 7.2 are from four years of sixth grade students, so it's true that each bar represents a different set of students. This is often a concern for teachers, especially those who survived statistics courses designed to prepare experimental design researchers rather than to equip practitioners for responsible decision making. It *is* sound practice to use data from different groups of students to reflect on the role of the school and engage in program improvement. Unless the size of the school and the group tested is very small, or unless there have been major demographic changes in the student population in a short period of time, student performance will remain relatively stable when compared to a nationally normed, random population. When the population is reasonably stable and the reference point is a large national sample, the school can infer that improvements are due to its efforts.

The plural of *efforts* in the previous sentence is intentional. In our daily life in schools, we do not have a laboratory where cause-and-effect relationships between one specific strategy or invention can be isolated and "proved" or where a matched control group and experimental group can be identified. That's why Chapters 12 and 14 refer to multiple strategies and assessments. We will never know the specific step we took on a given day with a specific student that improved learning. We *can* see student scores improving and know that the holistic effect, the synergy of our combined efforts, does indeed elevate the overall performance of our students.

Figure 7.2   California Achievement Test Scores for the Sixth Grade

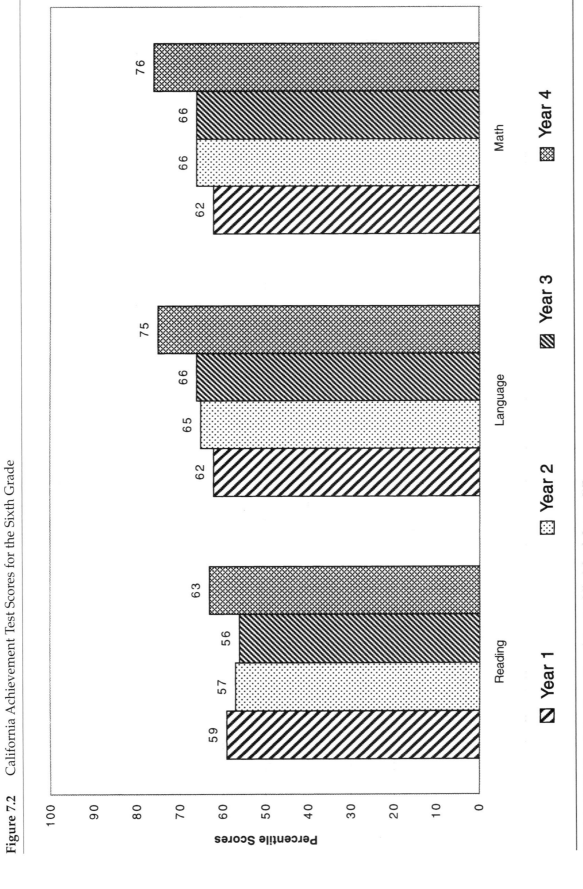

The Same Students

In some situations, perhaps for you, this holistic effect is not a good enough answer. Longitudinal data can be gathered for the same cohort of students as they move through their schooling in a district, but it takes time and money that most of us don't have. The same tests would have to be administered every year, and the scores of every student who was not in the initial group removed from the analysis. This assumes that the district has complete control over its assessment program, which is not true in most states. In Wisconsin, the four-year history of state assessment includes two different test companies, three forms or levels of the test, and a shift from fall to spring testing.

I know of two approaches that schools are using to account for changes in assessment programs. Bob Armstrong (1998), research consultant for the North Central Association of Colleges and Schools, recommends use of a formula to convert all scores into standard (z) scores. This requires statistical computations at the local level.

A more convenient method is the use of normal curve equivalents (NCEs).[1] Figure 7.3 is an example from the U.S. Department of Education's Blue Ribbon Schools nomination packet. It illustrates the use of NCEs to compensate for a change from use of the CAT to the Degrees of Reading Power test. Since most test companies include NCEs in their reports, this does not require use of a conversion formula.

Figure 7.4 illustrates another approach to tracking cohort data. State assessments are given in Grades 4, 7, and 10, so a three-year span of time elapses before we know how the fourth graders perform when they get to the middle school test, and how the seventh graders score on the high school exam. The plus and minus signs in the cells representing change provide a quick visual sense of gains and losses without requiring the reader to do any mental math.

Color Coding Proficiency

Plus and minus signs are used in Figure 7.4 to make it easier for school staff and constituents to identify areas of gain and loss easily. Figure 7.5 illustrates the impact of color and simple pie graphs. (Because this book is published only in black and white, the color *words* are printed on the graphs and the impact is diminished here.)

Many standards-based or criterion-referenced tests are reported in proficiency levels, such as *beginning, developing, proficient,* and *advanced.* In these pie graphs, the color blue represents the highest level—"blue ribbon" performance. Then, the stoplight colors represent the other three levels. Green represents proficiency, because students at this level are "good to go." Yellow represents students near standard, for whom the "caution" sign must be raised. The color red signals those who are in greatest danger and it insists that we *stop,* attend to their learning needs, and provide academic intervention.

Figure 7.3 M. T. Bailey Middle School California Achievement Test and Degrees of Reading Power Test

Arrows indicate a class as it goes from seventh to eighth grade. In all cases there is an increase in student performance when they go from seventh to eighth grade. The DRP in 94-95 is slightly lower, which we believe is attributed to the new style of the test.

Reading Scores - Grades 7 & 8

		92-93(CAT)	93-94(CAT)	94-95(DRP)	95-96(DRP)	96-97(DRP)
GRADE 7	NCE	60.5	60.1	59.2	60.6	61
	Enrollment	188	192	219	210	215
	% Tested	97%	96%	98%	97%	97%

		92-93(CAT)	93-94(CAT)	94-95(DRP)	95-96(DRP)	96-97(DRP)
GRADE 8	NCE	63.5	64.1	62.7	63.1	64.5
	Enrollment	176	198	189	190	193
	% Tested	96%	97%	97%	98%	97%

CAT=California Achievement Test. DRP=Degrees Reading Power

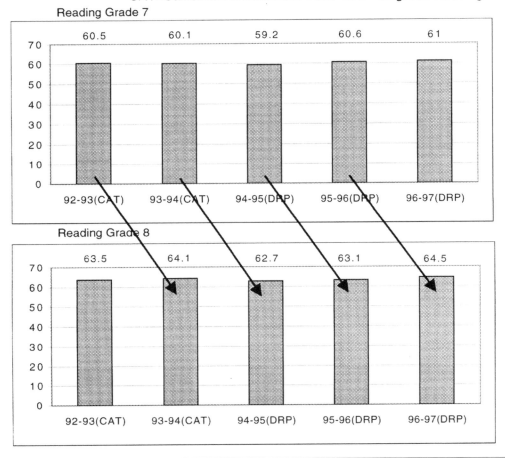

Results from norm-referenced tests can be displayed in similar fashion. The blue segment would illustrate the percentage of students scoring in the top quartile, the 76th percentile and above. Green would represent scores between the 51st and 75th percentile. Yellow and red would identify the distribution of students in the lower two quartiles.

Figure 7.4 Change in Percentage Meeting Standards for Grade-Level Cohorts

1998-1999 to 2001-2002

	Reading			Math			Writing			Listening		
	1998-1999	2001-2002	Difference	1998-1999	2001-2002	Difference	1998-1999	2001-2002	Difference	1998-1999	2001-2002	Difference
Grade 4 to 7 Cohort	64.2	56.5	– 7.7	44.8	39.2	– 5.6	39.8	61.8	+ 22.0	76.4	87.0	+ 10.6
Grade 7 to 10 Cohort	55.3	64.7	+ 9.4	36.5	45.3	+ 8.8	45.9	61.3	+ 15.4	91.0	86.4	– 4.6

1997-1998 to 2000-2001

	Reading			Math			Writing			Listening		
	1997-1998	2000-2001	Difference	1997-1998	2000-2001	Difference	1997-1998	2000-2001	Difference	1997-1998	2000-2001	Difference
Grade 4 to 7 Cohort	64.2	52.2	– 12.0	40.4	39.3	– 1.1	48.4	54.2	– 5.8	78.5	90.9	+ 12.4
Grade 7 to 10 Cohort	50.6	72.7	+ 22.1	33.0	51.0	+ 18.0	35.6	54.8	+ 20.2	85.9	88.6	+ 2.7

Figure 7.5 Percentage of Students in Proficiency Levels

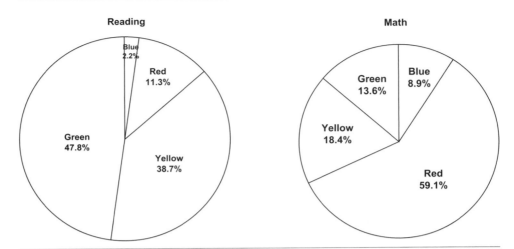

These color-coded pie graphs are not only easier to read than a list of percentages, they provide more information than a single percentage indicating those who do or don't meet standards. Information on the distribution of students in performance levels helps balance perspectives. For example, the school represented in Figure 7.5 could easily overlook the students who score in the advanced level in both reading and math. To do so, however, could mean that success might not be celebrated and appropriate learning experiences might not be provided.

The visual benefit of these color-coded pie graphs is evident when you have them printed in color. It is very clear that the priority for improvement is math. There is also a benefit in terms of simplified communication. It takes fewer words to ask, "Who's in the red zone?" than "Which students are performing at the lowest proficiency level?" It also reduces the number of times that words like *lowest, failing,* and *minimal* are associated with these students.

The No-Numbers Approach

Visual appeal and simplicity were provided by plus and minus signs in Figure 7.4 and by color coding in Figure 7.5. A completely no-numbers approach is illustrated in Figure 7.6. Here, at a glance, the viewer gets an overall perspective of how students at three grade levels performed on four tests, compared with their counterparts the year before. In a district that has focused on improvement in writing, the good news is immediately apparent and easily summarized—scores up for all grade levels.

Other topics of discussion would be generated by using a no-numbers approach. For example,

- Listening scores are down at all grade levels. How much do we value this test? Do we have other evidence of students' listening skills?
- Scores for tenth graders slipped in reading, math, and listening. How much? Is this a significant concern?

Figure 7.6   Comparing Two Years of Test Scores

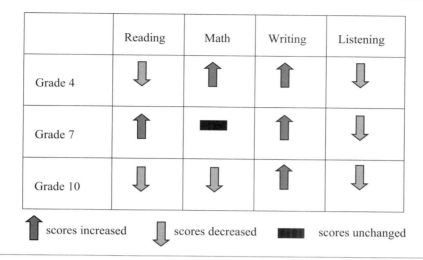

As the discussion continues, the interest and need for numbers will emerge and the complex array of score reports can be tackled in small increments. Thus begins the snowball approach discussed in Chapter 6.

Displaying Perceptual Data

Chapter 6 includes questions that should be addressed through the range of data compiled in the school portfolio. Perceptual data is needed to answer our questions about whether students feel connected, whether teachers collaborate, and whether parents and community members have confidence in their local schools. It's a challenge to display and summarize this data from surveys, interviews, and focus groups.

One caution in selecting a display format is not to report survey data by listing all the survey items and all the responses with a number or percentage next to them. Such a list may go on page after page, and then there may be even more pages that list every comment made in response to open-ended questions. No reader is going to invest enough time to discover which items have the highest and lowest levels of agreement and satisfaction. (If the raw data goes on page after page, the survey was probably too long to start with.) I suggest that all of this data belongs in the principal's 4-inch binder, but only a synopsis belongs in the school portfolio for discussion. Perceptual data can be displayed as graphs, as seen in Figures 7.7 and 7.8.

Figure 7.7 is a pareto chart that shows the percentage of students in an elementary school that answered *yes* to a short yes-or-no survey of 17 items. What makes it a pareto chart is that the items are organized from the one receiving the strongest affirmation, "Grownups at school care about me," to the item receiving the least affirmation, "I have time to eat lunch." This arrangement makes it easy to condense survey data and readily identifies the items of least satisfaction that may need to be addressed.

Figure 7.7 Results of Student Survey

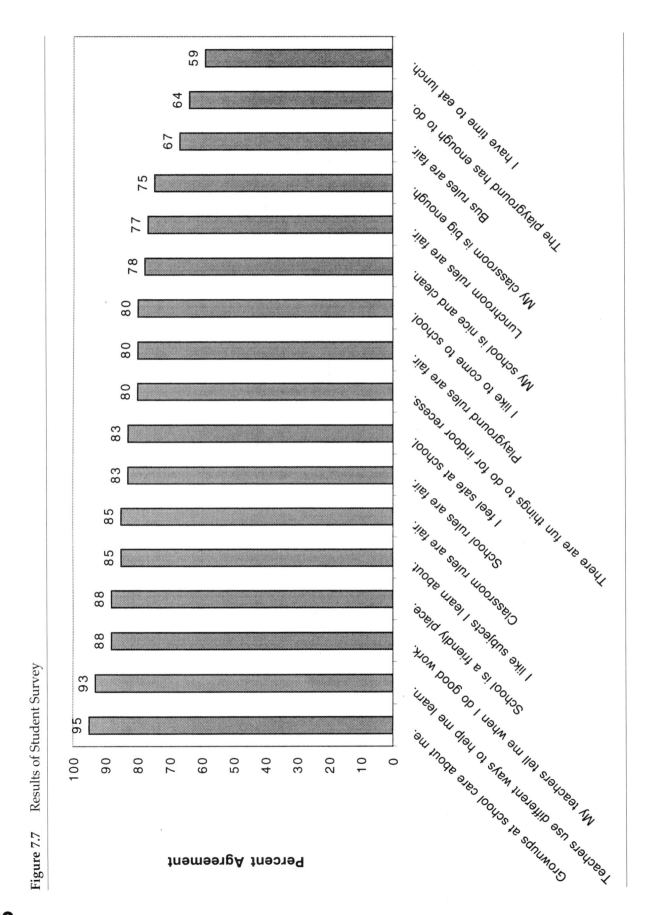

Figure 7.8 illustrates a way to display perceptual data from various role groups. In this example, a survey of 25 items included 5 items that related to each of five categories: Feelings of Safety, Focus on Teaching and Learning, Individual Help for Students, Fair Rules Consistently Enforced, and Home-School Communication. The detail of responses by item would be available for those interested in an in-depth look. What the data display can capture is a sense of which group is most pleased with which aspect of the school and where there is highest and lowest agreement among the responding groups.

The Whole Portfolio

This chapter began with a wide range of sources and kinds of data and then offered questions and activities to help focus on a smaller set of meaningful information. Figure 7.9 presents a complete school portfolio—or *effectiveness profile*—consisting of five pages. Data on *student learning* includes reading, math, writing, listening, and science from the Iowa Tests of Educational Development (ITED) and the Washington Assessment of Student Learning (WASL), as well as cumulative grade point averages. These scores are disaggregated for five racial/ethnic groups.

Data on *student engagement* is represented by discipline suspensions and expulsions, including a ratio calculated to check for disproportional disciplinary action by race.[2] Information on continuation rate, dropout rate, graduation rate, attendance, and truancy also reflect students' connectedness to the school.

This school portfolio includes *staff* attendance and survey data. The school used *parent and community* surveys in conjunction with accreditation and planning cycles, but they are not standardized and reported at the district level.

The request for "no snapshots, please" is reflected in graphs containing three years of data. Interpretation of the data is assisted by a solid line across the graph, which represents the district standard, and by brief captions under each graph. Preparation of materials like this for use by the schools is one of the support roles of the district described in Chapter 13.

Making It Public

The school district of Oregon, Wisconsin, is one I hold in high esteem for many reasons. Quality management folks would point to it as an example of constancy of purpose. It has retained the same superintendent for 10 years—a soft-spoken, tough-minded woman who is now president of the state administrators' association. The school district survived the "outcomes wars" without changing terminology or abandoning the effort to identify clearly the cognitive goals it has for its students. It simply took a very heads-up approach to communicating what *we* mean by outcomes-based

(Text continues on p. 110)

Figure 7.8   Survey Responses From Teachers, Students, and Parents

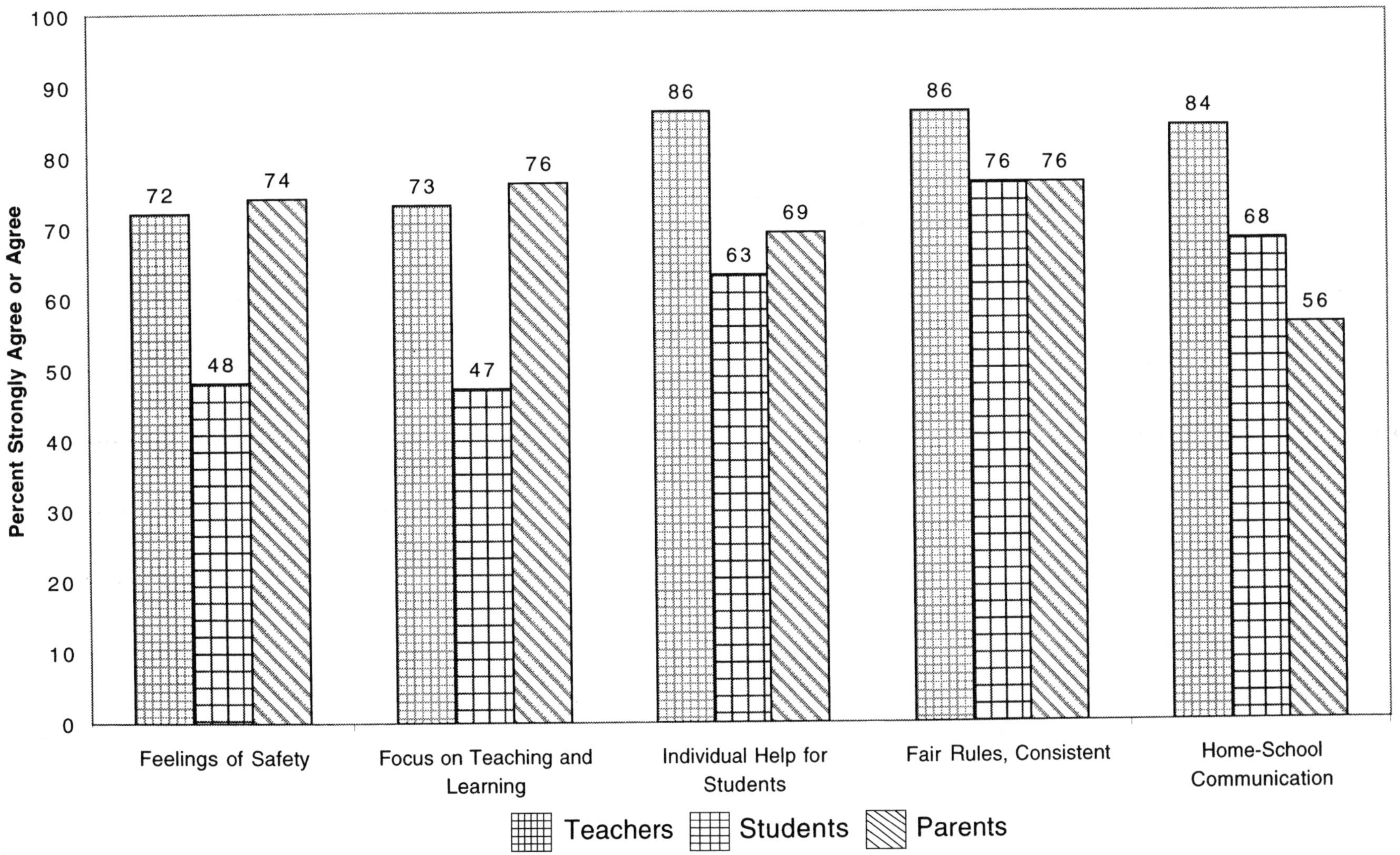

Percent Strongly Agree or Agree

Feelings of Safety
- Teachers: 72
- Students: 48
- Parents: 74

Focus on Teaching and Learning
- Teachers: 73
- Students: 47
- Parents: 76

Individual Help for Students
- Teachers: 86
- Students: 63
- Parents: 69

Fair Rules, Consistent
- Teachers: 86
- Students: 76
- Parents: 76

Home-School Communication
- Teachers: 84
- Students: 68
- Parents: 56

Legend: Teachers | Students | Parents

Figure 7.9   School Effectiveness Profile

NATHAN HALE HIGH SCHOOL
2001-2002 EFFECTIVENESS PROFILE

Mathematics

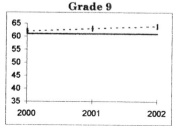

ITED Mathematics NCE Grade 9

School trend is level
At District Standard

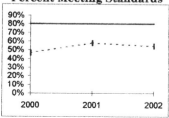

WASL Grade 10 Mathematics Percent Meeting Standards

School trend is positive
Well Below District Standards

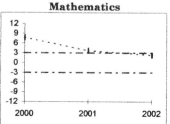

Value-Added School Effect Mathematics

Reading

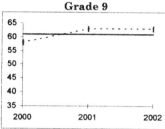

ITED Reading NCE Grade 9

School trend is very positive
At District Standard

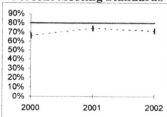

WASL Grade 10 Reading Percent Meeting Standards

School trend is level
Approaching District Standards

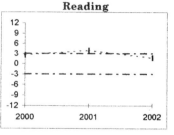

Value-Added School Effect Reading

Writing

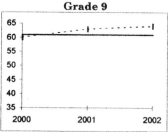

ITED Language NCE Grade 9

School trend is positive
At District Standard

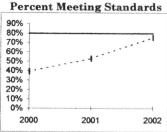

WASL Grade 10 Writing Percent Meeting Standards

School trend is very positive
Approaching District Standards

LEGEND: ---◆---   School
          ——   2004 District Standard

(Continued)

Figure 7.9 (Continued)

NATHAN HALE HIGH SCHOOL
2001-2002 EFFECTIVENESS PROFILE

WASL Grade 10 Listening
Percent Meeting Standards

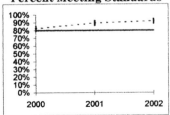

School trend is very positive
Above District Standards

Percent of Students with
Core and Cum GPA => 2.0

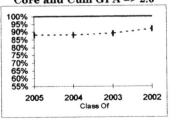

Approaching District Standards

ITED Science NCE
Grade 9

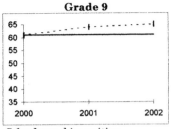

School trend is positive
At District Standard

LEGEND:
---♦--- School
——— 2004 District Standard

Disciplinary Action Rate
Long-Term Suspensions

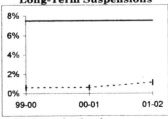

School trend is level
Above District Standards

Disciplinary Action Ratio
(Minority / White Rate)
Long-Term Suspensions

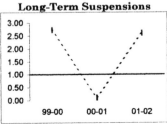

Below District Standards

Disciplinary Action Rate
Expulsions

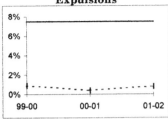

School trend is level
Above District Standards

Disciplinary Action Ratio
(Minority / White Rate)
Expulsions

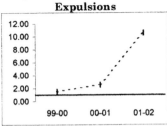

Well Below District Standards

NATHAN HALE HIGH SCHOOL
2001-2002 EFFECTIVENESS PROFILE

Achievement Gap for Five Ethnic Groups
ITED Core NCE

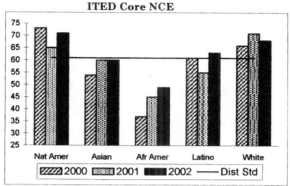

Achievement Gap for Five Ethnic Groups
WASL Reading Percent Meeting Standard

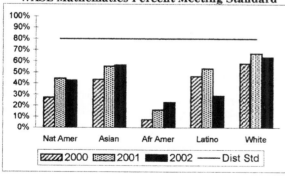

Achievement Gap for Five Ethnic Groups
WASL Writing Percent Meeting Standard

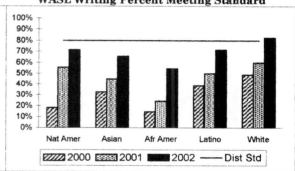

Achievement Gap for Five Ethnic Groups
WASL Mathematics Percent Meeting Standard

Achievement Gap for Five Ethnic Groups
WASL Listening Percent Meeting Standard

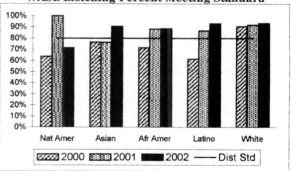

LEGEND: ---♦---   School   ——   2004 District Standard

(Continued)

Figure 7.9 (Continued)

NATHAN HALE HIGH SCHOOL
2001-2002 EFFECTIVENESS PROFILE

Continuation Rate

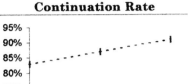
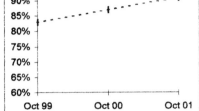

For Information Only

Truancy Rate

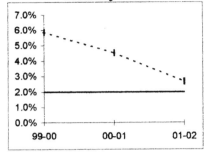

School trend is very positive
Approaching District Standards

Student Attendance Rate

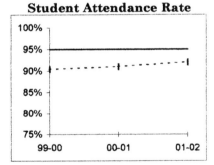

School trend is very positive
Below District Standards

Staff Attendance Rate

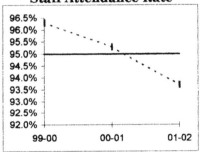

School trend is level
At District Standard

Dropout Rate

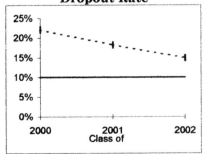

School trend is positive
Approaching District Standards

Graduation Rate

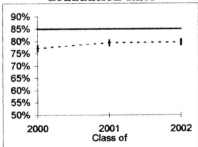

School trend is level
Approaching District Standards

LEGEND: ---♦--- School ———— 2004 District Standard

NATHAN HALE HIGH SCHOOL
2001-2002 EFFECTIVENESS PROFILE

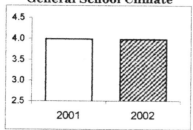

Staff Survey
General School Climate

Standard not yet established

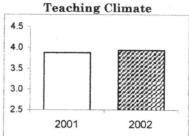

Staff Survey
Teaching Climate

Standard not yet established

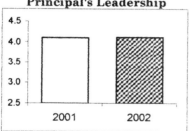

Staff Survey
Principal's Leadership

Standard not yet established

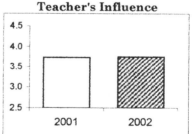

Staff Survey
Teacher's Influence

Standard not yet established

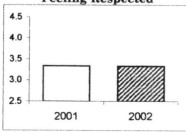

Staff Survey
Feeling Respected

Standard not yet established

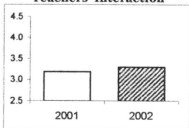

Staff Survey
Teachers' Interaction

Standard not yet established

LEGEND: ---♦--- School ——— 2004 District Standard

Reprinted With Permission From Seattle Public Schools, Seattle, WA.

education *here,* what we are *not* doing, and what we are able to tell you about your children. Moving quickly to data and documentation enabled the district to report percentages of students mastering outcomes, and the accountability the district was willing to provide spoke to the benefits of what it was doing. This history made the Oregon district better prepared than most for state standards and statewide assessments. It also made staff members more comfortable using data to demonstrate progress.

It was a new challenge to help parents and the community understand the relationship between national percentiles and state proficiency scores. School board members didn't want to hear about testing concepts in the abstract; they wanted to see numbers. So Cal Callaway, Director of Instruction, and Wayne Bellcross, High School Assistant Principal, decided to draw them a picture. Figure 7.10 shows mean national percentile scores—the numbers people are used to—as a solid line superimposed across stacked bar graphs that show the distribution of students rated as *minimal, basic, proficient,* and *advanced* in the new structure. This "double exposure" helps parents and constituents see that their students continue to score just as well as usual compared with the national sample. It also illustrates how dramatically Wisconsin—like other states—has raised the bar for student performance.

With increased use of technology and electronic files, more data is being provided on school, district, and state Web sites. The school effectiveness profile shown in Figure 7.9 is accessible to the world on www .seattleschools.org. As No Child Left Behind mandated additional kinds of reporting, state departments of education generated the data and posted it on their Web sites. Sometimes schools are unaware of the data about them that is available online. One role of the data team could be regular monitoring of other Web sites, as well as continual reporting on their own.

The Acid Test

Let's assume that at this point your school has 15 pages of data. On each page, there is just the introductory section and a graph. Chapter 8 suggests a way to empower your staff by engaging all of them in interpreting the data. The acid test is this: Do your data displays look like something your teachers can understand—or will at least discuss—if it's a nice, warm afternoon and they've been teaching all week?

Notes

1. Since I have cited Gerald Bracey (1997) twice in support of my content, it is only fair to share his opinion of NCEs: "Avoid them unless the feds force you to use them" (p. 31). My position is that the normal curve equivalent is an available alternative to the greater danger of neglecting to examine our students' progress over time.

2. Technical notes, including formulas used in calculations, are available on the Seattle Public Schools Web site (www.seattleschools.org).

Figure 7.10 Comparing Proficiency Levels With National Percentiles

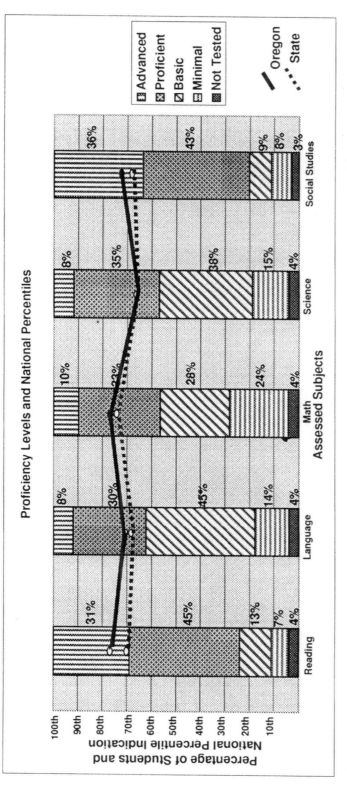

Proficiency Levels and National Percentiles

Subject Areas Assessed	Reading	Language	Math	Science	Social Studies
Not Tested	4%	4%	4%	4%	3%
Minimal	7%	14%	24%	15%	8%
Basic	13%	45%	28%	38%	9%
Proficient	45%	30%	33%	35%	43%
Advanced	31%	8%	10%	8%	36%

WSAS Percentile Ranks			
	Grade 10		
	Oregon	Wisconsin	Nation
Reading	76%ile	71%ile	50%ile
Language	71%ile	68%ile	50%ile
Mathematics	76%ile	75%ile	50%ile
Science	66%ile	66%ile	50%ile
Social Studies	73%ile	68%ile	50%ile

*Figures based on students in the school for a full academic year.

8

Interpreting the Results

Spring break had come and gone, and the countdown was under way. It wasn't the last day of school we were anticipating. It was the release of the test scores. Principals and teachers knew they had arrived in the district, because the corner window of the Research and Evaluation Department was lit up until the wee hours for two nights straight. It meant that the test expert was poring through the printouts, preparing them for dissemination to the buildings.

When we received them a few days later, we knew what mattered. The areas of student performance that would have been listed as concerns on Figure 1.1 were highlighted on each report. A memo was attached directing us to study them carefully and respond within two weeks with an improvement plan. It wasn't motivating and it didn't increase interest in working with data for several reasons:

- The implication was that not all staff members at the school were willing or able to identify areas of concern for them.
- The absence of acknowledgment that our students did very well in some areas created resentment and added to the emotional barriers described in Chapter 3.
- The expectation that a two-week window during the last month of school was either adequate time or the appropriate time to develop a sound improvement plan was ludicrous.

Carousel Data Analysis

Figure 8.1 outlines the structure of a staff development activity—Carousel Data Analysis—that engages staff in discussion, empowers them to

Figure 8.1   Carousel Data Analysis

Preparing the Materials

- Enlarged copies of the data displays
- Questions for discussion on flip chart paper
- Colored markers
- Post the data displays and questions at stations around a large room with blank wall space

Preparing the Participants

- Structure groups of 5 to 11 that cross department or grade-level boundaries
- Have groups designate a facilitator and recorder
- Colored marker travels with the recorder

Questions for Reflection

- What do these data seem to tell us?
- What do they not tell us? What else would we need to know?
- What good news is here to celebrate?
- What needs for school improvement might arise from these data?

interpret what the data means, and allows them to express reservations about its use. My ground rule for interpreting data is, "Let them do it themselves"—that is, let teachers be involved in interpreting the data about their own schools. My message to teachers is, "Do unto the data before the data gets done unto you."

Preparing the Materials

Materials for the Carousel Data Analysis are data displays, such as the graphs in Chapters 6 and 7. These are enlarged to poster size so they can be displayed on the wall and discussed as a small group. (It is much more effective to keep the discussion focused in this way, rather than by providing multiple paper copies of a packet of information to each individual around a table.) The School Effectiveness Profile in Figure 7.9 could yield displays for stations about reading data, writing, listening, science, and grade point averages (GPAs). Each station would include the disaggregated data for that content area and might incorporate school-based data as well. One station could include all the discipline, attendance, and other student-related data. Survey data from students could be at yet another location.

Two factors to consider in preparation are space and time. The room to be used should be large, with plenty of blank wall space for posting graphs and questions. This is one professional development activity that *does* work fine in a lunchroom or gym. People can think on their feet and move about, which is an important way to release tension, if this is an unfamiliar task.

The time needed is related to the amount of data ready for staff review and the number of staff members who will be participating. A general guideline is that this activity takes about 1 1/2 hours. That would accommodate a staff of 50, with 15 data displays to consider. They would be divided into 15 groups of three to four. There would be 15 stations to visit. At 5 minutes per station, the data review would take 75 minutes. Similar arithmetic will help you plan your time and groups.

Variations can be made for a group of 100. One is to have groups of seven or eight people. Another is to have two sets of graphs and operate two sets of stations. A third is to have larger groups and cluster several related data displays at each station.

Preparing the Participants

Groups should be structured before the event to help cross the natural boundaries of grade level or department that people naturally adopt. This structuring can be done in a straightforward manner, such as by posting the rosters, or a lighthearted approach can be used, with methods such as putting colored dots on nametags or numbers on the sticks of lollipops or bases of ice cream cones.

Take the first 15 minutes to explain the purpose of the activity and the reasons the participants have been placed in groups. The purpose is to give everyone an opportunity to view all the data that has been prepared for the school portfolio. The participants are being asked to contribute to the interpretation of the data and provide input to complete the data displays. The groups are a way of encouraging new discussions with people they may not see often and sharing various perspectives. Their activity models the collaborative culture that looks at the big picture of the whole school (rather than how the department is doing) and they will experience a sense of the collective responsibility that a school staff should share.

The numbers or color codes of the groups will help participants find the other members of their group and the station where they will start. Give them a few minutes to get located and to choose the facilitator and recorder for each group. The group will have a designated time at each station. The task is to discuss the data that is shown and react to each of the questions. The recorder will write members' reactions on the flip chart paper that is posted at the station. After the designated time, at a signal announced in advance, each group will move to the next station to review another type of data.

The kinesthetic value of moving from station to station has already been mentioned. Another benefit is that each group reviews the reactions of other staff members, increasing the shared perceptions in another way. A less interactive alternative is to have groups seated at tables and provide each table with a set of all the data displays for discussion. The same input may be provided, but the interaction of the groups with each other and the awareness of what other groups have said will be missing.

Questions for Reflection

The questions for reflection and discussion in Figure 8.1 have been carefully worded. The first question does not say, "What do these data tell us?" but, "What do these data *seem* (or *appear*) to tell us?" People will see different things in the same data, and someone is sure to quote Mark Twain's comment, "There are lies, damn lies, and statistics." Words like *seem* or *appear* acknowledge that the conclusions may not be cut and dried.

The second question provides further acknowledgment that a single snapshot of data may not tell the whole story of what we need to know to make decisions. Asking, "What else would we need to know?" sends a clear message that these are not the only data we will ever see.

The third question, "What good news is here to celebrate?" highlights the positive results and reminds us not to overlook the progress that is being made. Although student needs are urgent, we will not become more skilled or dedicated by focusing only on what is not yet done.

The last question, "What needs for school improvement might arise from these data?" raises awareness of the fact that these data will guide goal setting, decision making, and planning in the future. Including the word *might* reminds us that these are tentative conclusions at this point.

Figure 8.2 is a graph of cumulative GPAs that was posted at one station of the Carousel Data Analysis at Templeton Middle School in Sussex, Wisconsin. The interpretations recorded by staff members are listed in Figure 8.3. The principal, Patricia Polczynski, reports, "The experience of gathering information, putting it in graph form, and then allowing the staff to 'pick it apart' and determine what it means to us has been eye opening and powerful."

Listening In

During the Carousel Data Analysis activity, groups are primarily self-directed, but some listening in to assess the quality of the dialogue is critical. This may occur by having a member of the leadership team within each group or by having some facilitators moving about the room and observing the process. These leaders/facilitators need to be sensitive to comments that may be made and briefed on some strategies for guiding them in a productive direction. As Ruth Johnson (2002) points out,

> Inevitably, some of the discoveries that the school and district make regarding their beliefs, practices, and outcomes will be painful. The school community must be prepared to work through some hard times. Self-knowledge is the first step toward self-improvement. There will be conflict and debate, and some members of the school community will not be pleased with the data process. The knowledge, beliefs, values, and experiences that we bring to the table influence how data are interpreted. Others can interpret one person's analysis of the data picture very differently. Without opportunity for dialogue, problems and misunderstandings can fester. In the long run, the question should be:

Figure 8.2 Cumulative Grade Point Averages by Grade

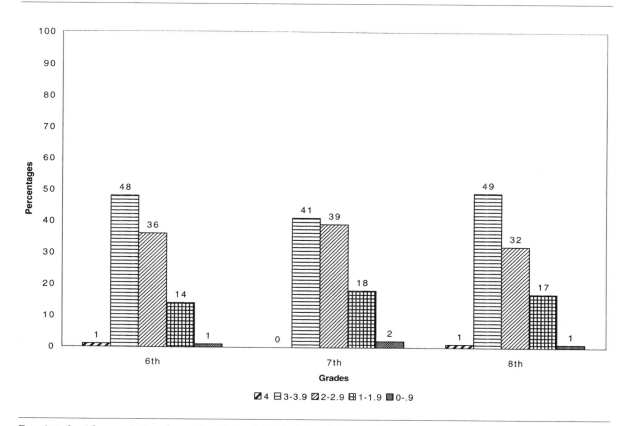

Reprinted with permission from Templeton Middle School, Sussex, WI.

"How can we use the data to build a common agenda for student improvement?

If data regarding achievement of various groups of students are particularly disturbing, there will be lots of finger pointing, and the familiar excuses will be heard about why things are the way they are. The responsibility for poor achievement may be placed solely on students and parents and the conditions in which they live. Policies and practices within the school or district may be skirted, and there is likely to be an abdication of the school's responsibility for outcomes. Without thoughtful dialogue, the same old tired solutions continue to occur, such as adding on more programs rather than fixing core problems. (pp. 49–50)

As groups discuss the data before them, especially disaggregated data, facilitators should listen in to hear if comments are being made that reflect or convey stereotypes and low expectations. Statements such as "Well, what can you expect? All [such students] are always low performers and unmotivated" cannot be ignored. If they are not addressed, silence becomes consent, and these beliefs go unchallenged and spread within the culture. The Carousel Data Analysis activity provides an opportunity to redirect such statements toward the "What else would we need to know?"

Figure 8.3   Carousel Data Analysis of Cumulative Grade Point Averages

1. What do these data seem to tell us?
   - 80% of the students in each grade are average or above.
   - The plateau of seventh grade brain growth correlates with this graph.
   - Small percentage of low GPA.
   - 70% fall at or above C level.
   - Only 1% are at 4.0 or better.
   - 30% to 40% or better are 2.0 to 2.9.
   - Eighth grade has highest with B averages—81%.
   - Seventh grade has highest failure rate:
     - lowest percentage of B or above and no one with 4.0 GPA
     - more "clumped" with 80% achieving 2.0 or higher
   - No drastic differences in grade levels overall.
   - Decline a bit in seventh grade.
   - Percentages are close.
   - Seventh grade achievement is relatively lower in all grade points except for 2.0 to 2.9; has the highest number of students with the lowest grade point average.
   - Less than 20% of each grade has a cumulative GPA between 1.0 and 1.9.
   - Seventh grade has the lowest percentage of high GPAs.

2. What do they not tell us? What else would we need to know?
   - Academic ability of students
   - Specific information as far as courses (elective vs. academic), teachers, etc.
   - Group dynamics of each grade
   - What they actually know versus grades
   - Teacher expectations/grading expectations
   - Attendance information
   - Gender differences
   - Doesn't reflect grade scales by teacher or grade
   - Doesn't reflect weight of time frames (some classes are 1/4 as long, etc.)
   - Seventh and eighth can choose electives
   - Motivation, effort, parent support
   - How this compares to other districts in terms of breakdown per grade level

3. What good news is here to celebrate?
   - There is a very high percentage in the 3.0 to 3.9 range.
   - Majority fall within 3.0 to 3.9 range.
   - 40% or better are 3.0 to 3.9 for all Grades 6, 7, and 8.
   - At least 40% of each grade level has a cumulative GPA between 3.0 and 3.9.

4. What needs for school improvement might arise from these data?
   - Create common criteria and expectations for A, B, C grades
   - Improve vertical curriculum articulation 6 → 7, 7 → 8
   - Better counseling for seventh grade courses and electives

question. Asking the speaker how we might follow up and check the accuracy of a negative statement conveys that it is not being accepted at face value, but does so without creating an adversarial stance or passing moral judgment on the individual.

Using the Responses

The four reflection questions in Figure 8.1 have specific application for use as the school moves forward with its school improvement process. Responses to the first question, "What do these data seem to tell us?" will be synthesized to form the summary statements under the graphs in the school portfolio. They are also used to compile the overall data summary, as shown in Figures 8.4–8.7. Reference to these summary statements is an important part of narrowing the focus to a few priority goals.

The second question, "What do these data not tell us?" prompts the further analysis described in Chapter 11. In this way, the Carousel Data Analysis starts the snowball rolling for data work (see Chapter 6). The needs for additional data also support indicators that may serve as the evidence of implementation and impact required by Chapter 14.

Question 3, "What good news is here to celebrate?" focuses on positive accomplishments and highlights data the school will want to emphasize in both public and internal communications. Answers to the fourth question identify possible needs for school improvement. These needs will be verified through additional data work, and strategies will be selected to match.

Making It Public

As pointed out in Chapter 4, the administrative team, data team, and leadership teams must have a working familiarity with all the school's data. In comparison, the whole staff needs a big-picture overview of their school's results. Moreover, involved parents and community members will admire and appreciate the school that provides them with a user-friendly summary of their data.

The Data Summary

Figure 8.4 provides an example of a data summary for two assessments given at the elementary and middle school level. Figure 8.5 provides an outline for summary statements from the types of data recommended in Figure 6.2. Two to three bulleted statements, as in Figure 8.4, would be provided under each subheading. This narrative data summary should not exceed a maximum of two pages, so it could be produced as a single two-sided sheet of information.

Figure 8.4   Summary of Student Performance Results

Direct Writing Assessment

- 85% of all students at or above standards in 2002 compared to 81% in 2001—a gain of 4%; a gain of 18% since 1998
- Significant increase in students performing at the advanced level— 22% in 2002 vs. 25% in 2001
- Substantial progress made toward meeting standards among cohort groups

Iowa Test of Basic Skills (ITBS)

- Elementary—slight decrease in reading and language; remained constant in math
- Grade 6—students scored above the national average in all content areas
- Grade 8—slight increase in reading and math; remained constant in language
- District scores above state averages in all content areas for Grades 3 and 6

Data at a Glance

Chapter 7 included a school portfolio that provided line graphs of three years of data, referenced to a district standard. One school further summarized its data into a one-page chart shown in Figure 8.6. The headings on the columns match the captions that accompany the graphs. A more generic template for this data-at-a-glance is shown in Figure 8.7. These headings can be used to describe trends in numerous types of data. Such summaries help to develop a common vision of the reality of the school and serve as a ready reference for decision making.

Figure 8.5   Summary of School Portfolio

Student Learning

Reading

-
-

Writing

-
-

Math

-
-

Science

-
-

Student Engagement

Discipline

-
-

Attendance

-
-

Graduation

-
-

Survey

-
-

Staff Productivity

Professional Development

-
-

Surveys

-
-

Parent/Community Support

Surveys

-
-

Figure 8.6   Three-Year Data Summary

School Trend Is Level/Positive & at or Above District Standard	School Trend Is Level and Approaching District Standard	School Trend Is Very Positive and Well Below District Standard	School Trend Is Level and Below District Standard	School Trend Is Level and Well Below District Standard	School Trend Is Negative and Below District Standard
Truancy Rate	ITBS Language	WASL Reading	ITBS Reading	WASL Writing	ITBS Math
Attendance Rate	District Writing Assessment—3rd Gr.			WASL Math	
Disciplinary Action Rate—Short-Term Suspensions	District Writing Assessment—5th Gr.			WASL Listening	
Student Survey—Staff Relations	Student Survey—Student Relations				
Student Survey—Learning Climate	Student Survey—Safety				
Staff Survey—Team Cohesiveness					
Staff Survey—Leadership					
Staff Survey—Climate					
Staff Survey—Curriculum					
Staff Survey—Public Relations					

Figure 8.7 Data Summary Template

School Name _____

Data Summary for 20 ____

Performance Is High and Consistent	Trend Is Significantly Positive	Performance Is Consistent but Low	Trend Is Downward

123

9

Designing a Data Day

There are opposing schools of thought about visibility and magnitude of change. One is that change should be introduced and should occur in small increments to maintain a sense of continuity and not exceed organizational capacity. Another is that people don't get excited about little changes, that gradual change doesn't generate energy and enthusiasm, and that people can hide behind their classroom doors thinking, "This, too, shall pass." Neither approach is an antidote for natural resistance. Resistance to the incremental approach may take rather passive forms, but it can be just as detrimental as active resistance. Introducing change as a major new focus with lots of visibility may generate more overt resistance, but that may be easier to handle when it's out in the open.

I have seen both approaches work when the choice was made intentionally after thorough discussion of the history and current situation of the specific district. The leadership team in East Troy, Wisconsin, chose to build on its past successes and took more of the incremental approach. The team started its data-driven school-based efforts by providing a timeline of the curriculum and instruction work already done in the district and introduced this new focus as the next logical phase in an ongoing, evolving improvement process (Larsen & Bresler, 1998).

The school district of Fort Atkinson, Wisconsin, looked at its current situation and saw a number of factors that created a readiness to introduce the use of data as a major new initiative. A new high school building would be opening soon. One round of district strategic planning had occurred and a commitment had been made that this cycle would be more data-driven than the previous one. The requirements for school accreditation included an increased focus on documenting student success. The year's statewide assessments would be reported in proficiency levels for the first time. All these changes were occurring anyway. Why not capitalize on their common need for data?—especially since participation in a Goals 2000 consortium focused on school improvement provided resources to help answer the "Who's gonna do this and where will we get the time?" questions. Fort Atkinson's decision was to be very direct about accountability issues and to engage all 200 teachers in a kickoff event—a Data Day.

I have helped other districts design Data Days, but will use Fort Atkinson as the model for this chapter. Three leaders deserve special acknowledgment: Dr. Jerry McGowan, District Administrator; Dr. Mabel Schumacher, Director of Instruction; and Mr. Joe Overturf, Director of Special Education and Strategic Planning Facilitator.

Purpose

A district might choose a highly visible approach such as the Fort Atkinson model for several reasons:

- To make everyone aware that using data is an important focus
- To convey the expectation that all will support and participate in using data
- To ensure that all staff members receive common information about why they are doing this, what will happen, and how it will affect them

The Fort Atkinson district also had unique local purposes:

- To strengthen this cycle of strategic planning with greater use of data
- To provide an opportunity for all staff to provide input to the Strategic Planning Team

Preparation

You don't plan an event of great magnitude and visibility just by setting a date and contracting a consultant to "come in and kick it off." I already had some prior understanding of the district, because I had worked with some of the local leaders for more than five years. Even so, we scheduled an advance day for planning and preparation. Almost two weeks before Data Day, I met with a group that included the superintendent, curriculum and instruction staff, all principals, and the facilitator of strategic planning. (The presence and participation of the district administrator in key instructional issues is a powerful modeling tool that I request at all times and reinforce vigorously.)

Figure 9.1   Agenda for Data Day

8:15–8:30	Opening Remarks by Superintendent
8:30–9:00	Using Data for Alignment and Achievement
9:00–9:30	Why We Need to Use Data More
9:30–10:15	What Data Will We Use?
10:15–10:45	Break
10:45–11:05	Monitoring Our Mission: The First Critical Question
11:05–11:30	The Other Four Questions
11:30–11:45	Swapping Stories
11:45–12:00	What Happens Next
12:00–1:00	Lunch
1:00–1:15	Overview by the Principal
1:15–2:30	Carousel Data Analysis
2:30–2:45	Break
2:45–3:10	Reporting Out
3:10–3:30	Messages for Strategic Planning Team

We began our planning by discussing the purposes of the Data Day. I asked each group to express what we would need to accomplish for participants to consider the day a success. This joint list became our set of desired outcomes and our criteria for planning.

After clarifying the purposes, we developed the agenda for a morning session that would include all district staff. Because students would not be in attendance, constituents were informed of how the day would be used and were invited to attend. The morning session would also be videotaped so it would be available for anyone interested who could not participate (see Figure 9.1).

We then planned school-based activities for the afternoon so principals could build on the momentum of the general session and staff members could be immediately engaged in authentic work with their own data. Our last task was to develop our respective To Do lists in preparation.

The handout packet for the morning district session included Figures 1.1, 5.4, and 6.1. We also prepared overhead transparencies of the district and school mission statements. The biggest task—preparing the data that staff members would analyze in their schools in the afternoon—fell to the Office of Curriculum and Instruction. Principals worked on the logistics of the Carousel Data Analysis, organized the groups, and prepared the reflection questions for each station (see Chapter 8).

District Session

Following a continental breakfast, teachers gathered in an auditorium-style room. I worked from the floor, not from a stage, and used a wireless microphone. These are important considerations, because they gave me the opportunity to move into and through the audience and to chat directly with participants. The following sections correspond to segments of the agenda in Figure 9.1.

Opening Remarks by the Superintendent

Superintendent Jerry McGowan opened the session with greetings and humor. His style cannot be captured in text—you had to be there! He then moved quickly from the ridiculous to the reality, describing recent state and local events that generated a sense of urgency for the work of the day: new laws offering public school choice, requests to move in and out of the district, data about the upward trend of home schooling, Youth Options legislation allowing for two years of technical school training after the tenth grade, and district comparisons being made in the media and by citizen activist groups.

To emphasize these realities, he cut to the quick with dollar figures on revenue lost for each student exercising another alternative and compared these losses with the average cost of a teaching position. He ended on a note of optimism, however, describing the purposes of the day and asserting his belief that there were data to demonstrate the high quality of the school district and his faith in the staff to help pull it together.

Using Data for Alignment and Achievement

The second segment of the district session focused on the concepts of alignment outlined in Chapter 1 and illustrated on Figure 1.1. To foster active participation, I engaged the group in a musical performance assessment so that I could collect some data to use as an example. Tongue in cheek, I described the controversy about phonics and whole language and the accusations leveled by some citizen groups that students do poorly in reading because they haven't had enough phonics. I said that, as a result, I felt I needed to know whether the teaching staff actually knew their phonics and would focus on the long vowel sounds for an experimental test.

Their task would be to sing the familiar song, *Row, Row, Row Your Boat*, changing position each time they sang or heard a long vowel sound. We would stand for the first "row," sit down on the second "row," stand for the third "row," and continue with our ups and downs for all long vowel sounds (*boat, -ly, stream, -ly, -ly, -ly, -ly, life,* and *dream*). After reciting the long vowel sounds to activate our prior knowledge and a little humming to practice the tune, we had administrators model and then we gave it a try.

I then announced my conclusions that, based on multiple observations, about 5% of the group were advanced, 20% were proficient, 55% were at the basic level, and 20% were only minimally proficient. (These were the four proficiency levels introduced with the statewide assessment for the first time that year.) I prolonged the satire by commenting that I was in a district the previous week that had 10% advanced, 30% proficient,

50% basic, and only 10% minimal and by asking them to speculate on reasons why District X was doing so much better.

I used these mock data to bring relevance and humor to a discussion of the alignment between the components in Figure 1.1. First, these data wouldn't mean anything unless we actually cared about whether students could identify long vowel sounds (the content standard) and respond to them by sitting or standing while also singing (the performance standard). If "basic skills" was in the mission statement of a given elementary school and long vowel sounds was one of the essential learnings, these would be important data. It might appear as one of many concerns and surface as a priority learning goal. Then we would study best practice and further analyze our local performance to select strategies.

We might identify the students who were advanced and ask how they learned to perform so well. We might even have them tutor the rest of the group. Or we might practice other songs with vowel sounds, have drills of the vowel sounds themselves, or make little kits for more practice at home. Perhaps the music department could help with rhythm, and the physical education department could set up clinics for deep knee bending. We would repeat this same assessment in hopes of better results and might design other forms of assessment to provide alternative demonstrations of the essential learning. Then we would identify who was responsible for carrying out the strategies and administering the assessments and develop our action plans.

Spoofing a little kept the large group curious and engaged and still conveyed the concepts of alignment and the big picture of what else happens once data are compiled.

Why We Need to Use Data More

Chapter 5 describes the live Motivation Continuum that was used during the next segment of the district session. Audience participation was noisy and energetic. After the applause contest reinforced the factors that would make data meaningful to the participants, I mentioned that "to keep our accreditation" or "to get our Goals 2000 money" were not on the list. They are important considerations, but should not be the driving force behind our professional commitments.

What Data Will We Use?

One page of the handout packet included a list of data corresponding to the categories described in Figure 6.2. During the segment examining what data to use, I showed examples of graphs from each category and told the story of the school that developed them, and how they do so and why. I also showed them the list of data Wisconsin districts must report annually and had them star those items on their handout. This would let them know which data are readily available and also foreshadow the data they would discuss in the afternoon at their school sites.

Break

As Figure 9.1 indicates, we worked for two hours before taking a break. As a rule of thumb, I try to take frequent, short 10-minute breaks, but a group size of 200 means longer lines for emptying and refueling, so we needed a long break in the middle. Plan your breaks according to group size and access to personal needs.

Monitoring Our Mission: The First Critical Question

When the teachers assembled at the beginning of the district session, no attempt was made to structure the seating arrangement. Before the break, I asked the participants to raise their hands by building to see where they were and asked them to sit as close as possible to most of the other people from their school after the break. Chapter 5 describes the activity we used to answer the question, "What evidence would demonstrate that we are fulfilling the commitments embedded in our mission statement?" Staff members stood and faced each other over the backs of their seats to work in small school-based groups. The transparencies of district and school mission statements were available for review.

The Other Four Questions

Figure 6.3 lists the other four questions for reflection on data selection. During the segment on them, I used the height example to illustrate disaggregation. One petite woman grabbed a chair to stand on, saying she "always wanted to be one of the 6-footers." This was gratifying evidence of the group's comfort level and participation. I encouraged staff members to chat briefly about each question with their neighbors, because in the afternoon they would be asked what else they might need to know.

Swapping Stories

The last activity of the morning—Swapping Stories—is described in Chapter 5. By this time, I had spotted some performers in the group and recruited them to read the book excerpts.

What Happens Next

We concluded the morning by telling the participants that a first batch of data had already been prepared for them to review in the afternoon. We described the process for engagement at their individual schools and emphasized its importance as an opportunity to provide input for strategic planning and to be proactive in determining the data to include in their school's portfolio.

School-Based Activities

Staff met at their respective buildings in the afternoon. Principals prepared for data interpretation by arranging the room, the materials, and the groups as described in Chapter 8.

Overview by the Principal

Each principal created a bridge from the morning to the afternoon by repeating the purposes of the day and using Figure 1.1 to help explain. The principals pointed out that the afternoon activities related to the *School Portfolio* box and also the column of *Concerns*. Participants would review data that would be in the portfolio and identify concerns that might arise from them. They would also identify other data they wanted added to the school portfolio for review before focusing on *Priority Goals.*

Carousel Data Analysis

After the introduction, the school groups utilized the Carousel Data Analysis process of group data interpretation from Chapter 8.

Reporting Out

After completing the round of stations in the Carousel Data Analysis, each small group shared its overall reactions to the complete set of data. Common observations from all groups were highlighted. A list of desired data was also compiled from the sheets at each station. These requests were forwarded afterward to the Curriculum Office and district staff would help compile the lists from all schools and provide as much of the desired data as possible.

Messages for the Strategic Planning Team

Each school had a representative who would be participating in the strategic planning process in the next few days. The afternoon discussion concluded by identifying the input this representative should provide from the building.

Follow-Up

The Strategic Planning Team met a few days later. The external consultant was very cooperative and incorporated references to Data Day and the schools' input as the process moved forward. One participant commented that "the information came back and really jelled" in the strategic plan. Joe Overturf, Director of Special Education/Pupil Services and internal facilitator of strategic planning, shared with me these helpful comments on the interface between district strategic planning and school improvement:

This demonstrated how data analysis could be used to complement and enrich our model of strategic planning. It's my belief that information contained within school portfolios should be used to validate the acknowledgment of weaknesses identified during the internal analysis phase of planning. Currently, sites or districts are asked to develop a database, but there is not an emphasis on the analysis of the data. In my experiences to date, cited weaknesses are more intuitive on the part of individual planners. I believe that data analysis of preexisting information would strengthen the basis for identifying critical issues (which is the culmination of the internal and external analysis of the organization).

While data-driven objectives may address the critical issues of the day, they fail to address the objective of dreamers. If objectives are to be strategic in nature and are to be driven by dreams, then the planning team has a responsibility to identify assessment measures and apply them to those objectives over time to monitor the impact on student learning.

Regardless of the origin of the strategic objectives (i.e., addressing the critical issues of the day or the dreams of the future), there needs to be a conscientious effort to gather data to see if our school improvement efforts via strategic planning are making a difference. I would suggest and hope that some of the information in a school portfolio be directly aligned with strategic objectives and that progress be closely monitored on a periodic basis. This could occur every time there is a periodic review of the site plan. This would provide the vehicle to monitor and demonstrate growth over time to determine if we are having a positive impact on kids.

Other comments on Data Day included these reactions:

"It went just perfectly and we are so happy with the level of participation."

"This was a wonderful staff development day."

"The activities worked so well with that setting of 200 people. It made them all feel involved and even made them laugh."

"The morning gave people a sense of purpose and they went away happy to return after lunch and do something that matters."

Of all the activities discussed in the first edition of this book, I have received the most gratitude for information on designing a Data Day. Readers report that it was exactly what they needed for their building (or district) kickoff of data work. "It let people know we were serious about using data, but yet it was a lot of fun."

Making It Public

One of the scarcest resources in schools today is time for collaborative professional work. Making such work possible during the regular work-day typically means having students stay home or sending them home early. This creates a change in routine for families and an interest on their part in what the teachers are doing. One principal uses the school news-letter to create transparency around early-release days. A typical message reads, "Thank you for your support in providing for your children's care on Wednesday afternoon. Their teachers will be conducting student progress reviews so we can be sure every child is receiving appropriate support for learning success."

One district posted messages on the doors and school message boards reading, "2,100 staff hours devoted to learning literacy strategies." Signs in another district read, "Data Day Underway." One of the best ways to safeguard the precious commodity of collaborative professional development time is to be proactive in communicating how it is being used and how that benefits students.

10

Establishing Priorities

In the first edition of this book, this chapter began with the statement that, "depending on whose research you read, school reform either takes 3 to 5 years or 5 to 7 years." Since then, Michael Fullan (2003a) has referred to the "rule of 3-6-8." Based on his observations of educational change, an elementary school can improve performance in about three years, while it seems to take six years to get changes in achievement at high schools, and more like eight years to create change districtwide.

One reason it takes so long is that the school improvement process isn't the only thing going on in a school. That's why it's critical that change efforts focus on a few goals that are systemic and substantive enough to motivate sustained attention and have an impact on student learning. This chapter describes a process through which students, staff, and constituents can generate all their concerns and then participate in identifying priorities and sharpening this focus. We will then address how to phrase goals so they keep the focus on student learning and point out the danger of confusing goals with strategies.

Getting It Out and Narrowing It Down

The goal-setting process that has been effective in many settings is a combination of the traditional nominal group process and the use of a decision matrix. These two techniques are described separately in *Asking the Right Questions* (Holcomb, 2001). What I've discovered is that the nominal group process, when used alone, can result in agreement on goals derived solely from the opinions of the group. If reference to data about the school's and students' performance is lacking, people end up wondering why they went to all the trouble of compiling the school portfolio.

Without baseline data, schools also end up with no basis for comparison to show progress. Use of the decision matrix brings both objective and subjective data to the table. As Doris Thompson, principal of Lake Mills Middle School said to me, "Teachers do think about students' needs when they plan, but they will like being able to verify that by looking at the real evidence."

The steps in this hybrid process are

1. Review of the data
2. Individual reflection
3. Round-robin listing
4. Individual rating on three criteria
5. Adding individual ratings
6. Individual ranking of five priorities
7. Group ranking of five priorities
8. Discussion
9. Repetition of individual ratings and rankings as needed

Note how many steps occur before discussion. This sequence was developed to provide an opportunity for participants to share all concerns, engage in personal reflection, and observe how their ratings compare to the rest of the group before becoming verbal.

Review of the Data

In the previous chapter and in Chapter 8, we discussed Carousel Data Analysis, in which participants moved in groups from station to station, discussing compiled data and responding to critical questions. The last question asked was, "What needs for school improvement might arise from these data?" The kickoff for the data review process is to examine those responses. It is certainly appropriate to have the list typed and provide copies for the participants, but sometimes a more powerful connection occurs if the actual flip chart sheets from the earlier activity are saved and displayed again.

Individual Reflection

After participants have a chance to review the tentative concerns previously identified, stimulate further reflection by posing a question such as, "What are all the things that anyone might say could be improved about our school?" As the question is displayed, underline the word *all* and emphasize that this is the participants' opportunity to create a comprehensive list for consideration. They should be candid and jot down any concern they have on scratch paper provided.

Then, call attention to the word *anyone* and remind them to present not only their own viewpoints, but also the concerns of others they have discovered in survey data or private discussions. Stress that the word *could* expresses our commitment to continuous improvement and does not imply that the current situation is so awful. We're simply expressing our openness to look closely at all aspects of our school.

Observe the individual reflection and allow time for most participants to finish writing. Emphasize that every one of their concerns will be included and that it will be helpful if they look them over to be sure they are specific and easily understood. Suggest that longer statements be reduced to a short three- to five-word phrase. Omitting verbs from the list of concerns keeps the focus on the issues rather than what action should be taken.

Mention that a concern like "student test scores" will be more helpful if it is broken down into specifics, such as "reading achievement" or "math problem solving." Even if that makes the lists longer, it is good to sub-divide such general items, because reading scores and math scores would be approached differently if they were to become the school's goals.

Round-Robin Listing

If the group consists of 25 or fewer participants, serve as recorder and conduct the round-robin listing yourself. If you are working with a large group, divide it into smaller units and have each group select a recorder. Group members designated as recorders can give their concerns to another participant, who will ensure that the items are included.

Round-robin listing means that each person states one concern from his or her list, and this is repeated around the circle. Emphasize that everyone must listen carefully and cross off items that other people mention to avoid duplication and keep the process moving quickly. The recorder should assign a letter to each item as it is listed to facilitate ranking and discussion later. In addition to the public recording, each participant should jot down the items on the form you have provided (Figure 10.1). Unless participants create their own lists as you go, use of the decision matrix will be complicated and confusing.

If you have facilitated a small group, you now have one list of all members' concerns. If you divided a large group into smaller groups that actually represented different schools, each group has its own total list and will rate and rank those items. However, if everyone in a large group is from the same school, take a break and combine the separate group lists into a master list. This can be done quickly during a break for the large group, either by repeating the round-robin exercise on flip charts or by word processing all the responses and then printing the master list for each participant. If you use a laptop to do this, participants will not need to write in the concerns on Figure 10.1.

Individual Rating on Three Criteria

People get more motivated to work toward goals if there is clear evidence of need (proof), an intrinsic sense of their importance (passion), and a feeling that the goals are achievable and within their reach. The three

Figure 10.1 Goal-Setting Matrix

Area of Concern	How Severe? Rate each item 1–5. 5 = greatest dissatisfaction with results (i.e., lowest test scores, worst problem, etc.).	How Crucial? Rate each item 1–5. 5 = most important issues; needing most immediate attention; most essential to the mission.	How Responsive? Rate each item 1–5. 5 = most amenable to change; within power of school.	Total of Individual Ratings	Individual Ranking Rank order 5 items only with 5 as highest priority.	Group Ranking

criteria of the decision matrix reflect these characteristics of goals that get done. Ask participants to deal with just one column at a time so you can clarify the directions and keep the group in about the same place.

The first question, "How severe?" provides one more opportunity to connect with the data. Participants give ratings of 5 to any concerns they feel are severe, especially areas of student performance with the lowest test scores or survey items with high percentages of dissatisfaction. Remind participants that they can give the same rating—whether 5, 4, 3, 2, or 1— to as many items as they wish.

The second question, "How crucial?" emphasizes the need to establish goals that are closely linked to the mission of the school or that are particularly urgent and important. Urge participants to ignore the ratings they gave in the first column and rate each item according to this criterion only.

The third question, "How responsive?" allows participants to acknowledge that some concerns may be severe and crucial, but outside the scope of influence of the school. Use of this column addresses reality and feasibility. Ratings of 5 are given to those concerns that the school can address most independently; a rating of 1 indicates that the participant feels the school really can't do anything about it.

Adding Individual Ratings

The column in Figure 10.1 labeled *Total of Individual Ratings* is provided so participants can add together the three ratings they gave to each item. Point out that an ideal goal would have a total of 15, because that would identify a severe need that is crucial to the effectiveness of the school and that the school can address. True 15's are rare. The principle is that the higher the total, the more priority the item deserves.

Individual Ranking of Five Priorities

Based on the individual ratings, each participant is to choose his or her top five priorities, with 5 being the highest priority. A helpful tip is to provide stick-on notes and have the participants put the letter code of each of their top five priorities on a note. If a group member is most concerned about items labeled A, E, J, M, and P, there would now be a slip of paper with a letter A, another with E, a third with J, and so forth. The participants can move the stick-on notes around in case they want to change their priorities, but should end up with a 5 on the same card as their *top priority*, a 4 on their next, and so forth. Double check to be sure all have 5 for their top priority (usually someone does this ranking backward).

Group Ranking of Priorities

When participants have ranked their items, ask them to alphabetize their stick-on notes to speed up the group ranking. As you call out a letter, go quickly around the circle and have each person who ranked it state the numerical value he or she gave it. Write down each ranking rather than just adding them mentally and recording a total. When discussion takes place, it will make a difference whether one concern has a total value of 20 because 10 people ranked it a 2 or because 4 people ranked it a 5.

After all concerns have been recorded, total the numbers. In most cases, there will be a group of concerns that cluster together with high scores and then a drop down to another set or the rest of the list.

Discussion

Now is the long-awaited, intentionally postponed opportunity for discussion. Set a few ground rules, which may include the expectation that only advocacy statements will be made. This means that people express why they think a concern is of great importance and should be one of the top priorities for goal setting, but that speeches *against* specific items will not be heard at this time. Sometimes, it's also necessary to set the number of times that any individual can speak or the length of time for any individual comment.

Repetition of Ratings and Rankings

In some cases, a second round of rating and ranking is unnecessary, because the priorities become very clear and the discussion does not indicate strong disagreement with any of them. If there is disagreement or if questions are raised about some items, ask if those who gave it a 5 would share their reasons for being so concerned about it. Sometimes, their responses will provide new information for other participants and cause them to shift their priorities. On other occasions, questions will raise the need for more accurate information before a final decision is reached. In such a situation, help the group decide what information is needed, who can provide it, and what time will be needed to get the information. Then, schedule another meeting to look at the information before a second round of ranking determines the school's priorities. The process should continue until between two and five priorities have been determined.

Variations for Participation

All interested parties should be invited to participate in the goal-setting process, but it may not be feasible to do it all at once, because of group size and scheduling considerations. The process can be broken into phases, and multiple groups can participate and have their input added. For example, staff might generate their list of concerns during a faculty meeting, students might contribute theirs during homerooms or in a representative fashion through a student council meeting, and parents might engage in the round-robin listing at a PTA meeting. If these three events are held in the same week, Figure 10.1 can be prepared as a synthesis of the concerns raised by all three groups. The items could even be coded as to origin. For example, *TSP* might mean that teachers, students, and parents all generated this concern. Each group could meet again the next week and do the ratings and rankings, which would then be combined, and so forth.

Participants who come to a goal-setting session expecting arguments and tension are relieved to see that there is a safety net in the form of a structured but inclusive process. Jeanne Anderson of Jim Falls Elementary School in Chippewa Falls, Wisconsin, put it this way: "I have done many kinds of goal setting and this is the best. It's slick and easy but very sound. It takes the stress out of this important step in school planning."

Wordsmithing Works

Once the few priorities for improvement are identified, the next opportunity for engagement is to develop a goal statement for each one. I admit that I, too, become frustrated with interminable wordsmithing. At the same time, careful thought and conversation should go into the language of such powerful statements as a mission and goals. Common understanding of "what we really mean," is critical, and individual support flows from hearing "my own voice" in the statement. It's also essential to hear/see the student voice in the goal.

Here are two sample statements I use to generate discussion by asking groups to comment on differences between them:

- To increase computer access and develop an integrated technology curriculum
- All students will increase their application of computer skills across the curriculum

Participants observe that the first one doesn't mention students. It's a statement of what the teachers and district will do. The second one says what the children will do. Is it possible to do the first goal without students being affected at all? Sure. The district could buy more computers and hire teachers to write curriculum during the summer and report to the board that the goal was accomplished—with no impact on students at all.

The second statement is systemic enough to drive change in a whole school. Fulfilling it would involve acquiring hardware and software; dealing with facilities and location for access; and identifying the computer applications students should be able to use, how they would be integrated into each discipline, and what products would be created. Staff would also have to develop performance assessments that students would do to demonstrate the computer skills and determine when students could do them. Would they be assessed in classes or would students sign up at a computer lab to test out?

The emphasis of this book is on the use of data. Once goals are set, it should be possible to look backward and forward from the *Priorities* spaces on Figure 1.1 and see the data connections:

- Do the improvement goals accurately reflect data that were reviewed? Is there evidence to support the need for this goal as a priority to sustain several years of effort?
- Will the indicators that demonstrate achievement of the goal be evidence of what *more* students can do *more* of, do *better*, do *differently*?

Goal setting should not be simplistic and formulaic, as witnessed by the purposeful, structured process offered earlier in this chapter. However, for those who find a guideline helpful as a starting point, this template may be useful:

By _____, students will _____ [do more or better on a specific skill] as evidenced by an increase [or decrease] of _____ as demonstrated by or on _____.

For example: *By June 2005, students will improve the quality of their written work through better organization, as evidenced by a score of 3 or better on each trimester schoolwide writing prompt.* This goal narrows the generality of writing performance to a specific area of improvement and foreshadows the evidence that will demonstrate progress (see Chapter 14).

A prosocial goal might read: *By January 2002, students will resolve conflicts appropriately, as evidenced by a decrease in referrals for fighting and loud arguing and an increase in "catch-em-being-good" notes.*

Most schools have issues that need to be addressed that are unrelated to student performance. It may be more accurate to say these are issues that relate to learning *indirectly*, because it's hard to imagine anything occurring in a school that would be of concern to a large number of staff, students, and constituents and yet be so isolated it would have no connection to learning or the learning environment. These issues can be handled as additional goals or may be considered as strategies to help meet a goal. On a few occasions, I have had to stop after the round-robin listing and address the fact that many items on the list would not qualify as student-centered improvement goals. I point this out before the individual ratings are done and ask which items we could code with an *S* because they are actually strategies. We set these items aside and save them for consideration later in the planning process.

An example that could be an additional goal is "relations between staff and administration." If this is a major concern, it certainly affects the teaching-learning environment and needs to be addressed. I would call it an additional goal to emphasize that it is not a substitute for goals aimed directly at improving student performance.

Parent involvement is an example of a *Concern* that might become a *Strategy* in service of one of the student learning goals (see Figure 1.1). If there is a goal that relates to improving students' reading achievement, part of the planning may involve how to engage parents specifically in helping their children with reading. Or if there is a goal that aims to increase students' responsibility for their learning and behavior, parents could be involved in developing strategies to help parents teach and reinforce students for taking responsibility.

The Ends or the Means?

In the goal-setting process, we suggested that noun phrases without verbs be used to express the area of concern. This is because verbs are action words and imply what action should be taken. The actions are the *Strategies* section on Figure 1.1, and a lot of things need to occur in the previous box, marked *Study*, before strategies are selected. When people become committed to a strategy rather than a goal, the focus becomes fuzzy.

One day, I received a call to meet with members of the leadership team of an urban elementary school. An out-of-state consultant had returned their school improvement plan, criticizing their goals. They didn't understand the feedback, and I was nearby and free, so they asked me to help them sort this out. These are the goals they had:

- To set up a writing-to-read computer lab
- To use the Degrees of Reading Power test
- To implement James Comer's school development/mental health model

I began by asking team members to describe their school and their students and how they reached these goals. Then, I asked them to be patient as I probed with "why" questions:

"Why do you want to set up a writing-to-read lab?" "Because IBM will give us the computers."

"Why is it worth the trouble of writing the grant to get the computers and find a place for them and get them set up?" "Because then the kids can use them."

"Why do you want the kids to use them?" "Because there is research that shows that the computer makes it easier and more exciting to write, and when they write more, they learn to read better or faster."

"So what is it you really want?" "For students to read better."

Ah, ha! The goal is that students improve their reading performance. The computer lab is a strategy. Technology is one of the means; it's not the end in and of itself.

Next, we tackled the Degrees of Reading Power test:

"Why do you want to use the Degrees of Reading Power test?" "Because the standardized test we give now just has subtests of phonics and alphabetizing and discrete skills like that, but it doesn't really tell us if they can *read*."

"Why do you like the Degrees of Reading Power test?" "Because it has real passages for students to read and gives us a better measure of comprehension."

Bingo! The goal is that students increase their ability to read and comprehend. The Degrees of Reading Power test is one source of evidence (see Figure 1.1) that will be used to monitor accomplishment.

Similar discussion about Comer's mental health model revealed that the school had a diverse racial and ethnic population, and team members worried about low self-esteem and lack of pride among the students. They wanted to get social service agencies and churches involved with the school to build self esteem and pride in the students. The model was the strategy—not the goal. To keep our school improvement plans aligned, we must be clear about *what* we want to accomplish, before we identify *how* to achieve it.

Mandates and Motivation in Goal-Setting

Although state accountability systems and the No Child Left Behind Act virtually prescribe goals for every school in the nation, most of this chapter remains as it was written for the first edition. I still believe strongly that change occurs through authentic, local participation in expressing concerns, setting priorities, and identifying targets for accomplishment. School improvement does not occur because a bureaucracy provides a graph with a trajectory plotted from current performance to 100% student success, divided into equal increments between 2002 and 2014. These mandated goals (or accountability requirements) have good intent—to serve every child with equity and excellence—and it is an interest that we share with urgency. However, these mandates intimidate more than they inspire. They lack the characteristics of goals that arouse passion. They are certainly specific and are measurable on an also-mandated assessment. They are certainly attainable for every child—but whether that means attainable at a single given point in time, with reference to a single cut-off score, on a single measure is a legitimate question, especially in schools with complex student needs that are in constant flux. The immigrant child who arrives in September speaking no English is not likely to pass a test in April that requires the equivalent of seven years of academic language acquisition.

We would, however, be irresponsible to ignore these accountability requirements, even if we could. Those of us who work in public schools are public employees, and, at this time, mandated goals represent the will of the public. How can we respect mandated goals and still maintain a personal sense of efficacy that fosters local participation and builds professional commitment?

One answer may be found in the example of the School Effectiveness Profile shown in Figure 7.9. In those graphs, a solid horizontal line represented the district standard for performance on a measure. Graphs of school performance might use a similar visual aid to represent accountability requirements. For example, a back-shadowed trend line could represent the trajectory of improvement needed to meet the 2014 targets of No Child Left Behind. Meanwhile, staff and constituents of the school must still engage in the authentic dialogue needed to make meaning of their own situation and forge commitment to challenges that are both rigorous *and* within the vision of the most optimistic and idealistic among them. These targets would also be superimposed on the graphs that show improvement.

How steep can a trajectory for improvement be and still be rigorous but not ridiculous?

There are no literal answers, but I find these three perspectives to be helpful:

1. No morally defensible goal (or plan) creates improvement for some at the expense of others.
2. No self-respecting goal sets a target that is statistically insignificant.
3. No school community should settle for less than "best in class."

Improvement for All

The positive intent of No Child Left Behind is that schools will increase the achievement of all students. In other words, the school will add value to every child's progress, with some accelerated more than others in order to close the gap. Seattle Public Schools, among other districts nationwide, is implementing an analysis methodology known as "value-added" to measure the impact the school is making on its students based on each student's individual starting points. Figure 10.2 shows the value-added student achievement data in reading and math from Brighton Elementary School.

The area in the middle represents a calculation of the progress students could be expected to make, based on a combination of each individual's prior assessment history. Any point above the designated area represents more or faster progress than would have been predicted and thus is a measure of extraordinary value added by that school. An index of 1.0 would be normal progress or growth. One way to set a rigorous goal to accelerate the learning of students in complex schools would be to state that every child will progress at a faster-than-normal pace. In personal conversation with Dr. William Sanders, originator of the Tennessee value-added accountability system, he stated that the highest measure of added value he has seen a school attain on a consistent basis is about 1.25—or a year and a quarter's growth in one year's time. A school should certainly generate passion for a goal to move its lowest-achieving students at a pace that will help them close the gap.

Statistically Significant

During the 1990s, when the Blue Ribbon Schools program was beginning a more research-based and data-driven process to identify exemplary schools, a panel of assessment experts was convened to discuss a rigorous but realistic challenge in terms of improved performance. The criterion that evolved was movement of one third of a standard deviation over a period of three years. Rough approximations might describe a standard deviation on a typical norm-referenced test as about 21 normal curve equivalents (NCEs)—in which case, improvement of 7 NCEs over three years would be considered significant. A school feeling totally overwhelmed when faced with the need to move from 12% to 90% of students meeting the state-determined standard should at least be excited and able to generate energy around a goal that represents true change. On the other hand, no self-respecting school should set a goal of 1–3 NCEs over three years, a goal that is statistically *in*significant and subject to the whims of standard error.

Figure 10.2 Value-Added School Effects

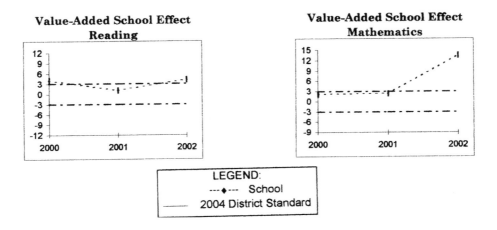

Reprinted With Permission From Seattle Public Schools, Seattle, WA.

Best in Class

The line between explaining why and whining is a narrow one. The boundary between facing reality squarely and making excuses is a slippery one. I have never been known to tolerate avoidance of our responsibility to provide equity and excellence for all students. However, I am also known as an advocate for fair treatment of educators, which means recognizing that the task is harder for some than others, requires more resources for some than others, and requires more time for some than for others.

Just for the Kids (www.Just4theKids.org) is a way of looking at school data that originated in Texas and is now emerging in numerous other states, including Washington. It creates a comparison group of schools with similar challenges and selects those that are top performers within that group. Figure 10.3 is a graph of results for continuously enrolled students in a school with a low-income population of 9%, and only 1.1% receiving bilingual education services. These 10 schools have the highest achievement with similar populations—in other words, they are "best in class." Although 79.4% of students meeting standard may seem impressive, similar schools are doing even better. No school should settle for a goal that is less than best in class for their students.

Mandated accountability requirements are part of our reality and responsibility. However, our goals must be our own. As Susan Rosenholtz stated in *Teachers' Workplace* (1991),

> If there is any center to the mystery of schools' success, mediocrity or failure, it lies deep within the structure of organizational goals: whether or not they exist, how they are defined and manifested, the extent to which they are mutually shared. Indeed, the hallmark of any successful organization is a shared sense among its members about what they are trying to accomplish. (p. 13)

Figure 10.3 Just for the Kids

Washington
Just for the Kids

Table Explanation
Multi-Year Summary

Bar Charts
How Top Ten Comparable Schools Were Selected

Choose Another Subject,
Ch

Comparison Of Top Schools For Grade 03 Reading 1999

ITBS Results Campus ID 310064164 Campus Name Campus ID (District)	Continuously Enrolled Tested Students National Percentile	Student Characteristics		Counts for Selected Grade				School Size	How Selective is the Group?	
		Schoolwide Percent Low Income	Percent in Grade Receiving Bilingual Services	Total Students	Number not tested (Absent, IEP, ESL, or other)	Total # Tested	Number Continuously Enrolled 3 years		% of Students Excluded from Testing	% of Students Continuously Enrolled
Your School: MUKILTEO ELEMENTARY MUKILTEO SCHOOL DISTRICT	70	9	0.0	103	(3)	100	80	544	2.9	77.7
BRYANT SEATTLE SCHOOL DISTRICT	81	21	5.4	92	(1)	91	75	556	1.1	81.5
CHAUTAUQUA ELEMENTARY VASHON ISLAND SCHOOL DISTRICT	81	12	0.0	95	(1)	94	82	721	1.1	86.3
LOWELL ELEMENTARY SCHOOL BELLINGHAM SCHOOL DISTRICT	79	22	3.8	53	(2)	51	36	271	3.8	67.9
BAY VIEW ELEMENTARY BURLINGTON EDISON SCHOOL DISTRICT	79	16	2.0	51	(2)	49	42	487	3.9	82.4
HIGHLAND TERRACE ELEMENTARY SHORELINE SCHOOL DISTRICT	79	14	0.0	63	(0)	63	49	486	0.0	77.8
ISOM INTERMEDIATE LYNDEN SCHOOL DISTRICT	78	30	9.4	149	(3)	146	10	439	2.0	6.7
ROGERS SEATTLE SCHOOL DISTRICT	78	26	1.8	55	(1)	54	48	356	1.8	87.3
EDMONDS ELEMENTARY ED EDMONDS SCHOOL DISTRICT	78	14	0.0	56	(5)	51	37	413	8.9	66.1
VIEW RIDGE SEATTLE SCHOOL DISTRICT	76	33	0.0	64	(9)	55	35	410	14.1	54.7
S WHIDBEY INTERMEDIATE SCHOOL SOUTH WHIDBEY SCHOOL DISTRICT	76	18	0.7	140	(7)	133	78	475	5.0	55.7
Average National Percentile	79									

Gifted
<=30%

10% less than target school
Low-Income
10% less than target school
Receiving Bilingual Services

Selection of Comparison Schools:
3 Year Continuously Enrolled
Less than 15% students
Untested Students

Number in pool:
739

Grade Size
>=40%
 # Eligible
>=10 Students

Washington School Research Center, Seattle Pacific University.

(Continued)

147

Figure 10.3 (Continued)

Washington
Just for the Kids

Table Explanation
Multi-Year Summary

Bar Charts
How Top Ten Comparable Schools Were Selected

Choose Another Subject A
Cho

Comparison Of Top Schools For Grade 04 Reading 1999

WASL Results Campus ID:310064164 Campus Name Campus ID (District)	Continuously Enrolled Tested Students		Student Characteristics		Counts for Selected Grade					How Selective is the Group?	
	Exceeded Standard	Met Standard	Schoolwide Percent Low Income	Percent in Grade Receiving Bilingual Services	Total Students	Number not tested (Absent IEP, ESL, or other)	Total # Tested	Number Continuously Enrolled 3 years	School Size	% of Students Excluded from Testing	% of Students Continuously Enrolled
Your School: MUKILTEO ELEMENTARY MUKILTEO SCHOOL DISTRICT	27.9	79.4	9	1.1	87	(0)	87	68	544	0.0	78.2
SUNSET INTERMEDIATE SCHOOL SHORELINE SCHOOL DISTRICT	22.9	94.3	16	16.9	59	(1)	58	35	456	1.7	59.3
OTIS ORCHARDS ELEMENTARY SCHOOL EAST VALLEY (SPK) SCHOOL DISTRICT	35.3	94.1	40	1.9	54	(3)	51	17	354	5.6	31.5
ENDEAVOR ELEMENTARY MUKILTEO SCHOOL DISTRICT	40.5	91.9	12	1.1	87	(3)	84	37	487	3.4	42.5
SIERRA HEIGHTS ELEMENTARY RENTON SCHOOL DISTRICT	33.3	91.1	28	8.7	68	(5)	63	45	447	7.4	66.2
FRANKLIN ELEMENTARY SCHOOL PULLMAN SCHOOL DISTRICT	38.9	88.9	32	2.1	47	(1)	46	36	287	2.1	76.6
MAPLEWOOD HEIGHTS ELEMENTARY RENTON SCHOOL DISTRICT	37.3	88.2	17	5.3	94	(2)	92	51	513	2.1	54.3
FRANKLIN ELEMENTARY SCHOOL VANCOUVER SCHOOL DISTRICT	32.4	88.2	24	2.2	46	(1)	45	34	224	2.2	73.9
LOUISA MAY ALCOTT ELEMENTARY LAKE WASHINGTON SCHOOL DISTRICT	44.0	88.0	12	9.5	73	(3)	70	50	476	4.1	68.5
BROADVIEW-THOMSON SEATTLE SCHOOL DISTRICT	31.8	87.9	38	8.4	95	(7)	88	66	564	7.4	69.5
OLYMPIC VIEW SEATTLE SCHOOL DISTRICT	30.6	87.8	24	4.3	67	(7)	60	49	489	10.4	73.1
Average Percentage	34.8%	89.5%									

Gifted <=30%

10% less than target school Low-Income
10% less than target school Receiving Bilingual Services

Less than 15% students Untested Students

Selection of Comparison Schools: 3 Year Continuously Enrolled

Number in pool: 407

Grade Size >=40%
 # Eligible >=10 Students

Washington School Research Center, Seattle Pacific University.

11

Drilling Down the Priority Data

Through the previous 10 chapters, we have moved about halfway through the process illustrated in Figure 1.1. We began with identifying the mission (passion) of a school and gathering available data into an initial school portfolio. We checked for discrepancies between the stated values and the actual accomplishments, which helped us identify all the concerns of staff, students, and constituents that might be addressed in our school improvement efforts. In Chapter 10, we explored a group process that used mission, data, and feasibility as filters to narrow those concerns into specific priority areas for further work.

The need for a limited set of priorities is conveyed visually by the presence of just three lines under the *Priorities* heading in Figure 1.1. This "limit of three" is intentional, not just a matter of how much can fit on a standard size page. As we move across Figure 1.1, each of these priority areas will need to be addressed through more than one strategy, and each of these priority areas will also need further data collection to monitor implementation and impact of the changes that are introduced. If you set too many different goals, planning for change will spin out of control. When everything is a priority, nothing is a priority. Schools that manage to stay on course and demonstrate increased student achievement have been able to capture their work on two copies of Figure 1.1. They identify three to five priority areas and stay on course. Under state accountability systems and the No Child Left Behind Act, reading and math are automatic areas of priority. In many situations, a third priority is a prosocial goal related to issues of student discipline, student interaction, and other aspects of school climate.

Chapter 10 also raised a caution about the tendency to confuse goals with strategies. One of the high schools in Chapter 1 confused a goal with a strategy when it tackled block scheduling as the goal itself—a change for the sake of change. The other high school had clear goals and chose block scheduling as one of the strategies to accomplish their goals.

The scarcity of time in the work of schools and educators increases the temptation to leap into a plan before looking closely enough at the existing reality of student performance and professional practice. The old adage "haste makes waste" applies very well. Time, money, and energy can actually be wasted, not saved, if we rush into practices that don't match our students' needs or our school culture, or that don't have any prior evidence of success in accomplishing goals like ours. It's not only our time that may be wasted. Each year that goes by without effective intervention is a year that our students move on and out of our classrooms and schools.

Near the middle of Figure 1.1, we encounter a box marked *Study* related to each of the priority areas we have selected. The three bullet points represent three different ways in which we need to pause and learn more before we select strategies and develop a plan for change. First, we need to drill down into data we already have, to get a closer look at which students have what specific individual skill gaps, and where we have gaps in the instructional program that affect all students. Second, we also need to study research and best practice so that we increase our probability of success by implementing programs and practices that really work. No Child Left Behind further emphasizes the utilization of scientifically research-based strategies. The third bullet point in the *Study* box requires the most courage and professional discipline. It emphasizes the need to gather data about the prevalent current practices in the school and classrooms that may or may not match up with research and best practice.

In Chapter 4, we described the configuration of the administrative team, leadership team, and data team. For the types of work described as study—drilling down data, researching best practice, and analyzing current practice—the entire staff of the school should be divided into study groups, one study group for each of the priority areas. A member of the leadership team and a member of the data team should be assigned to facilitate and support each study group and to coordinate the overall schoolwide work. As described by School B in Chapter 1, these study activities would constitute the focus and use of professional development time for a period of several months.

This chapter deals with the first bullet point of the Figure 1.1 *Study* box—drilling down the data for specific information about student skill gaps and program gaps. Chapter 12 addresses the exploration of research and best practice and provides tips and tools for capturing current practices that may be celebrated, strengthened, or abandoned.

Planning Forward
With Student-Specific Data

The school portfolio and the overall data summary typically reflect averages and large groups of students. For example, norm-referenced test results may be summarized in terms of a mean performance at the 73rd percentile. This tells us that the average of all the scores for all the students who took the test locally is better than the scores of 73% of all the students who took the test nationally in the year when the norms were established. Or the results on a criterion-referenced or standards-based test may be reported as the percentage of students above a set score or the percentage of students performing in four proficiency levels, as determined by three cut scores. Disaggregated data provides the same general information for various groups of students.

This level of generality meets mandates for public reporting, but it does not help with program evaluation and instructional improvement. Moreover, in many cases, the timing of the testing and scoring sequence makes use of the data even more difficult. In Washington State, for example, the good qualities of the assessment (many short answers and extended response items) make it difficult to score, and students have moved onto another grade—or even another school—before the results come back. The issues of data that are too general and timing that is too slow are conveyed in the book's subtitle, *Planning Forward With Student-Specific Data*.

Student-specific data is sometimes found only in the reports to parents, which the school has to retrieve and photocopy before they are sent home. Or these individual results may be included in a roster of student scores. New data warehousing systems are emerging that simplify the next steps needed—which are to *move* the data forward to the teachers who now serve the students. Only in this way can schools plan forward and target remediation and support programs for maximum effect.

When the school year starts, teachers should have access to a spreadsheet for each class that lists student names on the left, critical skills (e.g., standards, benchmarks, grade-level expectations) across the top, and that indicates which cells represent specific skill gaps for specific students. Whether in hard copy or electronically, the district or school data team should put these spreadsheets directly into the hands of teachers. Implementation of a new data warehousing system may provide instant access and capacity for teachers to produce this data set themselves, but technical capacity does not automatically translate into human capacity and motivation. Once teachers learn how to use this information and find that it is valuable and useful, they become interested in how they can generate it themselves and what other analyses they can do from their desk tops.

Student-specific information is needed at the start of the year to convey expectations about instruction and to utilize resources effectively. It's an expectation that teachers personalize and differentiate instruction, which requires specific information on what students do (and do not) need. When this information is not readily available, two bad things may happen. Days and weeks of instructional time can be devoted to pretests, which yield information already generated somewhere else and delay the introduction of new content. Or the course syllabus simply rolls right on, with no knowledge of students' previous learning until the first midterm exam yields winners and losers on the grading curve.

The specific information by skill for each individual student must be made readily available to teachers. The expectation that it will be used to allocate instructional time, differentiate instruction, and guide flexible grouping must be shared and clearly articulated. Chapter 14 includes a school example focused on staff agreements to group and regroup students for skill development and the principal's support and monitoring of those commitments.

Planning Backward With Skill-Specific Data

While cohorts of students move forward and skill information moves with them, other students are following them along the same instructional pathway. If the spreadsheets of student skills show empty cells down an entire column (representing a lack of proficiency for almost all students), it is likely to be the taught (or untaught) curriculum at fault, not the learners.

Drilling down the skill-specific data means looking at the item-analysis reports that provide a breakdown of skills or subtests. Three years of reports should be compared in order to see any pattern where many different groups of students have consistently struggled with the same skills. The next step is to consider how important these specific skills may be. Is this an area that is heavily weighted on a high-stakes test by being assigned many items or a disproportionate number of total points? Is it a skill that's essential for success on many other learning tasks? If the answer is, "No, this is a small item and we never use the skill again in life or learning"—then, not to worry. If the answer is, "Yes, a skill like separating main ideas from details to summarize material is an essential skill in all content areas," then further discussion must focus on when it is taught, by whom, in what ways, with what materials, and how it is assessed at the classroom level.

At the secondary level, another form of looking backward is to examine the courses taken by students who are successful with graduation tests (e.g., tenth-grade state assessments, New York Regents exams) and those who are not. This is especially important in mathematics, where, "among low-income high school students, 71% of those taking algebra and geometry enroll in college. Only 27% of those who don't take these courses go on to college" (Quattrociocchi, 2002).

Ruth Johnson (2002) explains how critical it is for students to have access to high-level courses and support so they can be successful. She cites many studies, including a national report by the College Board, *Changing the Odds: Factors Increasing Access to College* (Pelavin & Kane, 1990), which looked at the relationship between enrollment in college-level courses and college-going rates and whether African American, Latino, and white students participated equally in those courses related to college going. The authors found that low-income African American and Latino students did not enroll in geometry and foreign languages and did not aspire to a bachelor's degree at the same rates as white students did. However, when they had the opportunity to enroll and completed the courses, the likelihood of college enrollment increased, and the gap between minority students and whites decreased.

Regardless of race, students who are afforded the opportunity to study higher-level math score higher on the National Assessment of Educational Progress (NAEP) math test. Furthermore, research by Adelman (1999) concluded that the highest level of mathematics studied in secondary school has more continuing influence on completion of a bachelor's degree than any other precollege curricula. Finishing a course beyond the level of Algebra 2—for example, trigonometry or precalculus—more than doubles the odds that a student who enters postsecondary education will complete the degree.

According to Johnson (2002), there are promising results from increased emphasis and access for study of mathematics. For example, New York City made a concerted effort to increase dramatically the opportunities for students to take regents-level science courses. For all racial and ethnic groups, the numbers of students who passed in 1995 well exceeded the numbers who were even enrolled in 1994. Moreover, a large-scale initiative of the National Science Foundation, which includes 22 large urban districts, is yielding early successes. The Urban Systemic Initiative reports increased enrollments in mathematics gate-keeping courses (e.g., algebra, geometry) and in higher-level mathematics and science courses, as well as a reduced disparity of enrollments among African American, Latino, and white students. Gains in assessment outcomes and achievement gaps have been achieved among racial and ethnic groups (Kim, Crasco, Smith, Johnson, Karatonis, & Leavitt, 2001).

Chapter 12 discusses the importance of examining school practices that hinder student success. Educators need to rethink the gate-keeping practices that consistently prevent students with previous low scores from acquiring the opportunity to learn the essential skills and concepts of algebra.

The moral imperative must be to prepare all students for the college option, rather than using bureaucratic policies and prerequisites to certify who is or who isn't college material. This moral imperative is about educators, students, and parents understanding the consequences of under-preparation. As Johnson (2002) insists, "It is about pointing out how and why some groups are underprepared. Ultimately, it's about transforming the expectations and behaviors currently present in many schools and systems so that there are high-level options for all students" (p. 32)

Ramping Up the Roster

It can be discouraging to face a school year with many students below performance standards and a high-stakes assessment looming in the spring. Teachers in Oxnard, California, have been working with the California Center for Effective Schools (www.effectiveschools.education.ucsb.edu) and have used a strategy that provides them with a starting point to help them beat that overwhelmed feeling.

As soon as they become familiar with students and their current level of development, they list their students in order of performance on standards, from most advanced to those most challenged. Then, they draw a line across the list at a point that roughly separates those who are already "over the bar" and those below it. They begin by focusing interventions and individual help on the three students closest to the standard, knowing that their grouping strategies will also address the needs of other students at the same time. As these students move closer to and above the line that represents the standard, teachers move down the list and focus intensely on the next set of students. The results of "ramping up the roster" have been demonstrated in improved test scores and annual performance indicators for the last three years.

Slicing the Pie

In Figure 7.5, a pie graph illustrates the distribution of student scores in four segments representing quartiles of norm-referenced test data or proficiency levels on standards-based assessments. The current emphasis on disaggregating data has the benefit of creating visibility for students who deserve closer attention and more focused support. The danger of this disaggregated data may be the tendency to make decisions and plans based on assumptions and generalizations around identifiable groups of students. Figure 11.1 challenges us to slice the pie a different way and challenge our assumptions.

This pie chart of overall scores shows a distribution with 30.9% of students in the top quartile, 19.5% between 51st and 75th normal curve equivalents, 18.3% in the third segment, and 31.3% in the lowest quartile, below the 25th normal curve equivalent. This school is an urban district with racial and ethnic diversity, and teachers viewing this distribution were moving quickly to an assumption that research was needed to learn what instructional strategies and remediation programs worked best with African American males. They were surprised when the pie was sliced three more times—to break out the characteristics of students scoring in

Figure 11.1 Distribution of Low Reading Scores by Gender, Socioeconomic Status, and Race/Ethnicity

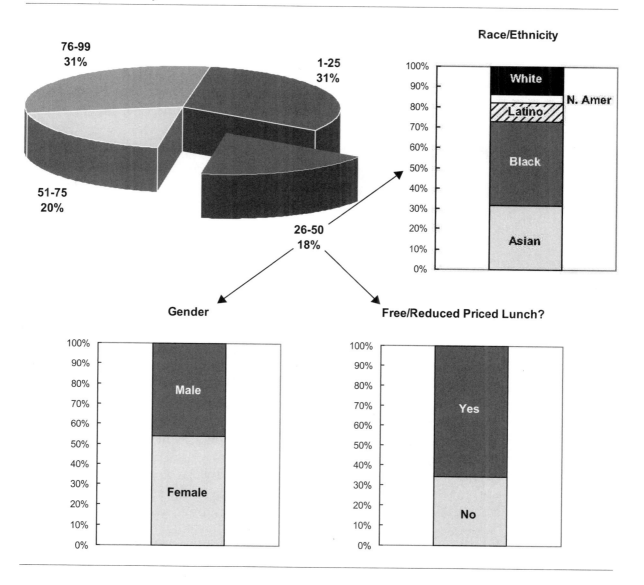

that bottom group. The low performers were not overwhelmingly male as expected. They were primarily—but not exclusively—of lower socio-economic status and actually represented a demographic distribution almost identical to the overall student population of the district.

This version of drilling down for student-specific data is a valuable technique to increase staff awareness and, at the same time, keep them from perpetuating inaccurate assumptions and spending time developing wrong-headed strategies to improve student success. A recent report by Texas researchers Confrey and Makar (discussed in Olson, 2003) describes a school's overreaction to a one-year drop in scores for African American students, which resulted in provision of academic interventions on race-based criteria and overlooked the needs of other students who were also failing to achieve the passing score on the state assessment. Reacting to scores on one year of one test, without adequate consideration of variation, sample size, performance over time, and overall distribution of scores can lead to errors in the allocation of precious resources of time, energy, and money.

Attacking Anonymity

Figure 11.1 illustrates the importance of testing assumptions about the characteristics of struggling students in your school and classroom. In that example, the expected gender difference was not found, and the low-performing students came from every racial/ethnic group in the school. The drilling down needs to go deeper still. We must do more than avoid attaching wrong assumptions to our students; we must attack the anonymity that causes us to see groups rather than individuals.

Figure 11.2 provides a profile of a class of 4th graders and describes their language status, gender, and whether they are served in Title I, resource special education, or gifted and talented programs. Their test scores from last year and this year are compared in reading and overall language. Just one year of performance data would help the teacher plan instruction and avoid making interpretations based on class. The comparison of these two years of performance data allows the teacher to see which students made the most progress in her class and which actually declined in achievement.

Only by looking at student performance by name and visualizing those students face by face are we able to focus on each child's learning needs as an individual. Furthermore, only by facing the reality that about one third of her students lost ground in reading and language can the teacher in Figure 11.2 make accurate and courageous decisions about her practice and professional growth needs.

Checking Out Perceptions

The previous two sections emphasized the importance of surfacing and challenging our assumptions about students who struggle in our schools and classrooms. It is also essential to drill down to clarify perceptual data that raise concerns and may give us helpful insights about how to move forward.

For example, a school leadership team that I worked with had administered a formal survey based on school effectiveness research and developed by a highly respected consultant group. Most of the responses made sense. There were no surprises except for negative parent responses regarding the format of parent-teacher conferences and student recognition. They were not too concerned about the parent conference item:

Figure 11.2 Fourth-Grade Class Profile

4th Grade Class Profile

ELL = English Language Learner **EO** = English Only **RD** = redesignated *Fluent English Proficient*

Student	ELL Level	Gender	Title I Y=yes	RSP Y=yes	GATE Y=yes	SAT9 NCE Rdg 2000	2001	+/-	SAT9 NCE Lang 2000	2001	+/-
1	FEP	M				41	41	0	29	31	+2
2	ELL	F				52	54	+2	64	48	-16
3	ELL	M	Y			29	35	+6	29	31	+3
4	RD	F				37	54	+17	47	45	-2
5	EO	M			Y	65	67	+2	67	50	-17
6	ELL	F				40	36	-4	29	35	+6
7	EO	F				46	35	-9	45	40	-5
8	ELL	F	Y	Y		19	13	-6	20	29	+9
9	FEP	M				21	32	+9	13	39	+23
10	EO	F				35	35	0	44	52	+8
11	ELL	F				38	44	+6	51	48	-3
12	EO	M				33	48	+15	43	50	+7
13	FEP	M	Y	Y		20	1	-19	13	18	+5
14	ELL	M	Y			36	47	+11	44	45	+1
15	RD	M				45	39	-6	64	46	-18
16	RD	M				39	41	+3	48	48	0
17	RD	F				44	41	-3	49	52	+3
18	ELL	F	Y			32	37	+5	32	37	+5
19	FEP	F	Y			29	35	+6	43	31	-12
20	FEP	M				42	28	-14	23	20	-3
21	RD	F				47	45	-2	38	45	+7
22	FEP	F	Y			30	37	+7	41	42	+1
23	RD	F			Y	65	49	-16	54	48	-6
24	EO	F			Y	65	70	+5	54	62	+8
25	ELL	F	Y			35	32	-3	38	39	+1
26	EO	M			Y	58	73	+15	47	56	+9
27	EO	F	Y	Y		21	15	-6	25	10	-15
28	FEP	M	Y			29	39	+10	38	50	+12
29	RD	M	Y			32	42	+10	32	48	+16

Data Analysis

Demographics
24% EO
27% ELL
24%RD
24%FEP
37% Title I
10% RSP
13% GATE

Reading
37% dropped
78%=RD/FEP/EO
66%=female

Language
34% dropped
80%=RD/EO/FEP
70%=female

New Teacher Center at University of California Santa Cruz.

Teachers had talked for some time about how they needed to make different arrangements for these important communication opportunities.

However, the team members *were* quite distressed about the student recognition item, and they began to list all the ways in which students were recognized for good work, good behavior, helping others, and so forth. They wondered what more they could do and were about to propose a subcommittee to explore ways to get funding from local businesses to provide more student incentives when one member said, "I wonder what *parents* thought *student recognition* means."

After a few moments of silent confusion, a first-year teacher timidly suggested, "Maybe we should ask them." It sounded like a pretty logical next move, and the principal helped identify members of a focus group, who were invited to come and discuss the items on the parent survey and what they were thinking as they read them. Through the focus group, school leaders discovered that the student recognition parents wanted was for the principal to know their children's names and for all teachers to get to know even the students who were not in their classes and to address them by name—or at least with more respect than "Hey, kid." The face-to-face communication of a focus group shifted the attention of staff from initiating more extrinsic reward systems to looking at the culture of the school and the interactions between staff and students.

Face-to-face communication is especially needed in schools where the demographics of parents and the community are in sharp contrast with the characteristics of staff. Johnson (2002) points out that "those in power often silence the dialogue when those who share the culture of poverty and children of color disagree with proposed solutions." Adults who share the culture of the students must be engaged in the search for promising practices and program changes to assist their children's learning.

Making It Public—*Not*

This chapter advocates more in-depth study of data and provides additional ways to analyze and display student-specific and skill-specific information. There is such a thing as being *too* specific. Barbara Tomasso, a colleague from New York State, returned from Hong Kong last August with a powerful *negative* example.

The English language newspaper there included a large notice that test scores would be reported the following day. The article cautioned parents to be attentive to their children and "comfort" their stress. The next day's special edition included page after page after page of small print—every score obtained by every child, listed by name.

We can, at least, take "comfort" in the reality that the privacy of individual children's performance records is still protected in America. Although students need to take assessments seriously and do their best, we must be vigilant and self-monitoring to avoid projecting our stress or reservations onto the innocent.

12

Looking Around and Looking Within

Chapter 2 described the importance of proof and the use of data as a characteristic of high-achieving and improving schools. Figure 2.2 listed five items that correspond to the *Study* stage depicted in Figure 1.1:

- Drill down for student- and skill-specific data in priority areas.
- Plan forward as students rise to respond to individual skill gaps.
- Plan backward to fill gaps in the instructional program.
- Look around at research, best practices, and exemplary schools.
- Look within to analyze curriculum, instructional strategies, and the culture of learning.

Chapter 11 provided examples of drilling down to plan forward and backward. This chapter focuses on adding a knowledge base about best practices and then analyzing current practices in comparison to what's been proven. The emphasis in Chapter 11 was the student; the spotlight here is on the classroom level and the teacher.

Kati Haycock (1998) of Education Trust, refers to research from Tennessee, Texas, Massachusetts, and Alabama that identifies teacher quality as a critical factor in student growth. She points especially to Bill Sanders' (1998) value-added approach, which yields information on gains students make from year to year. By grouping data according to the gains made in individual classrooms, it's possible to look at the impact of various teachers on high, medium, and low achievers. The impact of gains made by students in the classrooms of the most effective teachers compared to the least effective was found to be a difference of 39 percentiles (Sanders, 1998).

This dramatic difference in student learning will not be replicated through district curriculum writing or school restructuring. Chapter 13 will value those activities as the enabling factors that are needed, but in themselves—without a clear and close focus on the classroom environment and the instruction provided by the teacher—policy making and technical assistance would not extend to the desk of the student. School A in Chapter 1 focused on restructuring "to be progressive." School B started from what it wanted as student outcomes, backed up from there to what it would need to do differently, realized the schedule was a barrier, and changed it.

Examining Research

Like Benjamin Franklin's statement that a penny saved is a penny earned, time invested in the study of research and best practice can be time, energy, and emotion saved in the long run. This has always been conventional wisdom, proved by people's experiences with hasty selection and poorly managed implementation of the latest "hot" innovation.

The reauthorization of the Elementary and Secondary Education Act (ESEA) known as No Child Left Behind morphs this wisdom into mandate with a totally unrealistic definition of acceptable research. For example, No Child Left Behind strictly defines *scientifically based research* as experimental studies done with randomly selected, perfectly matched control and treatment groups, kept totally apart so they don't contaminate each other, the methodology, or the findings. And this is done in a real school setting where *all* parents want the "newest and best" for their children?! In a timely and transparent manner so positive findings can be swiftly disseminated and replicated?! Not likely.

The criteria I set for research that merits study on paid professional time are these:

- The authors/researchers are neutral and will not gain financially by favorable results.
- Objective measures are used to demonstrate effectiveness.
- The amount of improvement that is reported lies outside the standard error of measurement.

In other words, if there's no data, it isn't research. "I had a great idea and my friends loved it and my students loved it" signals an opinion article, not research. Learning can and should be designed so it's enjoyable and students can "love" it, but the test is the evidence of *learning*.

During the study phase depicted in Figure 1.1, requests to attend conferences and workshops should be approved based on their connection to the priority areas of improvement needed. Study groups could meet to discuss research obtained through such sources as the Educational Resources Information Center (ERIC; www.askeric.org) and the Educational Research Service (ERS; www.ers.org). These databases would be a starting point from which to pursue the original studies cited in bibliographies. Reviews by independent researchers, such as Ellis and Fout's *Research on Educational Innovations* (1997), are valuable resources to help evaluate the reports and studies offered by program authors and advocates. Cawelti's *Handbook of Research on Improving Student Achievement* (1999) and the recent work of Robert Marzano and others (Marzano, 2003; Marzano, Pickering, & Pollock, 2001) are particularly useful.

Some study groups have tried to select excellent articles and make copies to put in everyone's mailbox, but they have been disappointed with the lack of reaction to them. Other groups have told me about two strategies that seem to work better. Rather than reproducing the whole article, they prepare a summary on a 3" x 5" card that they distribute. They mention that the full article is posted in several key places in the school and invite anyone interested to talk to one of them about it or meet with them for breakfast on an appointed day.

Staff from another school told me that they post an article on a large piece of bulletin board paper in the lounge. They highlight the main points so it can be rapidly skimmed, and they hang markers beside it. Casual readers leave "graffiti" comments about the article, which prompt others to read and react as well. The informal reaction energizes the thinking of the staff and sometimes generates ideas for consideration that are brought to the school leadership team and then presented to the whole faculty.

Balanced Reading Programs

No Child Left Behind includes specific language about reading research and requires that recipients of Title I funding include all the components of "balanced literacy" in their instructional program. Figure 12.1 provides a visual overview of these components as synthesized by the National Reading Panel and referenced by the U.S. Department of Education.[1] It is a very useful tool as a one-page quick reference guide for discussion about reading instruction. Later in this chapter, Figure 12.7 demonstrates a way to convert these research findings into a data-gathering tool for examining current practices in your school.

The Power vs. the Promise

As study groups begin their exploration of research, they soon discover a plethora of promising practices identified through a sequence of studies over the past three decades. A technique known as *meta-analysis* can statistically aggregate the results documented in multiple studies of

Figure 12.1   Essential Components of a Balanced Reading Program

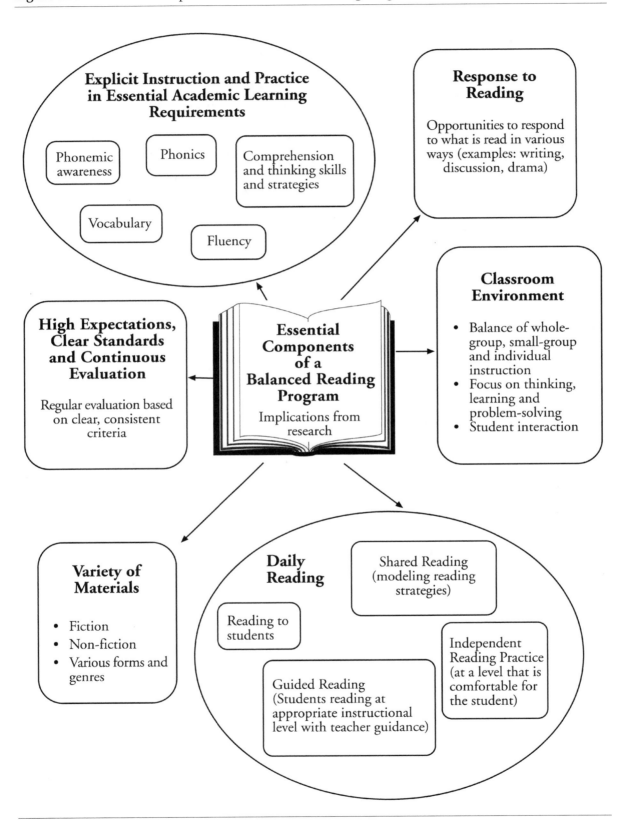

the same innovation. "Mega-power" would be represented by an effect size of 1.0, the equivalent of moving the mean performance of a group one entire standard deviation in achievement from pre- to post-test.

Figure 12.2 displays the results of a summary of meta-analysis research on a number of popular innovations.[2] These results represent the impact of the innovation as actually implemented, not necessarily the full potential as designed and implemented in the experimental setting. Brief comments capture critical attributes of success and potential pitfalls that limit effectiveness. As author Gordon Cawelti noted in personal correspondence,

> You ought to know the likely size of increases that can be expected from any single practice. Consultants or advocates of a particular practice tend to leave people with the general statement that "research shows achievement increases" or the inference that your achievement concerns will be over if you just use this.

The Essential Nine

The recent work of Marzano and others (Marzano, 2003; Marzano, Pickering, & Pollock, 2001) synthesizing research on classroom and school-wide practices was cited earlier. The summary provided in Figure 12.3 is an excerpt from the Association for Supervision and Curriculum Development (ASCD) *Curriculum Update,* used with permission and gratitude (Varlas, 2002). It describes nine essential instructional practices and includes suggestions for classroom application. Study of generic practices such as these can create common vocabulary and effort across grade levels and content areas. As such, they constitute a unique leverage tool for opening the chronically stuck doors of high school classrooms.

Exploring Best Practice

"Research and best practice" is a compound phrase in common usage as something we should know about, do, and use. Prompted by practitioners' questions about whether the terms are the same or different—and what the difference might be—I found no clear definition readily available. So, I made up my own, believing that they are indeed somewhat different.

Earlier in this chapter, I listed criteria for research worthy of consideration, including the objectivity of the researchers and/or authors. My definition of *best practice* allows for—perhaps depends upon—the voices of practitioners directly engaged in the improvement efforts. *Research* may be more distant and less timely; best practice is going on right now, in the real world. Both require data. It may be a promising practice when the principal says, "We're trying something new and we feel it's really helping." It's *best* practice when the principal can say, "We tried this, and our measures of student learning have gone from X to Y in the last _____ years."

Figure 12.2   How Effective Are Various Approaches to Improving Student Achievement?

Practices Resulting in Substantially Improved Student Achievement (effect sizes in 0.4–0.6 range)	Practices Producing Modestly Improved Student Achievement (effect sizes in 0.3–0.4 range)
Tutoring One-on-one over sustained period of time on skills relating to standards.	**Success for All** K–6 program uses a trained facilitator to provide staff development for teachers and aides, parental involvement, and an assessment program to record student progress; extensive use of cooperative learning and tutoring.
Early Childhood Programs Developmentally appropriate learning experiences for 3–4 year olds.	**Accelerated Reader Program** Specific skill development, wide reading and assessing comprehension on computers.
Behavioral Classroom Techniques Frequent use of teaching cues, active engagement, and reinforcement.	**Reading Recovery** Provides daily 30-minute lessons by trained teachers in a pullout program for 1st grade students performing poorly to ensure they develop the strategies used by good readers and writers.
Parental Involvement In activities designed to buttress the school's standards and curriculum.	**Staff Development** On specific teaching activities aimed at clear instructional goals.
Classroom Management Skills Good training for teachers on managing student behavior affords more time on task.	**Longer School Year** As judged from comparative international studies, extends time-on-task needed by many students.
Time-on-Task Achievement varies according to time spent on a particular subject.	**Computer-Assisted Instruction** To provide learning activities that supplement the teacher's work and focus on school standards.

Practices With Mixed or Controversial Results	Changes Rarely Showing Improved Achievement
Bilingual Education A major study shows advantage for late exit bilingual approach, but many dispute this; issue turns partially on what the dependent variable is—reading skills or science achievement.	**Site Based Management** Schools haven't focused sufficiently on improving achievement but do focus on peripheral issues, processes, etc.
Detracking Earlier known as *heterogeneous vs. homogeneous grouping* issue; some studies show consistently lower quality of instruction for students in low tracks, but others dispute the inevitability of this.	**State or District Policies** Tend to be far removed with little effect; may be changing as state agencies get better at leading and not regulating.
Class Size Clearly smaller classes create fewer problems and opportunities to give individual students more personal attention; however, lowering class size by 3 or 4 students rarely produces better achievement; unless class size is reduced to 12–15 students, achievement increases are very slight.	**Pupil Retention** Large number of studies that tend to show no improvement in subsequent years for those held back; may be necessary sometimes for very immature students.
School Size Research on this topic has been hard to control and has not produced reliable evidence on optimum size, but evidence is growing in support of smaller schools on matters such as achievement, attendance, participation, and climate for learning. More use of smaller "learning communities" within larger schools is gaining in popularity.	**Changes in Schedules or Organization** Rarely serve, in and of themselves, to improve classroom teaching and learning activities; may well serve other purposes, however.

Reprinted With Permission From Gordon Cawelti, Educational Research Service, Arlington, VA.

Figure 12.3   Getting Acquainted With the Essential Nine

Getting Acquainted with the Essential Nine

Researchers at Mid-continent Research for Education and Learning (McREL) have identified nine instructional strategies that are most likely to improve student achievement across all content areas and across all grade levels. These strategies are explained in the book *Classroom Instruction That Works* by Robert Marzano, Debra Pickering, and Jane Pollock.

1. Identifying similarities and differences
2. Summarizing and note taking
3. Reinforcing effort and providing recognition
4. Homework and practice
5. Nonlinguistic representations
6. Cooperative learning
7. Setting objectives and providing feedback
8. Generating and testing hypotheses
9. Cues, questions, and advance organizers

The following is an overview of the research behind these strategies as well as some practical applications for the classroom.

1. Identifying Similarities and Differences

The ability to break a concept into its similar and dissimilar characteristics allows students to understand (and often solve) complex problems by analyzing them in a more simple way. Teachers can either directly present similarities and differences, accompanied by deep discussion and inquiry, or simply ask students to identify similarities and differences on their own. While teacher-directed activities focus on identifying specific items, student-directed activities encourage variation and broaden understanding, research shows. Research also notes that graphic forms are a good way to represent similarities and differences.

Applications:
- Use Venn diagrams or charts to compare and classify items.
- Engage students in comparing, classifying, and creating metaphors and analogies.

2. Summarizing and Note Taking

These skills promote greater comprehension by asking students to analyze a subject to expose what's essential and then put it in their own words. According to research, this requires substituting, deleting, and keeping some things and having an awareness of the basic structure of the information presented.

Applications:
- Provide a set of rules for creating a summary.
- When summarizing, ask students to question what is unclear, clarify those questions, and then predict what will happen next in the text.

Research shows that taking more notes is better than fewer notes, though verbatim note taking is ineffective because it does not allow time to process the information. Teachers should encourage and give time for review and revision of notes; notes can be the best study guides for tests.

Applications:
- Use teacher-prepared notes.
- Stick to a consistent format for notes, although students can refine the notes as necessary.

3. Reinforcing Effort and Providing Recognition

Effort and recognition speak to the attitudes and beliefs of students, and teachers must show the connection between effort and achievement. Research shows that although not all students realize the importance of effort, they can learn to change their beliefs to emphasize effort.

Applications:
- Share stories about people who succeeded by not giving up.
- Have students keep a log of their weekly efforts and achievements, reflect on it periodically, and even mathematically analyze the data.

According to research, recognition is most effective if it is contingent on the achievement of a certain standard. Also, symbolic recognition works better than tangible rewards.

Applications:
- Find ways to personalize recognition. Give awards for individual accomplishments.
- "Pause, Prompt, Praise." If a student is struggling, pause to discuss the problem, then prompt with specific suggestions to help her improve. If the student's performance improves as a result, offer praise.

4. Homework and Practice

Homework provides students with the opportunity to extend their learning outside the classroom. However, research shows that the amount of homework assigned should vary by grade level and that parent involvement should be minimal. Teachers should explain the purpose of homework to both the student and the parent or guardian, and teachers should try to give feedback on all homework assigned.

Applications:

• Establish a homework policy with advice—such as keeping a consistent schedule, setting, and time limit—that parents and students may not have considered.
• Tell students if homework is for practice or preparation for upcoming units.
• Maximize the effectiveness of feedback by varying the way it is delivered.

Research shows that students should adapt skills while they're learning them. Speed and accuracy are key indicators of the effectiveness of practice.

Applications:

• Assign timed quizzes for homework and have students report on their speed and accuracy.
• Focus practice on difficult concepts and set aside time to accommodate practice periods.

5. Nonlinguistic Representations

According to research, knowledge is stored in two forms: linguistic and visual. The more students use both forms in the classroom, the more opportunity they have to achieve. Recently, use of nonlinguistic representation has proven to not only stimulate but also increase brain activity.

Applications:

• Incorporate words and images using symbols to represent relationships.
• Use physical models and physical movement to represent information.

6. Cooperative Learning

Research shows that organizing students into cooperative groups yields a positive effect on overall learning. When applying cooperative learning strategies, keep groups small and don't overuse this strategy—be systematic and consistent in your approach.

Applications:

• When grouping students, consider a variety of criteria, such as common experiences or interests.
• Vary group sizes and objectives.
• Design group work around the core components of cooperative learning—positive interdependence, group processing, appropriate use of social skills, face-to-face interaction, and individual and group accountability.

7. Setting Objectives and Providing Feedback

Setting objectives can provide students with a direction for their learning. Goals should not be too specific; they should be easily adaptable to students' own objectives.

Applications:

• Set a core goal for a unit, and then encourage students to personalize that goal by identifying areas of interest to them. Questions like "I want to know" and "I want to know more about . . ." get students thinking about their interests and actively involved in the goal-setting process.
• Use contracts to outline the specific goals that students must attain and the grade they will receive if they meet those goals.

Research shows that feedback generally produces positive results. Teachers can never give too much; however, they should manage the form that feedback takes.

Applications:

• Make sure feedback is corrective in nature; tell students how they did in relation to specific levels of knowledge. Rubrics are a great way to do this.
• Keep feedback timely and specific.
• Encourage students to lead feedback sessions.

8. Generating and Testing Hypotheses

Research shows that a deductive approach (using a general rule to make a prediction) to this strategy works best. Whether a hypothesis is induced or deduced, students should clearly explain their hypotheses and conclusions.

Applications:

• Ask students to predict what would happen if an aspect of a familiar system, such as the government or transportation, were changed.
• Ask students to build something using limited resources. This task generates questions and hypotheses about what may or may not work.

9. Cues, Questions, and Advance Organizers

Cues, questions, and advance organizers help students use what they already know about a topic to enhance further learning. Research shows that these tools should be highly analytical, should focus on what is important, and are most effective when presented before a learning experience.

Applications:

• Pause briefly after asking a question. Doing so will increase the depth of your students' answers.
• Vary the style of advance organizer used: Tell a story, skim a text, or create a graphic image. There are many ways to expose students to information before they "learn" it. *C//*

Source: Adapted from Classroom Instruction That Works *by R. J. Marzano, D. J. Pickering, and J. E. Pollock, 2001, Alexandria, VA: ASCD.*

—LAURA VARLAS

Schools function as true learning communities when they actually observe other schools in action—hearing the voices, feeling the energy, sensing the passion, and seeing the evidence. Face-to-face contact and interaction are still the most powerful forms of communication and collaboration, although electronic exchanges, telephones, and video-conferencing increase accessibility. Schools that are serious about studying their practices and that have the courage to compare themselves to peak performers should get acquainted with both high-achieving schools "like us" and with "gap-closing" schools. Few learning experiences are as stimulating as one-on-one opportunities to ask, "What do you do? Why do you do it? How did you make it happen?" and to hear the answers directly from those who overcame the obstacles.

Schools Like Us

Chapter 10 included a reference to the Just for the Kids analysis, which creates sets of comparable schools based on demographic characteristics, such as poverty, mobility, and English language acquisition.[3] Schools who participate in these projects can easily identify other schools with similar student populations, discover which schools have the greatest success with student achievement, and receive either reassurance that they also perform well *or* reassurance that there are things that will work. Figure 12.4 provides cause for celebration at Happy Valley Elementary.

Demonstrating top performance among schools that also have advantageous student demographics assures staff that their success is a result of their professional efforts. Kulshan Middle School, with a more challenging student population, can also take pride at being in the top five performers and can connect with a network of similar schools striving to progress even further (see Figure 12.5).

On the other hand, an affluent school that thinks it's successful because its scores mirror the state's may experience a rude awakening and urgent call to action when faced with an awareness of what the outliers in their group are accomplishing. Moreover, complacent adults who attribute low achievement to the characteristics of the learners may be enlightened to discover that the same types of students perform much better in other school settings. The most dramatic reactions of principals exploring the Just for the Kids database have been those that followed discovery of higher achievement than theirs in schools with even greater challenges. After serving urban schools of poverty, I'm often tempted to say, "Let me take you on a field trip."

Gap-Closing Schools

The increasing body of literature on gap-closing schools includes both research and best practice. The work of Ruth Johnson (2002) has been cited throughout this edition and contains an extensive collection of references and resources. Gap-closing schools have succeeded in eliminating or dramatically reducing discrepancies between the achievement of white

Figure 12.4 Just for the Kids: Happy Valley Elementary

Happy Valley Elementary, Bellingham
Top Comparable Schools for Grade 4 Reading 2002

School Name District Name	Continuously Enrolled Tested		School-Wide		Selected Grade				School Size	Selectivity*	
	% Exceeded Standard	% Met or Exceeded Standard	% Low-Income	% Biling.	Grade Size	# Not Tested	Total # Tested	# Cont. Enrl.	Total Enrl.	% Not Tested	% Cont. Enrl.
Happy Valley Elementary, Bellingham	70.2	93.6	23.3	2.9	68	4	64	48	403	5.9	70.6
Happy Valley Elementary, Bellingham	70.2	93.6	23.3	2.9	68	4	64	48	403	5.9	70.6
Coe, Seattle	62.1	93.1	23.4	13.3	45	2	43	29	293	4.4	64.4
Lynndale Elementary Ld, Edmonds	65.1	93.0	26.5	11.1	54	0	54	43	387	0.0	79.6
Hawthorne Elementary School, Kennewick	46.2	92.3	49.3	4.0	75	6	69	41	441	8.0	54.7
Madison Elementary, Everett	36.2	89.9	48.5	3.1	97	6	91	71	604	6.2	73.2
Sierra Heights Elementary School, Renton	46.8	89.4	25.9	10.4	67	4	63	47	526	6.0	70.1
Martin Luther King Elementary, Vancouver	43.2	88.6	68.8	17.6	85	19	66	52	581	22.4	61.2
Silver Lake Elementary School, Federal Way	48.1	88.5	23.3	14.7	75	3	72	52	553	4.0	69.3
Sanislo, Seattle	50.0	87.5	59.7	14.6	48	1	47	32	292	2.1	66.7
Parkwood Elementary, Shoreline	60.0	86.7	24.8	9.4	64	4	60	49	447	6.3	76.6
Average of Top Comparable Schools	51.6	90.1									
Opportunity Gap	18.7	3.5									
Number in Pool	332										

Washington School Research Center, Seattle Pacific University.

Figure 12.5 Just for the Kids: Kulshan Middle School

Kulshan Middle, Bellingham
Top Comparable Schools for Grade 7 Reading 2002

School Name District Name	Continuously Enrolled Tested		School-Wide		Selected Grade				School Size	Selectivity*	
	% Exceeded Standard	% Met or Exceeded Standard	% Low-Income	% Biling.	Grade Size	# Not Tested	Total # Tested	# Cont. Enrl.	Total Enrl.	% Not Tested	% Cont. Enrl.
Kulshan Middle, Bellingham	28.5	62.4	28.7	1.5	206	10	196	169	650	4.9	82.0
Roosevelt Middle School, Port Angeles	21.2	65.6	29.4	0.5	184	7	177	158	544	3.8	85.9
Rainier Middle School, Auburn	23.1	63.7	32.6	1.9	269	3	266	214	843	1.1	79.6
Kulshan Middle, Bellingham	28.5	62.4	28.7	1.5	206	10	196	169	650	4.9	82.0
Jefferson Middle School, Olympia	27.4	62.4	31.7	2.6	153	2	151	119	464	1.3	77.8
Blaine Middle School, Blaine	23.0	57.8	40.7	1.5	198	5	193	137	558	2.5	69.2
Average of Top Comparable Schools	24.5	62.6									
Opportunity Gap	4.0	-0.2									
Number in Pool	147										

Washington School Research Center, Seattle Pacific University.

students and students of color, a gap that is usually greatest for African American youth.

As more schools and communities remove their "color blinders," face the reality, and attempt to change their worlds, more examples of success are noted and correlated with specific changes. Teachers who had low expectations for student performance became "warm demanders" and insist on conscientious effort (Bylsma, Shannon, & Griffin, 2002). Changed beliefs and attitudes that result in a learning environment of caring and higher expectations nurture students with greater self-efficacy and persistence.

Cultural responsiveness is another aspect of gap-closing schools. Adults acknowledge the legitimacy of the cultural heritage of every child and learn enough about it to build meaningful bridges. The use of a wide variety of instructional strategies increases teachers' success at connecting with the diverse needs and styles of the learners. Students are actively taught to know and praise their own and each other's cultures, and multicultural information is incorporated across the subjects taught in the school—not just in Social Studies and on ethnic holidays.

Gap-closing schools provide greater opportunity to learn by extending learning time through before- and after-school programs, summer school, and sometimes even Saturday sessions and through acceleration opportunities during other breaks in the school calendar. Every moment is considered an opportunity to learn, from social instruction on the playground to "books on the bus," which makes productive use of time *en route*. Every child is exposed to a rigorous curriculum, including the scope and sequence of mathematics courses needed to keep the gate to college open for all who wish to pursue it. Programs are varied and enriched with learning experiences that challenge and stimulate learning beyond the basics.

Closing the achievement gap requires adherence to core learning principles and coherence in systems. The taught curriculum must be tightly aligned with essential skills and standards for high-quality intellectual performance, with support provided to ensure students can and do learn. Given the challenge of time and the urgency to accelerate learning to close the gap, teachers do not have the luxury of spending time on topics and activities *they* enjoy; they must find joy in effectively teaching what the students most need. The instructional program is planned to provide a balance of basic and advanced skills, ensuring the foundation, but also stretching students to higher-level thinking.

It is still the exception for staff to mirror the racial composition of the student population, so an essential strategy is to include adults who share the children's culture. This creates the need for a full range of strategies for family and community involvement. Epstein and Connors (1994) describe the benefits to be gained by various types of parent involvement, including supporting their children through good parenting, two-way communication, volunteering in the school, engaging in learning activities at home, participation in school decision-making processes, and collaboration with community groups and agencies.

The literature on gap closing refers primarily to the impact of attitudes, beliefs, and practices of teachers. Johnson (2002) devotes an entire section to the powerful role of high school guidance counselors as gatekeepers. Through conscious or subconscious assumptions about who will be able to handle particular courses, far-reaching decisions are made that close windows of opportunity for students. Johnson includes examples of data gathering to examine the practices of the counseling office at the same time that teachers are analyzing their classroom practices.

Probing Our Practice

Figure 1.1 has been our visual map through a process of affirming what we believe, reviewing what we achieve, admitting our concerns, focusing our priorities, and engaging in professional study. Chapter 11 provided guidance for deeper analysis of data related to our priorities, represented by the first bullet point in the *Study* component on Figure 1.1. The first part of this chapter relates to the second bullet point and has provided a sampling of the sources and activities that would constitute looking around at research and best practice.

The third part of the *Study* phase is a thorough, authentic analysis of the *taught* curriculum, the instructional practices *in use* in classrooms, and the characteristics of programs *as implemented* in the school.

Over the past 30-odd years, I have seen district and school reform efforts come and go. I've facilitated strategic planning at the district level and improvement planning at the school level. I've reviewed, audited, and accredited schools. But when it comes to the classroom level, I've signed off on far more individual, idiosyncratic, nonaligned, preference-based autonomous staff development "plans" than the short list of standards-based, goal-oriented, collaborative, professional learning initiatives in which I've been engaged.

We have begun to break down the isolated individualism of the teaching profession through negotiated collaboration time. We have still not, however, added the rigor of self- and peer-observation and challenge. We've implemented critical friends groups with the emphasis on being friends and an avoidance of being critical. It's time to challenge ourselves with the same criteria we use to demand higher-level thinking and intellectual effort from our highest-achieving students.

Mapping the Curriculum

Most of us remember our Curriculum 101 course, in which we learned that the origins of the word *curriculum* related to a racetrack or a course to be run. We learned the words *scope* and *sequence*. And we drew a Venn diagram with three circles representing the written curriculum, the taught curriculum, and the assessed curriculum. We were enlightened with the profound concept that students do the best on assessments if the assessment matches the written curriculum and if that curriculum is actually taught.

Over 10 years ago, in the *last* ESEA reauthorization, federal money was sent to states to distribute to schools with the requirements that the states must develop "rigorous standards and assessments." So, every state but Iowa—which passed the work along to local districts—did so. Then districts began to look at their written curricula and adopted materials and checked off the standards that were addressed. They created alignment documents, moved a course up or down a grade, or rearranged the sequence of chapters to be taught in the text so students would be exposed to the right content in advance of the testing window. The written curriculum was aligned to standards. "All is well" was reported to school boards. Meanwhile, the taught curriculum rolled right along its merry way.

After curriculum alignment came curriculum mapping. Teachers came together to look at the new academic standards and verify the ones they taught. Upon completion of the activity, people went home happy because they had checked off all the standards. It made sense at the time to start with the standards, and I led similar efforts myself. The activities did give teachers hands-on contact with the new academic standards and an awareness-level knowledge of the expectations for student performance. However, the work did not rigorously challenge how time and focus were actually allocated within the classroom.

Next time around, I will do curriculum mapping in two phases. First, I will have teachers map their taught curriculum by looking at their lesson plans *without* reference to the standards. The purpose would be data gathering—to capture what actually occurs as standard practice throughout a school year. At the elementary level, I would start by having them calculate the total number of hours students are scheduled to attend school, and then subtract lunches, recesses, "specials" (like music and physical education) taught by other teachers, assemblies, field trips, and predictable special events (like end-of-year track meets) to see how many teachable moments they control within the classroom. Then, we would estimate an actual time (*not* a time derived from the written schedule) allocated for reading, writing, and math. Teachers would list their science and social studies units, and the number of weeks and approximate time per week.

At the secondary level, teachers would identify the things that typically disrupt their schedules and reduce the number of actual class meetings for the courses they teach. This often differs by time of day, with more interruptions later in the day or more students not present to learn directly after their lunch period. Then, high school teachers would highlight their course syllabus with the lessons and activities that usually do occur as top priorities.

The academic standards—accompanied by student data—would be introduced after compiling this more precise and honest picture of the curriculum map in operation. This would be openly referred to as *redrawing* the curriculum map. I would push the question of "What will each of us put on the chopping block?" to make room for what students need most.

Unless there is a deliberate sense of giving something up, work to align instruction with standards will be seen as "stacking even more on our plates and never taking anything off."

Becoming Standards-Based

The development of academic standards during the 1990s resulted in a keener awareness and common understanding of what should be taught. Even the skeptics and resisters knew it was important to align instruction and be standards-based. But, as the discussion of curriculum mapping revealed, being standards-based was mainly perceived as a checklist to cover all the standards.

The attributes listed in Figure 12.6 were compiled to provide a more complete understanding of standards-based teaching and learning. In addition to conveying expectations for school and classroom practice, these characteristics can be used as a diagnostic instrument. School leadership teams consider each item and rate their progress from 1 (*aware, but no action*) to 4 (*implemented consistently in all classrooms*). Participants in one principals' workshop noted that they all had the same items ranked lowest—numbers 9 and 13–15. This prompted the realization that major new work was needed in the whole area of classroom-based assessment and that input was provided to the staff development coordinators. Just as students need clear expectations and models of what their work should look like, staff members need a clear picture of what it means to be standards-based.

Balancing the Reading Block

Earlier in this chapter, the components of a balanced reading program were displayed in Figure 12.1. Those components are duplicated on Figure 12.7, which is a diagnostic tool in the form of a *discussion guide*. Note that only the school and grade level are identified at the top. This tool should *not* be used as a reporting form given to each individual teacher to fill out and turn in. Rather, grade-level teams should use it to reflect on the past month of instruction, review plans they have made, think about activities and materials that were assigned to students, and analyze how each of these components are taught and how much time is devoted to them.

In the same way, schoolwide reading programs and interventions should be analyzed to identify whether all components are provided, including explicit instruction. Some school leaders have been dismayed to note that funds for improving student achievement have supported numerous strategies—all of which provided various formats for independent practice and none of which provided explicit instruction for new skill acquisition.

Surveying the Learners

Most of the examples in the following section on probing our practice gather data from the teachers about their own work. From an early age,

Figure 12.6   Indicators of Standards-Based Teaching and Learning

1. The district develops clear statements of what students should know and be able to do.

2. Standards apply to all students with high expectations for their success.

3. The teacher knows how each lesson relates to district and state academic standards.

4. Students know what they are learning, what standards are related to it, and why they are learning it.

5. Standards are constant; instructional strategies and time are the variables.

6. Planning begins with standards rather than materials.

7. Practice activities are clearly aligned to standard(s) with the student as worker and the teacher as coach.

8. Students know how the teacher expects them to show what they've learned.

9. Students frequently evaluate their own work before the teacher does, using the same criteria.

10. Feedback to students is related to performance levels on standards, not based on comparison with other students.

11. Student performance data is used to revise curriculum and instruction.

12. The assessment system includes a balance of external tests for program evaluation and classroom assessments for individual student diagnosis and instruction.

13. Students have multiple opportunities to demonstrate achievement of standards.

14. Assessment of student achievement is consistent across teachers and schools, using common performance indicators.

15. Teachers work with colleagues to share and compare scoring of classroom-based assessments.

Figure 12.7 Balancing the Reading Block

School _____ Grade _____

Essential Reading Components	Strategies/ Techniques	Materials	Approx. # of Minutes/Week
Explicit instruction in phonemic awareness			
Explicit instruction in phonics			
Explicit instruction in vocabulary			
Explicit instruction in fluency			
Explicit instruction in comprehension skills and strategies			
Explicit instruction in thinking skills			
Opportunities to respond in a variety of ways			
Whole group instruction			
Small group instruction			
Individual instruction			
Reading aloud to students daily			
Shared reading daily			
Guided reading daily			
Independent reading practice daily			
Experiences with fiction			
Experiences with nonfiction			
Experiences with other forms (e.g., lists, directions)			
High expectations and clear standards for all students			
Continuous evaluation			

students begin to compare teachers and teaching practices and come to conclusions about what's effective. At five years of age, my niece told me that her kindergarten teacher "wasn't very flexible or friendly." When asked about the former, Kacie stated, "She gave us a list of all the things we need to use to learn and we bought them. Now she says we have to leave them in our cubby at school and not take them home. Doesn't she think I might want to learn some things at home?" With regard to friendliness, she shared that the teacher "doesn't smile much," but acknowledged that "some of the boys are kind of naughty and maybe she'll get nicer after she gets them shaped up." These are powerful comments on teaching and the learning environment.

By middle school, students should be guided through conversation with adults, self-assessment, and group activities to develop an understanding of their learning styles and what they need to provide for themselves—or to ask from their teachers—as they take increased responsibility for their learning. By high school, students are an excellent source for data on prevalent teaching practices. Figure 12.8 is a survey given to students at Bellingham High School to gather data on classroom activities, much as Figure 12.7 gathered data about elementary reading activities.[4]

The first three questions in this survey capture student feedback on three goals set by staff to improve classroom instruction: clear statement of purpose, summarizing and connecting new learning at the end of the lesson, and increasing active engagement of students. Teachers also wanted to know what strategies students recognized and how students rated their effectiveness. When schools are willing to ask students what helps them learn, they are invariably impressed at the depth and accuracy of student responses.

Reinforcing or Replacing?

Figure 12.1 described components of a balanced reading program and Figure 12.7 was provided as the diagnostic tool to gather data and analyze how those components are delivered. I mentioned the disturbing discovery that intervention programs were providing practice but not explicit instruction to accelerate student learning and help them catch up with their peers, thereby reducing the achievement gap.

Major expenditures of Title I money, grants, and other funds are purchasing teachers and instructional assistants to deliver extra help to students. If these support programs are provided in pull-out models during the school day, they must be analyzed in terms of what classroom activities students are missing and who's teaching when they leave the classroom—compared to what they are being taught and by whom in their support program. If, for example, they are missing a stimulating discussion that involves higher-level thinking facilitated by a certificated teacher in order to have a rote memory practice session with a teacher aide, we are replacing one learning experience with another that has less to offer. This practice may actually result in the student having a weaker, rather than stronger, instructional program, thus increasing rather than decreasing the distance from meeting standard.

Figure 12.8 Student Learning Survey: Bellingham High School

Please take a few minutes to complete the following student learning survey. This information will help us better understand our strengths as well as identify areas where we might be able to improve our work in the classroom.

For the period just concluding, did the teacher share the learning goals for the class with you? ___yes ___no

For the period just concluding, was there a summary of ideas at the end of the period? ___yes ___no

For the period just concluding, rate the class from 1 (*low*) to 10 (*high*) on the following goal: "Classes at BHS will engage students and lead to deep understanding about significant ideas."

    1   2   3   4   5   6   7   8   9   10

For the period just concluding, use the categories below and approximate the amount of time you spent during the class period engaged in the following types of learning activities. Respond to as many as apply for <u>the preceding period only</u>. Your <u>total for all items should be 100 minutes</u>. If a certain type of teaching or learning did not occur this period, you should circle the '0.'

I listened to the teacher talk/lecture and took notes.
100   90   80   70   60   50   40   30   20   10   0

I worked independently on a short- or long-term research-based project.
100   90   80   70   60   50   40   30   20   10   0

I answered questions on a worksheet or from a textbook.
100   90   80   70   60   50   40   30   20   10   0

I participated in a class discussion.
100   90   80   70   60   50   40   30   20   10   0

I worked on an assignment with a small group of students.
100   90   80   70   60   50   40   30   20   10   0

I worked independently on a daily assignment.
100   90   80   70   60   50   40   30   20   10   0

I watched another student or small group give a performance or participated in one myself.
100   90   80   70   60   50   40   30   20   10   0

I did lab work or learned by experimenting with an idea.
100   90   80   70   60   50   40   30   20   10   0

I was given free time.
100   90   80   70   60   50   40   30   20   10   0

I was off task and not doing what the teacher expected me to do.
100   90   80   70   60   50   40   30   20   10   0

Please give your opinion about which teaching and learning strategies are most effective? Why?

Capturing Our Culture

Just as students have individual patterns of skill development and classrooms have idiosyncratic practices, every school has a feel of its own. Experienced practitioners who visit many schools sense the culture within seconds. It may be happy or stressed. It may be casual or purposeful. It may be civil or rude. Those who live in the culture may be too immersed in survival to be aware of how it differs from other schools or how it affects those entering the school for the first time. During the study phase, it's important to gather data on schoolwide phenomena as well as teaching practice and student performance.

It's Academic—Isn't It?

Have you ever been in a school that felt like a prison? Or one where the students seemed to think it was a social club? Somewhere between the two would be a school culture that is intentionally academic, purposeful about learning for both adults and students. Figure 12.9, consisting of four pages, provides a powerful tool for assessing the degree to which the schools' culture fosters high achievement.

Cause and Effect

Two schools were featured in Chapter 1. School A made a structural change simply to be progressive, and there was no evidence of positive impact other than fewer hallway incidents. (With half as many passing periods, one would hope there would be.) School B, on the other hand, started with students. They asked, "What do we want to see in our students and their work?" Then, they analyzed their own context and practices and concluded that the way they used time was a barrier to the kind of teaching they would need to do to see the evidence of student learning they sought. They might have used a technique like the cause-and-effect diagram to reach that conclusion.

A cause-and-effect diagram is a visual representation of the relationship between contributing factors and an issue or problem. Because the picture branches out like the skeleton of a fish, it has become known as a "fish bone."

The question, "What factors contribute to . . ." is stated across the top and the "head" of the fish represents the need or issue being analyzed. A horizontal line represents the spine of the fish. Some formal group process handbooks emphasize that causal factors fall into categories and that the categories should be identified first and the first "fish bones" should represent these categories. For example, quality management fish bone diagrams often start with the four categories of *procedures, people, policies,* and *plant*. I have left the process unstructured because I've seen too many groups get stuck figuring out what the categories might be. I'd rather have them dive into the discussion and attach smaller bones and "barbs" as

(Text continues on p. 183)

Figure 12.9   Assessing Institutional Reforms in the Academic Culture of Schools

Name (optional): _____		School: _____
Position: _____		Date: _____

(Fill in for postassessment *only*.)
Filled out instrument in 200 ___ ?   Yes ____   No ____

Directions: Please fill in the circle under the number that you believe best represents your school. One (1) is the lowest rating and five (5) is the highest.

Area	*Underachievement*	*Rating*	*Higher Achievement*
Leadership/Planning/ Decision Making	* Little or no collaboration between administrators and teachers about strategies to raise student achievement.	1 2 3 4 5 -O- -O- -O- -O- -O-	* Frequent and regular collaboration and joint problem solving to design and evaluate strategies to raise student achievement with a focus on access and equity.
	* Mostly top-down style of leadership; leadership teams function in isolation from colleagues; roles and commitment unclear;	1 2 3 4 5 -O- -O- -O- -O- -O-	* Frequent collaboration with administrative leaders; teams skillfully engage with each other and planning and decision-making involves all major stakeholders.
	* No use of data.	1 2 3 4 5 -O- -O- -O- -O- -O-	* Regular planning and use of data for inquiry; disaggregation of data.
	* No vision or strategic planning; add-on fragmented programs; no inclusion of stakeholders.	1 2 3 4 5 -O- -O- -O- -O- -O-	* Consensus on shared vision for school; focus on systemic issues that reform institutional policies and practices.
	* Meetings focus solely on operations, adult agenda.	1 2 3 4 5 -O- -O- -O- -O- -O-	* Meetings and activities have a clear focus on instruction.

What evidence supports your assessment? _____

Area	*Underachievement*	*Rating*	*Higher Achievement*
Professionalism/ Responsibility	* Low achievement and poor school functioning blamed on others.	1 2 3 4 5 -O- -O- -O- -O- -O-	* Staff views improved achievement and school functioning as its responsibility; analyzes institutional practices; highly committed staff; includes the entire school community.
	* 20% or more teachers lack credential.	1 2 3 4 5 -O- -O- -O- -O- -O-	* 90–100% of the teachers are fully credentialed.
	* Few teachers, counselors, and administrators are engaged in continuous meaningful professional development that will result in improved academic achievement.	1 2 3 4 5 -O- -O- -O- -O- -O-	* All professionals are continuously developing their professional skills.
	* Most professionals are not up-to-date in fields.	1 2 3 4 5 -O- -O- -O- -O- -O-	* Staff experiments; keeps up-to-date in fields; experiments with new strategies; evaluates progress and regularly uses data; teacher is a researcher; visitations to other sites with successful practices.
	* Nonrelevant, isolated, sporadic, or nonexistent staff development; in-service is the only form of staff development.	1 2 3 4 5 -O- -O- -O- -O- -O-	* Systematic, comprehensive, and tied to staff needs—up-to-date strategies, peer teaching, coaching, collegiality.

What evidence supports your assessment? _____

Figure 12.9 (Continued)

Area	Underachievement			Rating			Higher Achievement
Standards Curriculum	* Curriculum and courses are not aligned with state/national standards.	1 -O-	2 -O-	3 -O-	4 -O-	5 -O-	* Curriculum and courses are aligned with state/national standards.
	* Few students are engaged in standards-based tasks.	1 -O-	2 -O-	3 -O-	4 -O-	5 -O-	* All students are engaged in rigorous standards-based tasks; 90–100% of students score at levels demonstrating mastery.
	* Little or no agreement on consistent process to measure and report student performance.	1 -O-	2 -O-	3 -O-	4 -O-	5 -O-	* Consensus and commitment to ensuring standards-based rigor in curriculum and course work for all students; consistent framework for measuring student progress and providing feedback.
	* Curriculum actually taught is thin, fragmented.	1 -O-	2 -O-	3 -O-	4 -O-	5 -O-	* Students are taught a rigorous, balanced curriculum, rich in concepts, ideas, and problem solving.
	* Remedial instruction is isolated to low-level skills based on discrete facts.	1 -O-	2 -O-	3 -O-	4 -O-	5 -O-	* All students are taught a curriculum that is at or above grade level; students pushed toward higher-order thinking.
	* No technology included in the curriculum.	1 -O-	2 -O-	3 -O-	4 -O-	5 -O-	* Students have technology integrated into curriculum.

What evidence supports your assessment? _____

Area	Underachievement			Rating			Higher Achievement
Instruction	* Mostly lecture format; students passive, emphasis on low-level skills.	1 -O-	2 -O-	3 -O-	4 -O-	5 -O-	* A variety of successful, challenging, and interactive instructional strategies are used, such as cooperative learning, directed lessons, extended engagement time for learners; use of high-quality technology and software programs.
	* Multicultural issues and concepts are not integrated into standards-based instruction. No use of students' authentic learning outside of school to connect what is being taught in school.	1 -O-	2 -O-	3 -O-	4 -O-	5 -O-	* Multicultural issues and concepts are integrated into standards-based instruction. Use of students' authentic learning outside of school to connect what is being taught in school.
	* Repetitive low-level drills, heavy use of workbooks.	1 -O-	2 -O-	3 -O-	4 -O-	5 -O-	* Higher-level skills taught; progress assessed frequently; production rather than reproduction of knowledge is encouraged.
	* Lots of pullout programs isolated from regular classroom instruction; emphasis on remedial instruction.	1 -O-	2 -O-	3 -O-	4 -O-	5 -O-	* Students taught all subjects that lead to college entrance; addresses needs of diverse student populations.
	* Student abilities and achievement assessed solely on standardized skill-based tests.	1 -O-	2 -O-	3 -O-	4 -O-	5 -O-	* A variety of indicators are used to measure student performance.
	* No use of standards-based assessments.	1 -O-	2 -O-	3 -O-	4 -O-	5 -O-	* Appropriate and frequent use of standards-based assessments.

What evidence supports your assessment? _____

(continued)

Area	Underachievement	Rating					Higher Achievement
Expectations	* Academic goals are unfocused; no attention to access and equity.	1 -O-	2 -O-	3 -O-	4 -O-	5 -O-	* Goals are clearly focused on student achievement, access, and equity.
	* Students from low-income and certain ethnic backgrounds are viewed as not having the potential to gain high-level knowledge and skills.	1 -O-	2 -O-	3 -O-	4 -O-	5 -O-	* All students viewed as potential high achievers—staff believes all students are capable of mastering the high-level knowledge and skills.
	* Students considered not capable of taking required courses for 4-year postsecondary institutions.	1 -O-	2 -O-	3 -O-	4 -O-	5 -O-	* Students have access, are supported and prepared for 4-year postsecondary institutions.
	* Staff conversation reflects much negativity about children; staff assumes no responsibility for low levels of achievement.	1 -O-	2 -O-	3 -O-	4 -O-	5 -O-	* Staff constructively focuses on institutional and instructional practices that need changing and engages in discussions about ways to help students learn at high levels.
	* Students are informally and formally labeled in negative ways, e.g., slow, remedial, dropouts.	1 -O-	2 -O-	3 -O-	4 -O-	5 -O-	* Students are not negatively labeled.

What evidence supports your assessment? _____

Area	Underachievement	Rating					Higher Achievement
Learning Opportunities Grouping/Tracking/ Labeling	* Students separated by perceived ability into rigid homogeneous groups.	1 -O-	2 -O-	3 -O-	4 -O-	5 -O-	* Flexible grouping for short periods of time; most/all instruction in heterogeneous groups.
	* Lower-level and remedial groups get least-prepared teachers, watered-down curriculum.	1 -O-	2 -O-	3 -O-	4 -O-	5 -O-	* All students have opportunities to be taught by best-prepared teachers.
	* Only high-achieving students taught advanced-level information/ skills/technology.	1 -O-	2 -O-	3 -O-	4 -O-	5 -O-	* All students get same rigorous core curriculum—variety of strategies including technology are used.
	* Few options for low-achieving students.	1 -O-	2 -O-	3 -O-	4 -O-	5 -O-	* Students form study groups; extended days are provided, other student supports are introduced and implemented; practices are altered when necessary to better serve students.
	* Levels that students' function at is seen as unalterable.	1 -O-	2 -O-	3 -O-	4 -O-	5 -O-	* All students viewed as having the capacity to achieve at higher levels.

What evidence supports your assessment? _____

(Continued)

Figure 12.9 (Continued)

Area	Underachievement	Rating					Higher Achievement
Parent Involvement	* Parents are considered indifferent toward child's achievement.	1 -O-	2 -O-	3 -O-	4 -O-	5 -O-	* Staff, parents, and leaders use a variety of strategies to motivate and accommodate parents as partners in their children's education. Families learn to become effective advocates for their students.
	* Education viewed as a domain of professionals; little or no collaboration between staff and parents.	1 -O-	2 -O-	3 -O-	4 -O-	5 -O-	* Collaborative process where staff and parents assume joint responsibility for student performance, homework, communication.
	* Parent involvement limited to a few persons; insensitivity to cultural differences hinders participation.	1 -O-	2 -O-	3 -O-	4 -O-	5 -O-	* Parents, leaders, and staff use effective strategies to achieve broad participation and representation of all ethnic groups in activities.
	* Parents, students, and other community members are not aware of and rarely provided information about preparing students for higher education.	1 -O-	2 -O-	3 -O-	4 -O-	5 -O-	* Parents, students, and community partners actively participate in planning and implementing of programs.
	* Information rarely translated into the parents' dominant languages; communications seldom relate to achievement.	1 -O-	2 -O-	3 -O-	4 -O-	5 -O-	* Translation to parents' dominant languages consistently provides for effective school communication (oral and written) focused on student achievement.

What evidence supports your assessment? _____

Area	Underachievement	Rating					Higher Achievement
Support Services for Students	* Few or no tutoring services, tutoring usually in the form of a homework club; limited numbers of students utilize services.	1 -O-	2 -O-	3 -O-	4 -O-	5 -O-	* Ample support services closely integrated with instructional program; variety of tutoring programs offered with a flexible schedule; coordinated with core curriculum; regular participation of students who need assistance.
	* Little coordination among special programs; no mechanism to catch students "falling through the cracks."	1 -O-	2 -O-	3 -O-	4 -O-	5 -O-	* Special programs integrated into regular instruction; counseling programs aligned.
	* No agreed-upon plan for handling attendance, discipline, vandalism problems, uncaring environment; no review of implications on academic achievement.	1 -O-	2 -O-	3 -O-	4 -O-	5 -O-	* Agreed-on procedures for handling attendance and discipline problems, reduced referrals, suspensions, caring environment; monitoring impact on academic achievement.

What evidence supports your assessment? _____

they identify factors that contribute to the problem and are related to each other.

After the diagram is drawn, guide the group to think about the factors they have identified. Acknowledge factors over which the school or organization has no control. Then, focus in on the factors that most closely match their perceptions of their own situation and that they are able to influence and are willing to address. These become their entry points and will guide their selection of strategies or interventions.

The example that follows comes from one of the most powerful transformations I have observed as a consultant. It not only demonstrates how to do the activity; it also answers the question, "Won't all this emphasis on data make us less humane and forget about students' feelings?"

Ten school leadership teams had been selected to participate in a three-day workshop that would guide them through the process of developing a school improvement plan. They had been asked to bring student data and draft versions of any work they had already done on mission statements, goals, or action plans. It was fascinating to observe their approach to the day.

At one table sat a group of newspapers. It would have looked like a display at a newsstand, except that every now and then a hand would reach out and feel around for a coffee cup, which would then disappear behind the newspaper—more specifically, the sports section.

At another table, a group of early arrivals were poring over a stack of computer printouts. Heads together and unaware of the caterer's late delivery of the pastries, the participants were engrossed in a discussion of which subtests from a recent assessment matched their curriculum and mission closely enough to merit major attention as they set their improvement targets.

Another group entered carrying the lid of a copy-paper box with waves of green-and-white striped computer paper spilling haphazardly over the edge. Locating the table with the school's name on it, the carrier dropped the box onto the floor—*thud!*—and kicked it under the table with the side of his foot—*thwack!* Having thus dispatched the dreaded data, this group attacked the coffee and doughnuts table with great zeal.

I was beginning to have qualms about the day when another member of that group approached me and began a speech. "In all fairness, I really ought to let you know that there's no reason for us to be wasting three days at this workshop. We already have our school improvement plan done." Swallowing hard, I asked him what they had planned for the coming year. "Well, we got our biggest problem figured out. It's kids not coming to school. And we've got two plans for working on it. First, we got a business partner that's going to donate us some equipment so we can program it to call those kids and get them going in the morning. Second, we got a committee all lined up to work on our attendance policy so these kids can't get by with skipping. And we'd rather spend our time working on that than sitting in here."

I managed to thank him for his honesty and ask him to stick around for this first day, listen carefully, and think about his school's plan, and at the end of the day we'd talk again and see what could be worked out to honor his group's time. "Well, I guess we might as well. We're already here and, besides, it's raining."

During the first part of the morning, I engaged the group in a review of research on school effectiveness and provided an overview of the activities we would be doing over the three-day period. I gave each group some time to talk about whatever data they had available and to share the concerns that emerged from this discussion or others that had taken place at their school. During the report out, members of this group repeated that their attendance data showed a need for improvement.

Lunch was provided in the room right next door—and it was still raining—so we continued into the afternoon. That's when we began to discuss the importance of understanding the problem we're addressing and some of the causes or related factors so we know where to begin changing it.

The group began its fish bone of student absenteeism with "Parents don't care" and went right on to list items like "No transportation," "Baby-sitting younger kids," "Pretty low socioeconomic," and "Staying up too late at their night jobs." The other groups were getting along well, so I tried to coach this team a little. "You seem to have a pretty good handle on the students' family situation. Got any thoughts about the kids themselves?"

The next phase began with "Kids don't care either," "Unmotivated" (when they hold down night jobs?) and went on to "Discipline problems," "Low achievers," and "A couple of them are pregnant." About this time, I noticed one person digging around under the table, but it had a skirt around it and I didn't want to get too nosy, so I ignored him.

The work on the fish bone was bogging down again. I tried sympathy. "It's really too bad some kids are like that, but I'm glad to see you're aware of them. Could there be any other source of factors that relates to whether kids come to school or not?" A soft voice from the other end of the table said, "Well, they don't like school when they do come." Several people just stared at her, so I reached over with my own marker and wrote, "Don't like school" on a new fish bone. A few others added things like "Don't participate in anything," "Can't see the point of learning," and "Don't seem connected to anyone."

Just then, a head popped up with the copy paper box in his hand and a dazzling grin on his face. "Wait a minute. I've just been digging through here and it looks to me like there's no more than 20 kids in the whole school that are causing our attendance rate to look so bad." My challenger responded immediately. "Oh, yeah? So, who?"

As the analyst mentioned a name or two, other members of the group began to comment on individuals. "Well, if Joey can just make it from the bus to the door without a fight, he does pretty well in class." "Sam doesn't have any trouble getting here, but he's so interested in messing around the art room he doesn't follow his schedule." "If Suzy wasn't so worried about her weight, she might have time to think about her work."

Because of the data, the participants suddenly began to talk about students as individuals. As they did, one brave soul said, "You know, if they are so low income, do you think they'll have phones to call?" Another drew courage and said, "If they really don't care about school, what good will it do to suspend them for skipping?" My challenger shrugged and said, "Well, maybe our plan isn't quite right, but look at that fishy thing [Figure 12.10]. We can't do anything about that stuff."

I delightedly agreed. "You're right. There are a lot of things that are beyond our control. Let's mark them off and see what we have left that we could tackle." Check marks on Figure 12.10 show the items they eliminated. But they didn't check off very many because some members of the group began to argue that maybe the system *could* make some kind of provision for transportation and that they had heard of some schools that provided in-school child care. As the last step with their fish bone, they circled the items that could be entry points for a new action plan.

The next morning, this group got there first. By the end of the day, the group had developed a plan that would provide each of the chronic absentees with an adult in the school (a teacher, custodian, or volunteer) who would check in with him or her each morning before school and follow up at the end of the day to see if the student was taking work home. (The mentoring plan the group created is included in Chapter 14.) A year later, I met an administrator from that district at a conference and asked how things were going. He told me that this particular school had made the most progress with its school improvement plan and that it was easy to sense a dramatic difference in the culture of the school.

Go for the Green

Bob Garmston introduced an activity he called Go for the Green in a workshop called *Premier Presentation Skills*. It is one of the most valuable techniques I have found to help groups deal with subjective data. It can develop greater empathy and minimize blaming the victim. You will need large chart paper, and black, green, and red markers.

Start with a red circle in the middle of the paper. Let the participants know that you are using that color deliberately, because this is the target. It reminds us of a stop sign, because it prevents accomplishment of their task or goal. Maybe it angers them, so they "see red." Help the group decide how to phrase the concern and write it in red. The example shared in Figure 12.11 is from a group that had been discussing student disengagement and lack of motivation. Participants were making comments such as, "Why should we teach differently? It doesn't matter what we do if the students won't dig in and work at it. And their parents let them just slide by."

When the problem has been identified in red, switch to the black marker and write, "Under what conditions would I. . . ." I asked these participants whether they had ever been disengaged and unmotivated, perhaps in a course or workshop. After various smirks and guffaws, they began to generate some of the items shown in Figure 12.11. I recorded

Figure 12.10 Cause-and-Effect Diagram of Student Absenteeism

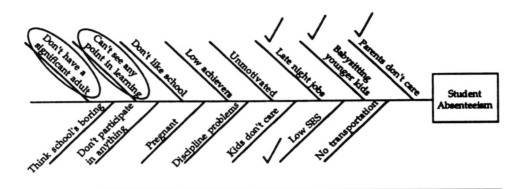

these thoughts in green on diagonal lines going out from the red circle, like rays on a child's drawing of the sun. Once the probable causes were recorded, I urged the group to "go for the green" rather than "rave about the red." After a long silence, one person sighed and said, "We're not so different from the kids, I guess. Those are about lack of skill and peer pressure and how the teacher teaches and what the assignments are like. I guess I need to change."

Professional Discipline

In the field of education, the word *discipline* is used in several ways. It may refer to a content area, such as mathematics or social studies, thus giving rise to derivatives like *interdisciplinary*. Or it may be used to describe methods of controlling or changing student behavior, yielding discipline policies and plans.

In this chapter, I challenge educators to submit to a professional discipline that involves courageous self-examination and willingness to sacrifice what we like to do for that which is most effective in meeting the needs of students. As Richard Elmore (2002) states,

> Improvement is a discipline. It requires picking a target that has something to do with demonstrated student learning, one that's ambitious enough to put schools in "improvement mode." . . . School improvement doesn't happen by getting everyone to come to the auditorium and testify to their belief that all children can learn—not if it means sending everyone back into the classroom to do what they've always done. Only a change in practice produces a genuine change in norms and values. Or, to put it more crudely, "grab people by their practice and their hearts and minds will follow." (p. 3)

Figure 12.11 Go for the Green of Student Disengagement

Under what conditions would I . . .

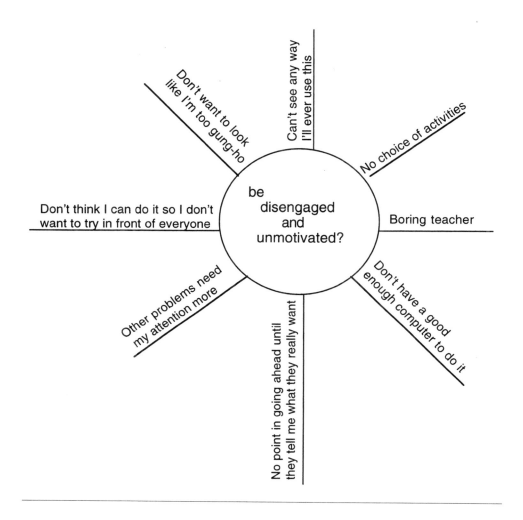

Notes

1. Thanks to Joan Dore and Charlotte Carr of Seattle Public Schools for their original work on the first version of this graphic.
2. Gordon S. Cawelti shared this material in personal conversation and a presentation at the College of William and Mary, Williamsburg, Virginia, in June 1999.
3. For more information on Just for the Kids, go to www. Just4theKids.org
4. Thank you to Steve Clarke, Principal, Bellingham High School.

13

Clarifying District, School, and Classroom Roles

The courageous examination of student outcomes and professional inquiry into instructional practices described in Chapters 11 and 12 will generate a long list of possible strategies for consideration. They will run the gamut from "we need a friendlier greeting on the answering machine" to "we need a new math program that matches the test" to "we need to refocus our building-based inservice time on a common objective." Strategies that are school-based and "within the power of the school" (see Figure 10.1) would be planned and implemented by the school leadership team, staff, and stakeholders. But should individual schools be doing curriculum development on their own? Do they have the time, resources, and expertise? Do they have the holistic view of a child's 13 years of experience from kindergarten to graduation?

Meanwhile, school districts are also looking at student performance, examining programs, and making plans for change. So, how does it all fit together? What about all the emphasis on state standards and assessment? If the school is the focus of attention on student achievement, what happens to K–12 continuity? It's not an either-or question. The district must engage in continuous improvement of the instructional program while every school works to strengthen the learning environment and its delivery of the instructional program to its unique student population.

Figure 13.1 Aligning and Improving Student Learning

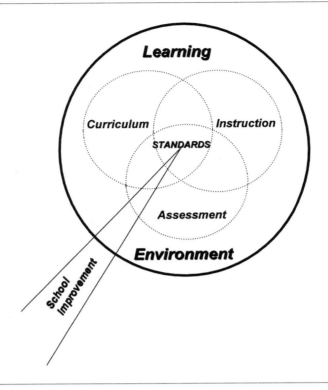

Going in Circles

Figure 13.1 illustrates relationships between district-level work on the instructional program and school improvement efforts. The three interconnected circles represent *curriculum, instruction,* and *assessment*. These are the three components of an instructional program. The overlapping areas of the three circles are referred to as *curriculum alignment*. The rationale behind curriculum alignment is that students learn more—or at least their scores are better—if there is a tight match between the content identified in curriculum documents, the content that is actually delivered, and the content that is assessed. I have placed standards at the very center of the figure, where all three circles overlap, because they are intended to increase student learning by tightening the alignment of the instructional program. We might consider the area marked **Standards** as a magnet, drawing curriculum, assessment, and instruction more closely together.

With regard to these three components of the instructional program, the district has responsibility for determining the curriculum, because public interest, represented through federal and state law, and direction from the school board dictate what children should learn. The assessment circle is now shared by the federal and state governments as well as the district, school, and classroom. Standardized assessments given to all children are mandated by the state, and additional tests may be selected by the district. Ongoing assessment for diagnosis and feedback to children occurs at the school and classroom level. Instruction refers to the way the curriculum is delivered and is generally accepted as the domain of the school and its teachers.

In addition to choices about instructional methods and materials, the school is responsible for the learning environment, or school climate. This includes expectations that are conveyed for student performance, how individual differences are recognized and met, and how safety and order are maintained.

The circles in Figure 13.1 representing curriculum, instruction, assessment, and the learning environment are like gears that interact and are continuously in motion. Budget considerations may drive a cycle of program review and textbook and materials adoption. External mandates, such as state standards, create a need to look at alignment and perhaps revise the scope and sequence of the curriculum. This is ongoing maintenance of the instructional program.

School improvement cuts across all of the circles. It looks at assessment results and identifies areas of concern where students aren't performing satisfactorily. Then, it considers the curriculum and the instructional methods and determines whether other kinds of assessment are needed to demonstrate what students know and can do.

In automotive terms, the inside circles represent routine maintenance, such as filling the car with gas, changing the oil, and topping up window washer and transmission fluids. These are done regularly to keep things running well. School improvement is more like what we do when something isn't working right—when we hear a sound we shouldn't, when things groan and grind. These symptoms demand attention, diagnosis, and repair.

Going With the Flow

Figure 13.2 provides another look at the relationship between district-level work and school improvement, with data on student performance as the driving force. Boxes with a dark border represent activities at the district level, and rectangles with thinner borders represent aspects of the school improvement process.

The district and individual schools identify areas of student success and need. For each area of need, the series of questions presented in Figure 13.2 is asked and answered, and plans are made accordingly. Let's use math problem solving as an example. Assuming that students' scores in this area are disappointing, the first question relates to having *processes* in place to address the need. If there are data to suggest a need to look at math problem solving, it's not appropriate to say, "Well, we'll look at that in 2006, the next time math comes up in the cycle." At the district level, there must be a process or forum in which to address needs as they arise. At the school level, data suggesting a student achievement need should be reflected in the school improvement goals that are set.

Figure 13.2A Using Student Performance Data to Integrate District Curriculum Work With the School Improvement Process

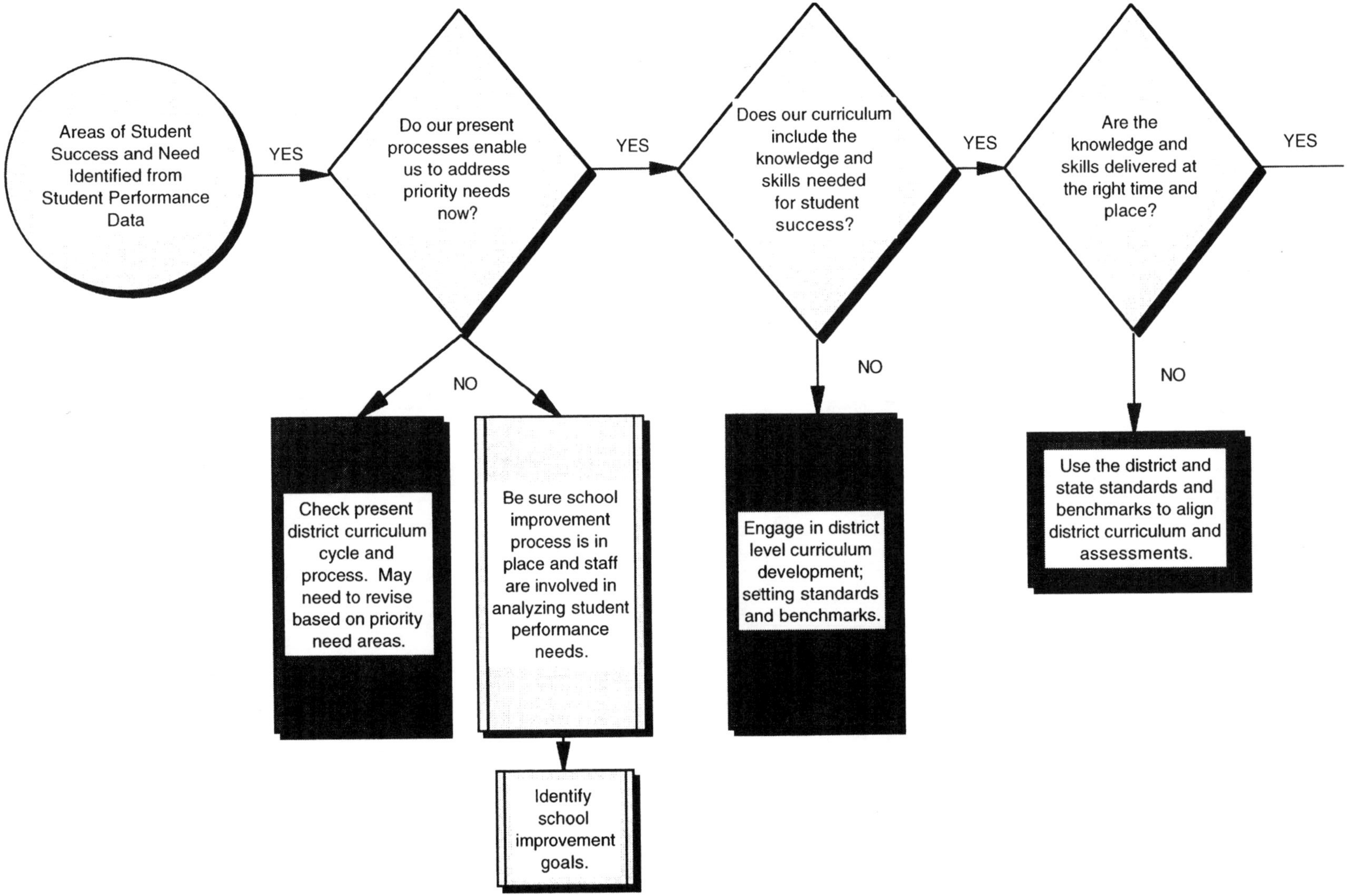

Figure 13.2B Using Student Performance Data to Integrate District Curriculum Work With the School Improvement Process

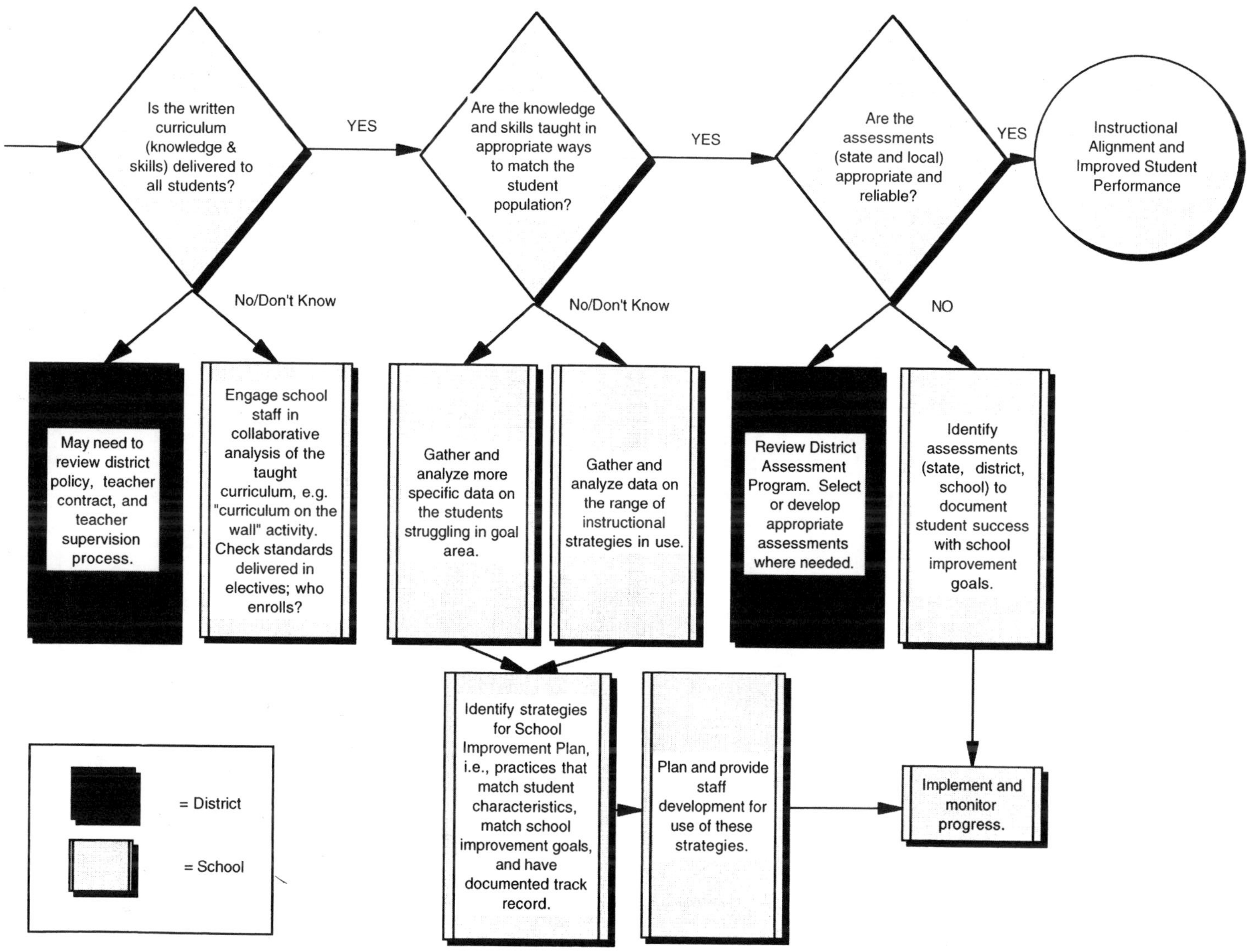

In terms of study (see Figure 1.1), schools ask questions about the area of student *need*. Is it in the curriculum? If not, the district's K–12 approach to revising curriculum needs to go into action. Math problem solving may turn out to be in the curriculum, but it may not be stressed until the next grade level after the major assessment is given. The same district-level process should be used to address needed realignment.

The real problem may be that the written curriculum is not actually being delivered. Most math programs include problem solving as a thread through all units and all grade levels. However, it may be a part that's omitted due to time constraints or teacher preferences for computation. The "curriculum on the wall" activity (see Figure 13.2) starts with teachers working by grade level to identify the main topics, units, or skills they teach along with time allocations and then clustering them in an affinity process. This activity may result in a more accurate picture than starting with the written curriculum guides would. If it reveals that some teachers are not delivering the curriculum, the district's policies, teacher contracts, and supervision procedures should be consulted and utilized to ensure that all students are being given the opportunity to learn the skills they need.

If math problem solving is in the curriculum and the curriculum *is* being taught, the next consideration may be the *methods* that are used and the characteristics of the student population. Further study at the school level would include gathering information on *how* problem solving is taught. Student performance data would be analyzed further to identify the students who are having difficulty to see if they have common characteristics that might provide clues about prior knowledge, learning style, or other barriers to learning that may be present.

School improvement plans should focus on strategies that match the students' needs, address the school improvement goal related to problem solving, and have been proven to increase student achievement of these skills. Once these strategies are selected, the school leadership team should develop plans that include staff development so teachers can utilize the strategies effectively. Meanwhile, the district curriculum process should also be scrutinizing the assessments that were the source of the student performance data. Their purpose is to analyze the degree to which existing assessments accurately measure learning expectations and to determine whether other types of assessment will be needed to measure all of the expected learning, provide ongoing information about student progress, and make decisions to strengthen the instructional program.

Cycling in Sync

Figures 13.1 and 13.2 are two visual ways of illustrating the relationship between district-level work and school improvement of the instructional program. The circles in Figure 13.1 may provide the best sense of ongoing motion and activity. Figures 1.1 and 13.2 appear more linear, limited as they are by the two dimensions of the printed page, but they repeat themselves in cyclical fashion. In fact, more than one of these cycles may be occurring at the same time, like several sheets of Figure 13.2 intersecting and spinning in a spiral.

Delivering the Data

The needs of schools for access to data and the time and technical assistance to use it are clear. External accountability systems demand it for schools to survive; internal capacity and motivation require it for educators and students to thrive. The data teams at individual schools need the help of a district data team. This district-level group should include district staff from curriculum, assessment, professional development, and technology areas, as well as representation of principals and teachers to connect district and school efforts.

The Learning First Alliance, a partnership of educational associations that includes the Association for Supervision and Curriculum Development (ASCD) and that represents more than 10 million Americans engaged in education efforts, conducted a two-year project to study what districts can do to improve instruction and achievement in all schools (Tagneri, 2003). The study focused on five districts that had free and reduced lunch eligibility ranging from 38% to 80% and exhibited at least three years of improvement in student achievement in mathematics and/or reading across multiple grades and across all races and ethnicities. District support for the use of data was one of the seven principal findings, which were as follows:

- Finding 1: Districts had the courage to acknowledge poor performance and the will to see solutions.
- Finding 2: Districts put in place a systemwide approach to improving instruction.
- Finding 3: Districts instilled visions that focused on learning and guided instructional improvement.
- Finding 4: Districts made decisions based on data, not instinct.
- Finding 5: Districts adopted new approaches to professional development.
- Finding 6: Districts redefined leadership roles.
- Finding 7: Districts committed to sustaining reform over the long haul.

The new approaches to professional development cited in Finding 5 included encouragement and assistance in using data. Based on this report, the responsibilities of the district data team would include identifying common sources of data for use by the district and by all schools, gathering the data, making it usable, and developing the capacity of principals and teachers to make use of it.

Like these districts, Bellingham, Washington has a data team on GUARD (gathering, using, and reporting data) duty at all times. One of their activities has been to survey principals and gather the "what I wish I could do with data" list to inform selection of an electronic data warehousing system. As this system is implemented to make student data available at each teacher's desktop, the GUARD team's role will include planning and delivering the professional development components for various groups of users. While individual capacity is being developed, the data warehousing system will enable them to create more user-friendly reports to place in the hands of principals and teachers so they can see what they could produce for themselves and learn how to use it.

This group has also developed a Data Handbook for schools that includes a timeline of the district-based and school-based assessment and data-related activities for each month of the year. This is referenced to the specific score reports that come from state and district tests and other sources, and explains the purpose and audience for each of the reports.

Coordinating the Common

As schools conduct their in-depth analysis of data in priority areas, examine research and best practice, and review their own practice, they begin to consider strategies for implementation (see Figure 1.1). This raises their awareness of needs for support with curriculum alignment; needs for formative, classroom assessments to guide instruction; and needs for professional development.

Rather than being directed from the top (i.e., the district) down, these needs should bubble up to the district level as school improvement plans are developed (see Chapter 14). District staff should identify the needs that are articulated in more than one school improvement plan and then coordinate responses to common needs. For example, when several schools identify the same topic for professional development, district coordination saves schools money as well as time and energy working out logistics. The focus is on improving student performance through the mutual efforts of the school and district. As Roland Barth (1990) wrote, "When the central office runs a service agency for principals, then principals are able to set up service agencies for teachers, and teachers for children. The chain of command can then become a chain of support."

14

Planning Your Work and Working Your Plan

Using Figure 1.1, the Achievement Plan, as a map, you've affirmed your mission, assembled baseline data to generate concerns, focused on a few priorities, drilled deeper into the data in those areas, studied research and best practice, analyzed current practices and programs, and selected strategies that will improve instruction and the learning environment and increase student achievement. Now, as with the new tires on my realigned car, the rubber meets the road. How will the new strategies and any new assessments and evidence of progress get implemented throughout the school? The right-hand side of Figure 1.1 illustrates a set of action plans that back up the overall achievement plan by providing the details of *what, who, when, where,* and *how will we know.* This chapter provides a format and recommendations for making sure that you're working your plan and your plan is working.

Developing Action Plans

A common characteristic of school improvement plans-that-never-happen is that they identify strategies they will use—for example, cooperative learning, a self-esteem program, or block scheduling—without analyzing what implementation of those strategies will entail. Any one of the strategies mentioned represents many substeps needed to provide training and support for implementation. When schools select popular options, such as learning styles and block scheduling, their plans often involve training in the content knowledge without sufficient consideration of changes that need to be made in the school itself to reflect and reinforce those concepts. Although plans will surely be adjusted during implementation, they must be sufficiently developed to represent clearly the magnitude of change they require and the demands they place on people, time, and budgets.

Because an action plan needs to identify specific steps, timelines, and resources, it is important to involve people who have access to information about the school calendar and budget, as well as a big picture perspective of all that is occurring in the organization. School teams often find it helpful to include a central office support person in the action-planning stage. If a major innovation, such as a shift to multiage classrooms, is being implemented, it is advisable to bring in a consultant or a team member from another school that is already using the approach. These resource people can provide advice on how they approached the change and can offer even more valuable insights about problems they didn't anticipate and what they might have done to avoid them.

The detail required in action planning often brings the realization that the strategy or approach to be used is a much more complex change than was anticipated. In some situations, it is helpful to identify major subtasks and to assign a small group to develop that part of the action plan. For example, the plan to implement a major change like multiage classrooms would need a parent education and communication component. Involvement of parents in this planning subgroup would be essential.

I've seen school improvement plans in many formats. Some are developed in chart form; others are written in narrative. Some work well; some look nice and accomplish nothing. The common elements of those I find useful are

- Steps to be taken and activities that will occur
- Persons who will be responsible to guide, coordinate, and monitor the activity
- Additional persons who will be involved
- Resources needed (money and materials)
- Time required and a schedule
- Indicators that will be monitored and used to evaluate effectiveness

Stepping Out

A simple way to begin drafting an implementation action plan is to use the six elements listed above as column headings on a large bulletin board or wall (see Figure 14.1). The sequence of planning is to work all the way down and then work across for each activity. In other words, first list all the steps that need to be taken. Because of their training in task analysis,

Figure 14.1 Action Plan Form

Activities: Steps to Be Taken	Persons Responsible	Persons Involved	Resources Needed	Timeline	Monitoring, Evaluation

special education teachers are valuable members of the planning group. Repeatedly asking, "What else will that involve?" helps the group to break down major tasks into their component parts. Continue to probe by asking, "What would need to happen before that?"

These questions will guide the group to identify missing steps and create a sequence, so the list of steps will need to be reorganized many times. This makes an awfully messy planning chart. It saves a lot of work if you do the first column with stick-on notes. If you write each step or activity on a stick-on note, and then realize you left something out or have things in the wrong order, it is easy to rearrange them.

Who's on First?

When the sequence of steps or tasks seems complete, have the group work across the chart horizontally for each step. Identify the person responsible for each step and the people who will participate.

Let's imagine that Our Town School identified these goals for its achievement (school improvement) plan:

1. Students will show improvement in reading and writing skills.

2. Students will demonstrate increased use of conflict resolution strategies and incidents of violent behavior will decrease.

3. All students will apply computer skills in their work in all subjects.

The school would then need to develop four action plans: one for changes in reading, one for writing, one for conflict resolution strategies, and one for increasing use of technology. As the leadership team compares those plans, it will look at the designated persons responsible to ensure that a few people are not carrying the full load for everyone else. The information from these columns will also clarify roles and responsibilities for keeping the process moving along.

Time and Money

After designating the human capacity for each part of the plan, budgetary implications must be considered. Time is money also, so there's a close connection between these two columns. If release time is needed, there will be substitute costs. If compensation for time outside the contract day must be provided, that cost must be estimated. Timelines should consider the school calendar and capitalize on any staff development days or inservice time to fit with the school's action plan for improvement.

Money is never in abundance in schools, and new funding is rare. As with time (see Chapter 4), existing resources must be clearly identified and scrupulously reallocated to match priorities. The three goals mentioned for Our Town School might be funded through a combination of federal Title I funds, state basic education allocation, a Safe and Drug-Free Schools grant, and a local technology levy. Without a master plan for school improvement, there might be multiple plans fragmenting the available resources.

In Chapter 12, I shared the story of a school leadership team's transformation as the members explored data about absenteeism and created the fishbone chart shown in Figure 12.10. Their decision to create one-on-one relationships for chronic absentees resulted in the action plan shown in Figure 14.2.

Note the careful breakdown of preparation steps that occur before any mentoring relationships are established. Also note the specificity of the timeline. Activities are designated by month and sometimes by week. I recently looked at school improvement plans with columns for "Start Date" and "End Date." The plans were already two years old when I was asked to review them because the project managers had a sense that nothing was happening. The first thing I noticed was that the timeline columns all had 1999 as the start date and 2004 as the end date. Given that broad time frame, no one felt much urgency in 2000; after all, there were still four more years to go. An implementation plan will never move along at exactly its planned pace and sequence, but unless we outline the sequence, there will be no way to know how far behind we are or what to adjust. The challenge is to strike a proper balance between flexibility and evolutionary planning on the one hand and patience and perseverance on the other.

Getting Proof of Progress

A most neglected but essential column on the action plan is the last one, often given the heading Monitoring or Evaluation. It corresponds to the *Evidence* component of Figures 1.1 and 1.2. Too often, this column is simply used to check off completion of the activity. For example, "All staff attended a workshop on cooperative learning." This is inadequate because it does not verify whether anyone actually went back to his or her classroom and applied the knowledge and skills that were learned in the workshop.

Take another look at Figure 14.2 and notice the Monitoring column. You may realize that there are two different kinds of indicators listed. They identify evidence that the strategies are being done *and* that the goal is being met. Various documents will be presented and approved, schedules will be turned in, and minutes of meetings will be recorded. This is proof that the plan is being carried out. However, the real proof will come when attendance and grades are graphed each month to demonstrate that the students are at school more and are learning more. This is evidence that the goal is being attained.

Evidence of Implementation

Many sound, research-based innovations have been initiated in schools, tried for a while, and then discarded because "they don't work" when there has been no way to know whether they *have been* worked. I have already

Figure 14.2 A   Action Plan: A Completed Example

School: _____ **School Year(s)** _____

Improvement Objective: To improve student attendance _____

Members of Team or Task Force: _____

Strategy: Develop 1:1 student-adult mentor relationships
for chronic absentees

Rationale: Research findings indicate that student engagement and personal bonding with adults in the school
are related to attendance and achievement

Activities: Steps to be Taken	Persons Responsible	Persons Involved	Resources Needed	Timeline	Monitoring, Evaluation
Develop criteria to identify the chronic absentees	Counselors	SIT Subcommittee	Part of June workshop time	During June workshop	Criteria approved by SIT @ August meeting
List the students who need to be involved	Counselor on SIT	Homeroom Teachers	-----	During June workshop	Presented & approved by SIT @ August meeting
Set expectations for students who participate	Counselor on SIT	Homeroom Teachers	-----	During June workshop	Presented & approved by SIT @ August meeting
Notify parents and get permission to contact students	Counselor	Counseling secretary	-----	Before registration in August	Parent permissions returned
Set expectations for adult mentors	SIT subcommittee chair	SIT subcommittee	-----	During June workshop	Approval by SIT @ August meeting
Develop training for mentors	Asst. Principal Staff Development Coordinator	SIT subcommittee Homeroom Teachers	Food for picnic	July	Approval by SIT @ August meeting

Figure 14.2 B Action Plan: A Completed Example

Activities: Steps to be Taken	Persons Responsible	Persons Involved	Resources Needed	Timeline	Monitoring, Evaluation
Recruit/select mentors	Asst. Principal	Homeroom Teachers	-----	July & August	List of mentors
Match students to mentors	Asst. Principal	Counselors	-----	July & August	List of possible matches
Hold mentor training and gain commitment	Asst. Principal Staff Development Coordinator	Mentors Homeroom Teachers	Stipends for 2-hour training session ($1200)	August	Mentors sign commitment forms
Hold meeting of students and mentors or make individual contact with students	Counselors Asst. Principal	Students Mentors Homeroom Teachers	-----	August	Students return commitment forms
Determine times & places mentors will contact students	Mentors	Students	-----	1st week of school	Schedules turned in to Asst. Principal
Schedule and hold mentor meetings	Asst. Principal	Counselors Mentors Homeroom Teachers	Early release time once per month	Monthly – October through May	Minutes of meetings Summary of student attendance and grades
Re-examine attendance data	Counselors	-----	-----	Weekly by student; monthly for all	Graph attendance and grades each month as run charts
Plan celebration for mentors and students	Asst. Principal	Students Mentors Families Homeroom Teachers	Budget for food, certificates, etc.	May	Progress certificates to students with % improvement

emphasized the need to select strategies that have documented data to back up their claims of improving student performance. However, to get the same results, they have to be implemented in the same way in your school.

A classic example of this is cooperative learning.[1] Schools have a one-day workshop for staff on cooperative learning and assume teachers are then ready, willing, and able to apply this powerful approach in their classrooms. A year later, test scores are the same; just as many kids are getting D's and F's, and someone in a formal leadership role asks, "Are we doing cooperative learning?" Various people reply, "Oh, sure, I moved my desks into circles." "Well, of course, I do group stuff once a week." And a serious skeptic is bound to chime in, "And they're even harder to manage because they talk more now." The point of this example is not to push cooperative learning, but to emphasize that, if you're going to choose a proven program, *use it as proven and prove you are using it*—or don't blame the program for your lack of results.

Once a strategy has been identified and staff members have made a commitment to learn and apply it, they must engage in a discussion of what it really looks like in action, how they will recognize it in their own work, and how the principal will observe it to provide reinforcement and support. They also must think about how these new practices or programs will show up in student work so that evidence of impact on learning can also be demonstrated (see the section on Classroom-Based Data Gathering, below).

Some evidence of implementation will be classroom-based and may be gathered by teachers and shared with each other in grade-level and team meetings. For example, Figure 14.3 provides a template for teachers to examine student work together. The work they bring may be students' responses to a schoolwide writing prompt or it might be a math problem-solving task including explanation of the approach students used to reach their answer. Teachers do a quick sort of the student work into four piles, and then compare the characteristics of each group of student work to identify common challenges with which students are struggling. They also discuss what supports are needed by each group of students. This information is used to guide the next instructional steps and suggest flexible skill groups with specific objectives.

Classroom-Based Data Gathering

At Alderwood Elementary, teachers made a commitment to use monitoring notes to observe students' successes and struggles and to use that information to group and regroup for differentiated instruction. The principal and staff discussed how the principal could support their efforts by providing feedback from informal observations. Figure 14.4 is an authentic artifact of Principal Nick Payne's log of visits to classrooms to observe grouping and regrouping. This data were then reviewed by the staff at the next early-release day. Teachers shared the classroom management challenges that discouraged them from working with small groups and gave each other ideas about selection of materials to support specific skills.

Figure 14.3 Analysis-of-Student-Work Template

Analysis of Student Work (Circle) SUMMER FALL WINTER SPRING

Name:_____ Advisor:_____ Date:_____

Describe your expectations for student work/performance in relation to the appropriate content standard:

Select samples for analysis:

Sort the students' work into four (4) piles and write the students' names in the appropriate column:

more than one year below standard	approaching standard	meeting standard	exceeding standard
_____%	_____%	_____%	_____%

Choose one sample from each pile for further reflection and respond to the prompts individually and/or with your advisor:

A. Describe the performance of each selected student:

more than one year below standard	approaching standard	meeting standard	exceeding standard

1 of 2

(Continued)

Figure 14.3 (Continued)

Analysis of Student Work (Circle) SUMMER FALL WINTER SPRING

B. How might you support each student to move forward?

more than one year below standard	approaching standard	meeting standard	exceeding standard

How will you use this assessment information to guide your planning and what are next steps?

2 of 2

New Teacher Center at University of California Santa Cruz.

Figure 14.4 Grouping and Regrouping for Instruction

Teacher	When Groups Meet	How Often Groups Change	Assessments Used	Walk-Through Notes	Evidence
Grade 3 Room 6	9:30–10:30	Change approx. 3 weeks	Running Records every 3 weeks; more often w/lower kids	5 Jan 03 Yes Reading	Observation Planning sheet
Kindergarten Room 1	M/W 9:00–10:30 T/TH/F 9:00–10:30 12:00–1:30	M/W/F Regularly	RRR Monitoring notes Screening	16 Jan 03 Yes Reading	Observation
Grade 5 Room 9	M–TH 9:30–10:30 F 10:00–10:30			17 Jan 03 yes reading	Observation
Grade 1 Room 10	10:45–11:30 12:00–1:00	No group (daily)	Draft books	15 Jan 03 No groups–sub Yes	Observation
Kindergarten Room 2	M/W 9:00–10:30			28 Jan 03 Yes	
Grade 2 Room 8	11:00–11:30	Monthly	Oral reading	15 Jan 03 Yes	Observation
Grade 1 Room 3	10:00–10:25 10:00–11:25	Every 3 weeks	RRR	21 Jan 03 Yes	Observation
Grade 2 Room 5	10:45–11:30	Weekly	RRR Monitoring notes	23 Jan 03 Yes	Observation
Grade 5 Room 11	10:00–10:25 10:00–11:30	Weekly	Monitoring notes	Weekly 15 Jan 03 Yes	Planning sheet
Grade 3/4 Portable B	M/T/TH/F 2:30–3:00 W 11:00–12:00			10 Jan 03 Yes Reading	Observation
Grade 4 Room 7	11:15–12:25	Every 2 weeks	Responses to guided reading	23 Jan 03 One group w/ teacher and one with aide	Observation
Grade 4/5 Room 14	10:00–11:30	Every 2 weeks		6 Feb 03 Groups listed with times on white board	

Teachers at Silver Beach Elementary studied their data on writing performance and realized that, in order to discuss student work, they needed to emphasize the use of common expectations and editing marks. Figure 14.5 lists attributes they would stress during the year. Principal Greg Holmgren took home a sample of student draft books and reviewed them for evidence of using the date-topic-audience-purpose format, skipping lines to make revising and editing easier, and completing the planning stage of the writing process. His handwritten notes, visible in Figure 14.5, indicated the variety of planning tools, including lists, illustrations, beginning-middle-end reminders, and categories.

Schoolwide Data Gathering

A powerful method for gathering evidence of implementation of best practice, specific new instructional strategies, or climate indicators is the walk-through. Some authors describe this as an audit process conducted by a team of external observers, such as central office administrators, consultants, or technical assistance staff (Ginsberg & Murphy, 2002; Richardson, 2001, 2002). It can also be "owned" by the school staff, as they identify desired characteristics from their new strategies, their mission statement, or attributes of schools they have studied who achieve high performance with similar students.

Figure 14.6 represents a set of indicators that Education Director Walter Trotter hopes to see when he visits elementary schools in Seattle, Washington. Figure 14.7 is the template being developed and revised for use with redesigned small high schools in West Clermont, Ohio.[2] Both include a lot of indicators, so schools who are just beginning to think about evidence of implementation should feel free to start with a shorter list of things to look for.

Evidence of Impact

Traditional reports of school improvement have included descriptions of the professional development provided, programs adopted, support staff hired, and materials purchased. All of these reflect the work of the adults in the organization. In some cases, the activities could take place, be celebrated as accomplishments, and yet make no difference at all to the experiences and learning of the students. Evidence of impact ties the work to results for students.

Staff at Sehome High School have been working to increase the success of entering ninth graders. Principal Jim Kistner provided evidence of impact in an e-mail to staff:

> It is exciting to note that the number of freshmen failing three or more classes is down 6% from last year. Even more interesting, the number of freshmen failing any classes at all for the first semester has been reduced by 9% this year. . . . Interventions we have made this year (peer support at the beginning of the school year,

(Text continues on p. 213)

Figure 14.5   Gathering Data From Draft Books

Grade 2—January   Editing Marks

Room/Student No.	Drafts/Collection	Date: (DTAP)	Skip lines	Planning	Underline "SP"	Paragraph "P"	Circle Punctuation	Caret Insert	Cross-Out Line	Change Case Dbl Line	Other
A/1	Y	DTAP	Y	Y—list				Y	Y		
A/2	Y	DTAP	Y	Minimal							
A/3	Y	DTAP	Y	Y—pictures				Y	Y		
A/4	Y	D	Y	Y—web					Y		
A/5	Y	DT	Y	Y—web					Y		
B/1	Y	DTAP	Y	Y—categories	Y			Y			
B/2	Y	DTAP	Y	Y—B-M-E (beginning-middle-end)				Y	Y		"Things I know how to do well"
B/3	Y	DTAP	Y	Y—list					Y		
B/4	Y	DTAP	Y	Y—web				Y	Y		
B/5	Y	DTAP	Y	Y—B-M-E				Y			
C/1	Y	DTAP	Y	Y—boxes-sequence	Y	Y					"I can & am learning to…"
C/2	Y	DTAP	Y	Y—4-box	Y			Y	Y		" "
C/3	Y	DTAP	Y	Attempt							" "
C/4	Y	DTAP	With help	Minimal							" "
C/5	Y	DTAP	Y	Y—categories				Y	Y		" "

Figure 14.6 School Walk-Through Look-Fors

SCHOOL WALK-THROUGH "LOOK FORS"	Evident	Partially Evident	Not Observed	Not Applicable
Learning Environment				
1. Academic standards are posted				
2. The hallways and classrooms are "print-rich" and intellectually stimulating, neat and attractive................				
• Student work is displayed everywhere................				
• Bulletin boards and display areas are done by students and for students........				
• Displays of student work have organization and are labeled................				
• Criteria for good work are prominently displayed (writing scoring, math scoring)................				
3. Seating arrangements facilitate collaboration................				
• Space for grouping students is available................				
• There is space for guided reading in primary grades................				
• There is space for large group shared reading................				
• There is space for students to develop group projects................				
4. Students know routines and procedures................				
• Students can solve a problem without the teacher................				
• Students know the routines for all parts of the day................				
• Students have responsibilities for operating some facet of school in ways that aren't controlled by adults................				
• Written rules are posted................				
• Routines are flexible and allow for discovery learning................				
• Evacuation plans are appropriately posted................				
5. Learning centers and materials are readily accessible to students................				
• All types of literature at different levels are available both in classrooms and in media centers................				
• Classroom literature is attractively displayed................				
• Pleasant reading areas are available................				
7. The grounds are clean				
8. The building is clean and organized				
9. The office staff is warm and welcoming				

SCHOOL WALK-THROUGH "LOOK FORS"	Evident	Partially Evident	Not Observed	Not Applicable
Students				
10. Students are actively engaged..........				
• Students are engaged in activities that require social interaction........				
• Students are engaged in discovery and independent thought about high-level problems and questions. Low-level recall is minimized.........				
• Work sheets are minimized				
• Hands-on activities are provided whenever appropriate.............				
• Students seem happy and engaged, not bored and uninvolved..........				
• Students write about what they read, think, learn, and feel............				
• Students write across the curriculum...........				
• Students serve in leadership roles...........				
• Students can articulate what they are doing and what they are learning.........				
Teachers				
11. Teachers are facilitators of learning............				
• Teachers facilitate discussion and group work........				
• Teachers give input, make presentation and model..........				
• Teachers listen, counsel in large groups and with individuals...........				
• Teachers create learning communities............				
• Teachers teach skills in the context of real events.............				
• Teachers display high expectations for every student...........				
• Teachers engage all students in higher order thinking............				
• Teachers engage students in the application of experiences and knowledge....				
• Teachers provide worksheets that avoid fill-in-the blank and literal recall.......				
• Teachers provide graphic organizers or other note-taking conventions for students...........				
• There is evidence of teacher collaboration............				
• Teachers align all classroom activities with standards and the attributes of the SPS graduate...........				

Signature: _____

Date: _____

Reprinted with permission from Seattle Public Schools, Seattle, WA.

211

Figure 14.7 West Clermont Walk-Through Feedback Form for Small High Schools

West Clermont Walk-Through Feedback Form for Small High Schools

School_____ Date_____ Time_____ Observer _____

The Students Were:

_____On task (80% or more)
_____Engaged in rigorous** work
_____Writing or creating original work
_____Taking a test or quiz
_____Completing projects
_____Completing worksheets
_____Using technology
_____Listening and / or responding
_____Answering rote or knowledge-level questions
_____Answering higher order questions
_____Initiating higher order questions
_____Working in groups
_____Self-directed, self-initiated
_____Completing or correcting homework assignment
_____At the overhead projector
_____Reading
_____Speaking in front of, or presenting to, class
_____In class, downtime
_____Transitioning between classes or activities

The Teacher Was:

_____Specifying expectations & desired behavior
_____Conveying high expectations
_____Lecturing or assigning to whole group
_____Helping individual students
_____Facilitating small groups
_____Demonstrating or modeling a task
_____Reading to or with students
_____Using multiple questioning strategies
_____Asking higher order questions
_____Asking knowledge-level or procedural questions
_____Using wait time effectively
_____Using or modeling technology
_____In front of class
_____Circulating among students
_____Sitting or standing behind desk (or podium)
_____Giving direct instruction
_____At the overhead projector
_____In class, downtime
_____Transitioning between classes or activities

Evidence of Schoolwide & District Expectations:

_____Objectives clearly stated or cited
_____Standards or curriculum objectives evident
_____Student data posted
_____Critical thinking / questioning skills used
_____Process or strategy charts in room and used by students
_____Reading: comprehension strategies
_____Emphasis on non-fiction
_____Writing process (e.g., prompts, conferencing)
_____Differentiation of instruction
_____Student agenda used & updated
_____Problem of the Day (DOL, DOM, OPT)
_____Character initiatives / respect
_____Cooperative/collaborative classroom
_____Personalization
_____Instruction focused on small school's curriculum
_____Curriculum integration
_____Rubrics in use

Evidence of Positive Climate & Teacher Efficacy:

_____High expectations for all
_____Appropriate student praise
_____Instruction appropriate to students
_____Student work displayed
_____Specific constructive feedback
_____Equitable, consistent application of rules
_____Respectful behavior / positive regard
_____Relearning or reevaluation of material
_____Room was without clutter
_____Effective time management
_____Efficient materials management
_____Real-world connections / student interests
_____Assessment (rubrics, student-generated)
_____Relearning or reevaluation of material
_____Cooperative/ collaborative classroom
_____Positive personal interactions with student
_____Procedures in place and being used

**Evidence that this was rigorous or challenging work:

_____

_____

_____

K:\ME Teaching\H.S. Walk-Through Obv. Form.doc
Revised February 2003

West Clermont Local District, Cincinnati, Ohio
Department of Instruction and Curriculum

Reprinted with permission from West Clermont School District, Cincinnati, OH.

community-building exercises during the opening days of school in all classes, special ed reconfiguration to provide increased support to teachers and students in classrooms, a greater focus on ninth grade challenges and needs, a common homework policy, beginning attempts to make connections across the ninth grade curriculum, a common writing rubric, introducing reading strategies into a number of classes across the content areas, etc.)—all may be having a positive impact on the lives and learning of our freshmen. (Personal communication, February 7, 2003)

Roosevelt Principal Steve Morse has been struggling to maintain a balance of instructional leadership while dealing with an array of discipline issues, so it's important for him to be able to see evidence of impact in improved behavior. He congratulated his staff with this message:

We only had 11 official office discipline referrals for February. . . . This compares to 17 last February and 36 in February 2001. The total for 2002–2003 is now 133, compared to 204 at this time last year. That is 35% fewer than last year, with only 24% fewer kids. (Personal communication, February 10, 2003)

The opening of a new school had reassigned some students, and it was important to verify that the improvements reflected the work of the staff, not just the change in enrollment.

Figure 14.8 provides examples of the link between strategic actions, evidence of implementation, and evidence of impact. Most of our work to increase student achievement will ultimately be judged by how our students perform on a state-mandated high-stakes assessment. However, schools need up-close, in-real-time evidence that they are making a difference. The number of students correctly using nonfiction text forms and features provides evidence of student learning that will, in turn and in time, translate into higher scores on the state test.

Both evidence of implementation and evidence of impact are needed to monitor a new program or initiative. In order to improve student writing, staff at Sunnyland Elementary drilled down into the data from all assessments—Iowa Tests of Basic Skills, the state standards-based test, and the district's six-trait writing tests. They decided that organization was a thinking, planning, and writing skill that would increase writing scores and also transfer into improvement in other content areas. Figure 14.9 lists the strategies they identified, the evidence of changes made in their own practice, and the resulting impact on student learning.[3]

Reaping Unexpected Benefits

There's a fringe benefit to monitoring implementation, as one junior high school discovered. Teachers had been concerned about the low self-esteem and disengagement of some students and what they perceived as an

Figure 14.8 Reporting Strategic Plan Progress: Middle School Examples

School: Our Town Middle School	Strategic Plan Area: Reading	
Goal: Students will comprehend a variety of non-fiction texts, as measured by classroom assessment and 6% increase in WASL scores.		
Strategic Action	**Evidence of Implementation**	**2002–2003 Report**
• Schoolwide Read-Aloud using high interest, nonfiction text. • Teachers will emphasize text forms and features in content area textbooks and supplemental materials.	• Grade-level teams planned activities to accompany schoolwide Read-Aloud. • Teachers used strategic questions to monitor use of text forms and features.	**Evidence of Impact** • 70% of students correctly used the nonfiction text forms and features according to teachers' monitoring sheets. • WASL scores in nonfiction improved from 73% to 79% meeting standard.

School: Our Town Middle School	Strategic Plan Area: Writing	
Goal: Use research-based strategies to improve WASL writing scores by 5% per year and improve ITED by 3% per year.		
Strategic Action	**Evidence of Implementation**	**2002–2003 Report**
• Teachers developed common rubric for writing in all content areas.	• All teachers trained in rubric on October 15 late arrival day. • Teachers analyzed the quality of a regular written assignment in teams on late arrival days in November and March.	**Evidence of Impact** • The quality of samples from regular written work improved from 39% getting 3's and 4's in November to 99% in March. • WASL scores improved from 62% meeting standards to 67% meeting standard.

School: Our Town Middle School	Strategic Plan Area: Learning Environment	
Goal: We will create a safe, supportive environment for learning by improving student conflict resolution skills and reducing playground incidents requiring referrals.		
Strategic Action	**Evidence of Implementation**	**2002–2003 Report**
• Implement Second Step curriculum. • Train and use peer mediators.	• All teachers took Second Step training and are teaching the lessons. • 25 peer mediators have been trained.	**Evidence of Impact** • 79 conflict resolution reports were written and turned in by students. • Discipline referrals down by 10% from last year.

Figure 14.9 Reporting Strategic Plan Progress: Writing

School: Sunnyland	Strategic Plan Area: Writing	2002-2003 Report
Goal: At Sunnyland School, teachers will develop competent writers who communicate effectively in a variety of genres.		
Strategic Action	**Evidence of Implementation**	**Evidence of Impact**
Teachers will provide regular demonstrations of written responses focusing on organization in a variety of genres.	Observable on chart paper in each classroom and teaching area.	33% increase in the number of students at standard in organization from fall to spring on the Sunnyland writing prompts; the 3rd grade writing score in organization increased by 13% from the previous year and the overall increase is 17%.
Teachers will score specific writing prompts 3 times each year using appropriate rubrics.	Copies of writing prompts and rubrics developed by grade level.	38% increase in the number of students at standard on all 6 Traits from fall to spring on the Sunnyland writing prompts; the average per student gain from fall to spring was 0.82 points.
Teachers will be supported by a coaching model that focuses on organization in writing.	17 teachers and 3 coaches participated in 1:1 coaching.	On the coaching evaluation, 65% of the participants felt a single focus was helpful and 85% of participants felt they had increased their expertise in teaching writing.
Teachers will learn strategies for teaching organization in writing.	The building focus and the coaching focus was organization in writing.	On the coaching evaluation, 85% of the participants felt they had increased their expertise in teaching writing. 45% increase in writing scores on the WASL over the last three years.
Teachers will learn how to assess student writing for organization.	Writing prompts; rubrics developed by grade levels.	33% increase in the number of students at standard in organization from fall to spring on the Sunnyland writing prompts; the 3rd grade writing score in organization increased by 13% from the previous year; the average per student gain from fall to spring was 0.59 points.
Teachers will develop appropriate grade-level prompts and rubrics for organization in writing.	Writing prompts and rubrics developed at all grade levels.	33% increase in the number of students at standard in organization from fall to spring on the Sunnyland writing prompts; the 3rd grade writing score in organization increased by 13% from the previous year; the average per student gain from fall to spring was 0.59 points.
Teachers will attend district 3rd or 6th grade writing assessments scoring to learn about organization.	6 teachers attended the scoring and 1 Title I IA attended.	33% increase in the number of students at standard in organization from fall to spring on the Sunnyland writing prompts; the 3rd grade writing score in organization increased by 13% from the previous year; the average per student gain from fall to spring was 0.59 points.

overall lack of respect for diversity in the student population. Some of the teachers had been reading about student engagement in learning and a few others had attended a workshop on cooperative learning. They felt that use of cooperative learning might seem more engaging to the students and thereby might increase achievement. Social studies teachers decided to work together to develop cooperative learning activities. Their goal was to have a cooperative learning activity every Thursday and see what would happen.

The data-gathering aspect of their project was overlooked at the time, but emerged as an "Ah ha!" for the entire school. After a month or so, the guidance counselor reported at a faculty meeting that, for some reason, attendance in seventh and eighth grade was showing an increase and was higher on Thursdays than any other day of the week. He wondered if anyone was doing something special on Thursdays. When the social studies teachers mentioned their experiment, the language art teachers decided to test it further. They chose Tuesday as a day to use cooperative learning and consciously set out to have the counselor help them trace the attendance patterns. At the time I lost contact with this school, the staff had not yet determined the effects on student test scores, but they had certainly made an impact on student interest and attendance. They had also stimulated the growth of a community of learners in their school.

Making It Public

Monitoring progress is not always a sophisticated and complicated endeavor. Sometimes, principals agree to conduct business on the roof or kiss a pig or sit in a dunking booth if students read a million pages—and parent volunteers construct a huge paper thermometer to count the pages read. This kind of public monitoring can motivate continued effort until the real results (higher reading scores) can be documented.

Notes

1. Cooperative learning has surfaced again as one of "The Essential Nine" cited in Chapter 13.
2. Thanks to Mary Ellen Steele-Pierce, Assistant Superintendent of Curriculum and Instruction, W. Clermont, Ohio.
3. Thanks to Jean Prochaska, Principal, Sunnyland Elementary School.

15

Sustaining the Struggle

I f you stay in education long enough, you can get hit on both sides of the head by the same innovation—because the pendulum swings back and forth, philosophies alternate, and next year's new thing replaces last year's new thing. One hallmark of Michael Fullan's body of work is his identification of the implementation dip as a predictable phenomenon of a change effort (see, for example, Fullan, 1993, 1999, 2001, 2003b). Something new is initiated with enthusiasm and energy, and there is upward movement toward the goal; then, we become tired, realize it's going to be harder than we thought, get distracted by yet more new things coming along, and there's a dip in the trajectory. When the focus is maintained and support is continued, people can push through the implementation dip and advance well beyond that first plateau.

Analyzing Implementation

The first strategy for coping with the implementation dip is to know about it, to expect it, and—when it hits—to help people understand what's happening and that it's natural. Then, take a close look at the dip and diagnose what may be contributing to the discouragement. Figure 15.1 provides a tool for such analysis.[1] This analysis consists of three stages and should not be rushed; it requires a minimum of 60–90 minutes with short breaks to stretch, debrief, and be oriented to the next phase.

Part I helps participants revisit the initiation stage of implementation and clarify the characteristics of the change that was intended. Confirming the reasons for the change, its purpose, and intended outcomes reconnects

Figure 15.1 Implementation Analysis

Part I: Initiation

What is the change?	What is its purpose, desired outcomes?	What were the expected/anticipated impacts?	On whom? (how many, specific)

Part II: Implementation Successes

What is going well? (being implemented, aligned with purpose)	For whom? (how many, specific)	What is the evidence? (of implementation, alignment with purpose)	Which strategies that worked well should be maintained?

(Continued)

Figure 15.1 (Continued)

Part III: Implementation Challenges

What is problematic?	For whom? (how many, specific)	What is the evidence?	What are their competing priorities or unmet needs? (specific, by name or group)	What strategies shall we revise or add?

the school to its mission and goals and concern for students as the impetus. Discussion of the impacts that were foreseen and who would be most affected reminds everyone that consideration was given to the realities of change. In Chapter 1, the leadership of School B intentionally created opportunities for those who would be most affected by aspects of block scheduling to serve on the committees that would resolve these issues.

At the same time, this discussion begins to create awareness of blind spots in the implementation. The leadership task at this point is to restrain the group from leaping directly to the last step in Part III and making quick decisions about how to "fix" the first few things that are missing. It's essential to spend time on Part II and discuss success as well.

Part II helps tired, disillusioned people see that there are implementation successes. At least some things are going well for some people. These need to be honored and celebrated. Evidence of success, such as the reports in Chapter 14 of increased ninth-grade success and decreased student discipline incidents, renews hope and energy and should be celebrated. Even more importantly, we must ensure that any revisions we make do not *undo* the aspects that are working effectively. Strategies that have worked must be kept in our repertoire for continued use.

In Part III, the problems of implementation are identified and their sources are clarified. Concrete, specific data on who is adversely affected or is resisting implementation is critical. Sometimes, the unrest of a very small group is being overgeneralized to "everyone thinks this was a terrible idea." The group should seek actual evidence of the problem. "Kids can't sign up for electives and they won't have enough credits to graduate" must be pursued in terms of the number of students affected, which students they are, what credits they may be lacking', and so forth.

Just as we want to keep the strategies that worked and generated success, we must identify the things we tried that weren't so useful. The fourth column of Figure 15.1 reminds us that it is particularly important to avoid blaming and casting judgment. Most of us have wants and needs that compete with other wants and needs within ourselves or within the organization. What looks like resistance may be a legitimate struggle to balance this conflict. Understanding what is missing for some may result in small alterations or additional individual support, rather than premature abandonment of the entire effort.

Integrating Programs and Practices

Careful work to sustain momentum doesn't mean a three-year plan will look exactly the same in Year 2 and Year 3 as it did when it left the drawing board. Better ideas may come along. The strategies that were selected and implemented may not be achieving the desired results. We need to scan the horizon all the time to be informed about new developments. However, we also need to be cautious consumers. The following questions can provide a helpful guide in discussion of whether something new can and should be synthesized with the ongoing efforts of the school or district.

1. What Are the New Program's Underlying Values and Beliefs? Do Those Values and Beliefs Fit Ours?

A lot of programs are packaged with materials and activities that look attractive and appeal to our instincts and intuition, but do they articulate their philosophy? Do they describe the theoretical foundation on which they are based? Is what they describe consistent with the discussions about mission and priorities that have occurred in the school and district? Even if this program is a good solution for some, will it simply dilute the mixture of energy and effort already under way?

2. What Results Does This Program Promise? Are They the Same Results That We Want to Achieve Through Our Goals?

"This is really great for kids" is a claim I hear so often, especially in the exhibit hall at national conventions. Because we care about children, we feel guilty if we don't listen—but how *carefully* do we listen? In what *way* is it great for students?

3. What Evidence Is There That This Program Has Achieved Those Results in Other Schools?

This question was also asked in Chapter 12. When we are trying so hard to produce proof of our effectiveness with students, why do we let consultants and companies off the hook so easily? "It sounds like something kids would like" is an inadequate reason to adopt a new model. Where's the data?

4. What Steps Are Required to Implement This New Program? Are There Other Processes in Place in Which We Do What the New Program Requires?

Several years ago, I worked with a group of districts that introduced school-based change and the use of data through the Effective Schools model. Suddenly total quality management (TQM) became the rage, and every national association's conference had multiple sessions in a TQM strand. The Q word was woven into every title to gain acceptance. One administrator who was a cautious consumer attended several and said, "These all seem to focus on teamwork, using data, and being oriented to the customer. Isn't that what we are already doing? The last thing I want to do is tell people who are now really committed to our process that we're going to throw it out and start something else!"

5. What Resources Are Needed to Implement This Program? Can We Afford It?

In Chapter 14, we addressed the reality of resources—not just money, but the time and energy of the human resources of the district. Just as individuals can burn themselves out doing good works and end up being unable to help themselves or anyone else, schools and districts can, with all good intentions and purposes, exceed their organizational capacity and end up in worse shape than they started. The question of "affording" it is not just a budget question; it's also an issue of commitment, credibility, and constancy of purpose.

Saying No

If a new approach can't answer any of the above questions to your satisfaction, the proper answer is "No, thank you." This can also be true for money. There are times when the best answer to a possible grant is also "No, thank you." If it doesn't match something that's already in your plan and if the time to generate the application, administer the grant, and write the necessary evaluation at the end exceeds the benefits it will bring the school or district, you can get along without it just fine. Recently, an administrator described a grant opportunity this way: "I was up at 4 a.m. trying to write this proposal when I realized that by the time the proposal was done, I would have put about $10,000 worth of time and energy into the needs assessment for it, and the planning, and all this work—in order to get a $5,000 grant. I threw the stuff away and went back to bed."

Celebrating

Most of us are comfortable with the phrase "nothing succeeds like success" and mentally apply it to teaching students at the appropriate level of difficulty so that they will be successful and motivated to keep trying and to make further progress. The same phrase and logic apply to organizational change. We can't keep on devoting energy above and beyond the call of duty without evidence that it is getting us somewhere. No school or district has the financial resources to provide extrinsic rewards commensurate with the amount of effort required to keep an organization focused on continuous improvement. We need evidence of progress to celebrate and rejuvenate our own energy.

The April/May 1998 issue of *Tools for Schools,* a publication of the National Staff Development Council, focused on celebration. In an article titled "Applause! Applause! Recognize Actions You Want to See More Often," Joan Richardson (1998) described a variety of mini-celebrations—from the Super Pat awards given at Adlai Stevenson High School to Golden Plunger Awards and Bungee Cord Awards given for risk-taking, innovative efforts by teachers. This issue includes a checklist for assessing the "celebration quotient" of your school and provides suggested activities and an annotated bibliography of resources about this important aspect of renewing school culture and sustaining focus. If everyone is at the band shell in the park celebrating progress on their current efforts, they won't be standing around on Main Street watching for the next bandwagon to roll into town.

Spreading a Little Cheer

Even the most passionate people, committed to truth and proof, need celebrations and cheerleaders. Just as change for the sake of change is illogical, crunching data for the sake of spouting statistics is inappropriate. The underlying and overwhelming purpose of this book has been to use data as *tools* to focus our efforts on the real *goal:* maximizing the success of our students. When benchmarks are reached or milestones achieved, call on the staff members who love drama—the former cheerleaders, the social organizers—and plan unique ways to celebrate!

In your study and analysis and planning, in your assessing and monitoring and celebrating, be guided by one teacher's version of a traditional cheer:

Give me a D	*D!*
Give me an A	*A!*
Give me a T	*T!*
Give me an A	*A!*
Who is it for?	*KIDS!*

Note

1. My development of the Implementation Analysis was influenced by Fred Wood's (1998) RPTIM model (readiness, planning, training, implementation, and maintenance) and by Fullan's (2003b) discussion of implementation dips. More recently, my awareness of unmet needs and desires perceived as resistance has been sharpened by the work of Kegan and Lahey (2001).

16

Leading With Relentless Resilience

"Leadership is to this decade what standards were to the 90's" (Fullan, 2003a). The focus of *Getting Excited About Data* has been on engaging people, creating shared leadership to build on and build up internal commitment—passion—for real change that can be sustained and yield proof of our accomplishments on behalf of boys and girls and young men and women. It greatly understates the important role of the formal leaders, the school principals, and their central office administrators.

I have touched upon these roles specifically in Chapters 4 and 13, discussing administrative teams, leadership teams, data teams, and district roles in support of data-guided decision making. In trying to describe some of the things they *do*, I have not shared my observations about who they *are* and *how* they go about the things they do—how they sustain themselves, maintain their focus, and create meaning for those around them. I close this book with a description of the relentless resilience I see in the everyday heroes in our schools and school districts.

Review

The first edition of this book was a Corwin bestseller, and readers attributed that success to its simplicity, its concrete practicality, its collection of ready-to-roll activities, and its voice from the trenches. In this second edition, I have tried to maintain those qualities while adding the complexity of our current context under federal and state mandates. Questions are now being raised about whether there should be a vision at all—or whether a collective consciousness can and should just evolve through dialogue.

There are constant reminders that change is far too complex to be viewed as a linear process or a set of steps. With each iteration of the events described in Figures 1.1 and 1.2, I change some of the terms and add more two-way arrows, trying to balance the practitioners' need for a picture of how data-guided instructional improvement looks with an increased reality that this is messy, cyclical work that constantly turns back upon itself. What we learn through in-depth study of our data and our own practices informs our goals; what we discover through the evidence we collect causes us to revisit our sense of mission.

In *Leading in a Culture of Change* (2001), Michael Fullan describes five themes that have developed independently, but that are deeply compatible and provide a comprehensive theory of leadership. They are

- Moral purpose
- Understanding change
- Developing relationships
- Knowledge creation and sharing
- Coherence making

Although I did not begin with these factors in mind, I hope the reader will find them embedded throughout the 15 previous chapters. Moral purpose is the overarching principle that encompasses my use of familiar terms like *mission, beliefs,* and *core values.* This theme runs through Chapters 1, 2, 4–6, and 9. Understanding the change process has guided my recommendations about engaging people in every aspect of the work, building a culture of collective responsibility for all students (Chapter 4), acknowledging the reality of a school's scope of influence in setting priorities and goals (Chapter 10), and dealing with implementation dips while sustaining the struggle (Chapter 15).

The principle of embracing resistance during change underlies the questions "What do these data not tell us?" and "What else would we need to know?" (Figure 8.1) and the consideration of who is resisting change (Figure 15. 1) and what needs they have that seem dissonant but are real and valuable. I hope that the many processes for engaging staff and constituents are perceived as ways to develop relationships, and that the importance of studying together, analyzing student work, implementing new strategies and looking at evidence of their results exemplifies knowledge creation and sharing. From the Motivation Continuum in Chapter 5 to the discussion of mandates and motivation in Chapter 10, the need for sense making and developing internal commitment are stressed.

Who are the people to lead such a complex process—one that demands such technical skills of assessment literacy and data use, such people skills to develop relationships and engage and motivate staff, and such strength of character in the midst of constant public pressure and criticism, the inevitable burdens of bureaucracy, and the flaws and foibles of human beings in their organizations? They are not a race of superheroes. They are, themselves, human beings facing their own flaws and foibles with admirable dedication and discipline to improve everything about them, starting with themselves. You may be one of them yourself.

Leading in a Culture of Change (Fullan, 2001) combines settings from business and education, and Fullan refers to the moral purpose of leadership as "acting with the intention of making a positive difference in the lives of employees, customers, and society as a whole" (p. 3). I am sure he would agree that the education version is making a positive difference in the lives of colleagues, students, and society as a whole. If you perceive your work as making a difference, you are a leadership work-in-progress, regardless of your job title.

Relentless Resilience

These everyday heroes like you possess something I've chosen to call *relentless resilience*. A technical definition of resilience includes characteristics like initiative, independence, insight, relationship, humor, creativity, and morality (Wolin & Wolin, 1993). Henderson and Milstein (2003) state that resilient educators exhibit

> the same basic resiliency factors—the desire and capacity for bonding; defining clear boundaries; developing and exhibiting life skills; seeking and communicating caring, support and high expectations; and capitalizing on opportunities for meaningful participation. (p. 40)

The element of "defining clear boundaries" is not to be overlooked. These resilient leaders do not build relationships through a permissive anything-to-please approach to their colleagues, supervisors, and staff. They seek clarity for themselves, and provide clarity to others on the expectations and parameters for their work together.

The components of resilience blend well with the personal and social competencies that constitute emotional intelligence (Goleman, 1998):

- Self-awareness (knowing one's internal state, preferences, resources, and intuitions)
- Self-regulation (managing one's internal states and resources, including impulse control)
- Motivation (emotional tendencies that guide or facilitate reaching goals)
- Empathy (awareness of other's feelings, needs, and concerns)
- Social skills (adeptness at inducing desirable responses from others)

The day-to-day heroes I admire are not charismatic and few would appear on the dais for a keynote speech or author a bestselling work. They are some teachers, many principals, and a few superintendents, whom I have observed in my own districts and have met in the consulting work I do across the country. These are people with a rare combination of technical expertise, people skills, and personal characteristics that keep them going. There are many, and those I mention here would be the first to say that they are just "ordinary people" who represent hundreds of their colleagues. They know themselves, reflect on their practice, and value relationships. They don't make excuses, they don't place blame, and they simply never, ever give up. Those are the attributes that I sum up in the term *relentless resilience*.

The best definition I can provide of this concept is the visual image of toys from days gone by. One was an inflatable figure with sand in the base, often a clown. The entertainment value of the toy was that it always returned to upright position, whatever knocks were administered. Another toy of the past was a set of wooden characters, best known by their advertising slogan. Do you remember "Weebles wobble but they don't fall down"? And, of course, still in commercials today, we have the Energizer bunny.

How does relentless resilience look in leaders? My still-favorite football hero, Brett Favre, has a relentless resilience that's respected by friend and foe alike. Hall of Fame quarterback Sonny Jurgensen describes him this way: "Just look at the way he plays the game, the way he always seems to be having so much fun out there. Even when he's sacked, he gets up and pats the guy on the rump. That's leadership, and it's so important when the other players see that" (Wood, 2001, 2-C)

Pats on the rump don't fit our education setting, so how does relentless resilience look for us? It shows up in the e-mail from the superintendent who invites principals to a study session on No Child Left Behind and acknowledges that "the weeks ahead are going to be filled with many anxieties and pressures. Probably talking about NCLB won't lessen that uneasiness. However, NCLB is a reality that we must all address and maybe learning about it together will help us support each other in this challenging work" (Dale Kinsley, personal communication, March 5, 2003).

Relentless resilience shows up in conversations, like this one overheard between two principals: "Do I know what will happen between now and 2014? No. But I know the next steps we need to take in my school to do what's right for our students. If we keep discovering that, and doing that, the right things will happen anyway."

Where does this relentless resilience come from? For some, it actually comes from data. My notes from a visit to Alderwood Elementary describe the enthusiastic greeting I received from Principal Nick Payne:

I'm so glad you came on a school visit today. What I'm excited to share with you is *data*! The district data might look like our trend line is flat, but we know better. . . . What I'm working with is "what's happening in the classroom" data. . . . We decided to quit

Figure 16.1   Success with Sunnyland's Kindergarten Cohort

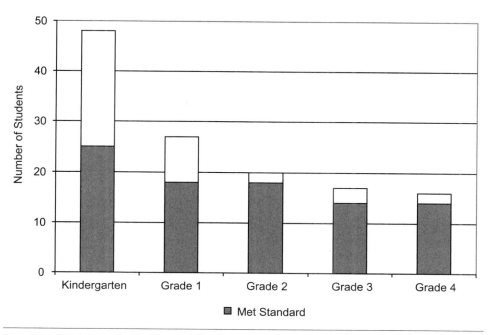

Reprinted With Permission From Bellingham School District, Bellingham, WA.

worrying about all the challenges our kids bring, and focus on what we control—our own understandings about learning.... As we worked on updating our strategic plan, we talked about what the evidence of impact on student learning would be, and we tended to delete the ideas we had that wouldn't contribute evidence.

Data also contributed to resilience at Sunnyland Elementary School, where the staff serve a regular population and two special education programs that draw students in need of service from across the district. Students are very mobile, and it's difficult to determine the effectiveness of the school's efforts on a single test, at a single point in time, at one particular grade level when the "target" population is constantly on the move. So Principal Jean Prochaska decided to "do her own data" and discover what she and her staff wanted to know.

She began with the first kindergarten cohort to be served under the schoolwide Title I plan. Figure 16.1 illustrates her discovery that Sunnyland's teachers and instructional program are successful with about 90% of the students who remain in the school. This data helps a school know whether to revamp its entire literacy approach or focus on specific strategies to support the short-term students.

Birchwood Elementary is another school with complex challenges: 61% of the students qualify for free and reduced lunch, and enrollment has grown about 20% over the last three years, even though 15%–20% leave each summer and don't return for the next year. This issue of mobility also plagued Birchwood's interpretation and use of test results for decision making and planning for instructional improvement. So, in preparation

Figure 16.2 Birchwood's Mobility Question

State Scores	Mean for Students 2+ Years	Mean for Students Less than 2 Years	Standard
Listening	401	305	400
Reading	398	359	400
Writing	9.4	7.6	9.0
Math	410	336	400

for a recent school board visit, Principal Dave Adams decided to discover for himself, the staff, and this audience what they might learn if they could account for the mobility factor. Figure 16.2 shows that the average scores of students who have attended Birchwood at least two years exceed the state standard in listening, writing, and math and, for all practical purposes, meet the standard in reading.

Digging out this data was labor intensive without the data warehousing and analysis capacity the district is seeking to provide. Staff members devoted hours of extra time to mine and combine multiple data sources by hand. For Sunnyland and Birchwood, it was well worth the effort. However, they didn't use this evidence of effectiveness as a reason to quit working for equity. Birchwood's presentation for the board ended with a set of Future Directions, and first on the list is "Find a way to respond to the needs of our mobile population." In addition, the principal's e-mail to staff reads as follows:

Congratulations! We just received summaries of the fall reading scores for the district. Ours look very good. Kindergarten: 93% met standard compared to 73% districtwide. First grade: 84% met standard, 90% districtwide. Second grade: 84% met standard, 82% districtwide. Third grade: 70% met standard, 72% districtwide. Fourth grade: 73% met standard, 74% districtwide. Fifth grade: 62% met standard, 78% districtwide. As we look at these numbers, we need to remember that in fifth grade we only have 8 students that have been with us from kindergarten, and a 130% turnover rate. In fourth grade, our turnover rate is over 200%. We have the highest free and reduced lunch count in the district. *Super work!* We know that when students remain with us, they are very successful. Our job now is to figure out how we can bring all of the students that move into our building up to standard also. That is a task that the Leadership Team is addressing now and will be working with you on as we look ahead to next year. (Dave Adams, personal communication, February 27, 2003)

When I visit the schools of resilient leaders like these, I don't hear complaints or whining. I once asked a principal about that, and he expounded enthusiastically at length about how lucky he is to have incredibly dedicated staff members who just keep doing their best to meet students' needs, whatever they are. He explained that they don't make excuses. I had to interrupt him to point out that one reason *they* don't make excuses is that *he* doesn't.

Reflection

Along with the encouragement these people derive from proactive use of data, I have observed another source for this relentless resilience. These everyday heroes are very reflective people. They focus on goals and test themselves against their priorities. Principal Steve Morse at Roosevelt Elementary struggles to balance time for instructional supervision with supporting teachers in student discipline issues. He evaluates himself against that criteria and heaves a sigh of relief when he checks his log. "I looked back on my chart this afternoon and found I have done 37 'drop-in' short observations in the five weeks since break, for an average of 7.4 with a low week of 5. Another good example of how objective data helps you keep perspective even when you 'feel' like the roof is caving in. I have actually found this observation data and the discipline data to be very simple to keep and quite helpful!" (Steve Morse, personal communication, February 28, 2003).

Chris Spence, principal of Lawrence Heights Middle School in Toronto, is one of many who use personal writing as a tool for reflection. His daily diary is "a collection of the good, the bad, and the ugly. Hope drives improvement. . . . By persisting, not getting discouraged, pouncing on daily problems, celebrating success . . . he moves the school forward—two steps forward, one backward"(Fullan, 2003, p. 38).

Some leaders are fortunate enough to have coaches that help them reflect. The greatest personal benefit that I have gained from district participation in a Bill and Melinda Gates' Foundation grant is the ability to meet for two hours monthly with an external coach. Judy Heinrich listens with patience as I describe recent leadership acts and upcoming leadership challenges. Then, she probes with the precise question that helps me stay in touch with my own core values, builds my confidence, and clarifies the next steps I will take. If I press hard for it, she'll give me advice—but she insists that I have the answers within myself. She employs a stubborn use of wait time while I think through skills I've learned, strategies that have worked in the past, and personal issues that may be driving my reactions to synthesize a solution of my own.

Other leaders I admire seem to prompt reflection by surrounding themselves with quotations that express and elicit their own sense of moral purpose. On the walls of their offices and in the privacy of their day-planners, I have seen examples that range from the scriptural to the irreverent, and from ancient to contemporary:

- "Run with patience the race that is set before you."—The Bible
- "I don't know about the key to success, but the key to failure is trying to please everybody."—Bill Cosby

- "If you are distressed by anything external, the pain is not due to the thing itself, but to your estimate of it, and this you have the power to revoke at any moment." —Marcus Aurelius Antonius
- "Courage does not always roar. Sometimes it is the quiet voice at the end of the day saying, 'I will try again tomorrow.'"

Everyday heroes with relentless resilience have a deep inner core with which they stay in touch so their personal grounding will help them keep their professional focus. They value relationships and value data, and have learned to use the two to create meaning and motivation in those around them—and thus we return once again to combining people, passion, and proof.

As the mandates and methodologies of No Child Left Behind play out in the coming days, the need and determination to tell our own story will be a strong driver of data use at the school and district level. Relentless resilience will be needed to stay the course, keep our eyes fixed on the real goal of achievement for all, and maintain our determination to do the right things for our staff and students.

The reculturing work to build collective responsibility for all students must occur rapidly in high schools across the nation. I specifically looked for high school examples to add to this second edition and wish I could disagree with Michael Fullan's (2003) conclusion that "there are no examples of high school reform in numbers, only the odd exceptional success" (p. 41). This reculturing of high schools may require structures and processes more radical than those described here, but authentic application and whole-staff engagement in even these simple processes would be a dramatic departure for most.

The opportunities for knowledge creation and sharing that this book describes at the school level must be replicated across and between districts so that principals and superintendents experience learning communities as well. My excitement about having a professional coach is dimmed by the disheartening reality that I was in the 34th year of my career before I got one!

It is up to us, today's leaders, to keep the data—and keep the faith: to lead with relentless resilience and to develop it in others. We must leave a two-fold legacy. For the students we serve now, we must produce evidence of increased equity and excellence. For an unpredictable future, we must leave a legacy of leadership—an exponentially increasing number of leaders at all levels who are ready, willing, and able to take up the torch. The ABC's of new leadership are three P's and three R's: *people, passion,* and *proof* carried out with *reflection* and *relentless resilience.*

References

Adams, D. (2003, April). What's the WASL look like? *The Birchwood Bulldog* [Newsletter].

Adelman, C. (1999). *Answers in the tool box: Academic intensity, attendance patterns, and bachelor's degree attainment.* Washington, DC: U.S. Department of Education.

Argyris, C., & Schon, D. A. (1974). *Theory in practice: Increasing professional effectiveness.* San Francisco: Jossey-Bass.

Armstrong, R. (1998, March). *Presenting the evidence.* Paper presented at the 103rd Annual Meeting of the North Central Association of Colleges and Schools, Chicago.

Barth, R. (1990). *Improving schools from within: Teachers, parents and principals can make the difference.* San Francisco: Jossey-Bass.

Bracey, G. (1997). *Understanding education statistics: It's easier (and more important) than you think.* Arlington, VA: Educational Research Service.

Bylsma, P., Shannon, S., & Griffin, A. (2002). *Addressing the achievement gap in Washington State.* Olympia, WA: Office of the Superintendent of Public Instruction.

Cawelti, G. (1999). *Handbook of research on improving student achievement* (2nd ed.). Arlington, VA: Educational Research Service.

Deal, T. E., & Peterson, K. D. (1999). *Shaping school culture: The heart of leadership.* San Francisco: Jossey-Bass.

Ellis, A. K., & Fouts, J. T. (1997). *Research on educational innovations* (2nd ed.). Larchmont, NY: Eye on Education.

Elmore, R. F. (2002, January/February). The limits of change. *Harvard Education Letter: Research Online,* p. 3.

Epstein, J., & Connors, L. (1994, August). *Trust fund: School, family, and community partnerships in middle levels.* Report No. 24. Baltimore, MD: Johns Hopkins University Center on Families, Communities, Schools, and Children's Learning.

Evans, R. (1996). *The human side of school change: Reform, resistance, and the real-life problems of innovation.* San Francisco: Jossey-Bass.

Fullan, M. (2003a, January). *Leading in a culture of change* [Handout]. Keynote Presentation, Office of the Superintendent of Public Instruction (OSPI) Winter Meeting, Spokane, WA.

Fullan, M. (2003b). *The moral imperative of school leadership.* Thousand Oaks, CA: Corwin.

Fullan, M. (2001). *Leading in a culture of change.* San Francisco: Jossey-Bass.

Fullan, M. (1999). *Change forces: The sequel.* Philadelphia: Falmer.

Fullan, M. (1993). *Change forces: Probing the depths of educational reform.* New York: Falmer.

Fullan, M., & Hargreaves, A. (1991). *What's worth fighting for in your school.* Toronto, Canada: Ontario Public School Teachers' Federation.

Garfield, C. (1987). *Peak performers: The new heroes of American business.* New York: Avon.

Ginsberg, M. B., & Murphy, D. (2002, May). How walkthroughs open doors. *Educational Leadership.* Alexandria, VA: Association for Supervision and Curriculum Development, pp. 34–36.

Goleman, D. (1998). *Working with Emotional Intelligence.* New York: Bantam.

Harvey, J. (2003, May 4). Nation's students still at risk. *The Seattle Times,* p. D-1.

Haycock, K. (Ed.). (1998, Summer). Good teaching matters . . . a lot. *Thinking K–16, 3(2).*

Henderson, N., & Milstein, M. M. (2003). *Resiliency in schools: Making it happen for students and educators.* Thousand Oaks, CA: Corwin.

Holcomb, E. L. (2001). *Asking the right questions: Techniques for collaboration and school change* (2nd ed.). Thousand Oaks, CA: Corwin.

Holcomb, E. L. (1995). To implement together, train together. *Journal of Staff Development, 16,* 59–64.

Holcomb, E. L. (1991). *School-based instructional leadership: Staff development for teacher and school effectiveness.* Madison, WI: National Center for Effective Schools.

Holloway, K. (2003, February/March). A measure of concern: Research-based program aids innovation of addressing teacher concerns. *Tools for Schools,* p. 3. Oxford, OH: National Staff Development Council.

Hord, S. M., Rutherford, W. L., Huling-Austin, L., & Hall, G. E. (1987). *Taking charge of change.* Alexandria, VA: Southwest Educational Development Laboratory.

Johnson, R. S. (2002). *Using data to close the achievement gap: How to measure equity in our schools.* Thousand Oaks, CA: Corwin.

Kegan, R., & Lahey, L. L. (2001). *How the way we talk can change the way we work: Seven languages for transformation.* San Francisco: Jossey-Bass.

Kim, J. J., Crasco, L. M., Smith, R. B., Johnson, G., Karantonis, A., & Leavitt, D. J. (2001). *Academic excellence for all students: Their accomplishments in science and mathematics* (USI Evaluative Study, funded by the National Science Foundation). Norwood, MA: Systemic Research.

Larsen, S., & Bresler, M. (1998, March). *Involving staff in an evolving process.* Paper presented at the 103rd Annual Meeting of the North Central Association of Colleges and Schools, Chicago.

Lezotte, L., & Jacoby, B. (1990). *A guide to the school improvement process based on effective schools research.* Okemos, MI: Effective Schools Products.

Marzano, R. J. (2003). *What works in schools: Translating research into action.* Alexandria, VA: Association for Supervision and Curriculum Development.

Marzano, R. J., Pickering, D. J., & Pollock, J. E. (2001). *Classroom instruction that works: Research-based strategies for increasing student achievement.* Alexandria, VA: Association for Supervision and Curriculum Development.

Olson, L. (2003, May 21). Study relates cautionary tale of misusing data. *Education Week,* p. 3.

Pelavin, S. H., & Kane, M. (1990). *Changing the odds: Factors increasing access to college.* New York: The College Board.

Quattrociocchi, S. M. (2002, Fall). Mathematics: the "gatekeeper" classes. *A Call to Parents* [Newsletter], p. 6.

Richardson, J. (2002, April). Reshaping schools from the top down. *Results,* pp. 1, 6.

Richardson, J. (2001, October/November). Walk-through's offer new way to view schools. *Tools for Schools,* pp. 1, 6. Oxford, OH: National Staff Development Council.

Richardson, J. (1998, April–May). Applause! Applause! Recognize actions you want to see more often. *Tools for Schools,* pp. 1–2. Oxford, OH: National Staff Development Council.

Rose, L. C., & Gallup, A. M. (2003). The 35th annual Phi Delta Kappa/Gallup poll of the public's attitudes toward the public schools. *Phi Delta Kappan, 85,* 41–56.

Rosenholtz, S. (1991). *Teachers' workplace: The social organization of schools.* New York: Teachers College Press.

Sanders, W. L., & Rivers, J. C. (1998, Summer). Cumulative and residual effects of teachers on future students academic achievement. In K. Haycock (ed.). Good teaching matters . . . a lot. *Thinking K-16, 3*(2).

Schmoker, M. (1996). *Results: The key to continuous improvement.* Alexandria, VA: Association for Supervision and Curriculum Development.

Senge, P. (1990). *The fifth discipline: The art and practice of the learning organization.* New York: Doubleday.

Shannon, G. S., & Bylsma, P. (2003). *Nine characteristics of high-performing schools.* Olympia, WA: Office of Superintendent of Public Instruction.

Sylwester, R. (1995). *A celebration of neurons: An educator's guide to the human brain.* Alexandria, VA: Association for Supervision and Curriculum Development.

Tagneri, W. (2003, March). *Beyond islands of excellence: What districts can do to improve instruction and achievement in all schools—A Leadership Brief.* Washington, DC: Learning First Alliance.

Taylor, B. O., & Bullard, P. (1995). *The revolution revisited: Effective schools and systemic reform.* Bloomington, IN: Phi Delta Kappa.

Varlas, L. (2002, Winter). Getting acquainted with the essential nine. *Curriculum Update,* pp. 4–5.

Wheelock, A. (2002). Foreword. In R. S. Johnson, *Using data to close the achievement gap: How to measure equity in our schools* (pp. xi–xiii). Thousand Oaks, CA: Corwin.

Wisconsin Education Association Council and Wisconsin Parent Teacher Association. (1997). *Understanding the new proficiency scores.* Madison, WI: Authors.

Wolin, S. J., & Wolin, S. (1993). *The resilient self: How survivors of troubled families rise above diversity.* New York: Villard.

Wood, F. H. (1989). Organizing and managing school-based staff development. In S. D. Caldwell (Ed.), *Staff development: A handbook of effective practices.* Oxford, OH: National Staff Development Council.

Wood, S. (2001, October 19). Favre is leader of the pack. *USA Today,* p. 2-C.

Index

**CORWIN
PRESS**

The Corwin Press logo—a raven striding across an open book—represents the union of courage and learning. Corwin Press is committed to improving education for all learners by publishing books and other professional development resources for those serving the field of K–12 education. By providing practical, hands-on materials, Corwin Press continues to carry out the promise of its motto: **"Helping Educators Do Their Work Better."**